from
HASTINGS
to
CULLODEN
(Battlefields in Britain)

Brigadier PETER YOUNG
DSO, MC, MA, FSA, FRHistS

Professor JOHN ADAIR
MA, BLitt, PhD, FRHistS

Kineton: The Roundwood Press 1979

First published in 1964 by G. Bell and Sons, London.
This new and enlarged edition first published in 1979 by
The Roundwood Press, Kineton, in the County of Warwick

Copyright © Peter Young 1979

Copyright © John Adair 1979

ISBN 0 906418 03 8

Set in Monotype Caslon series 128 and printed at
The Roundwood Press, Kineton, in the County of Warwick
and bound by Eric Neal, Welford, Northampton

Made and printed in Great Britain

Will no one tell me what she sings?—
Perhaps the plaintive numbers flow
For old, unhappy, far-off things,
And battles long ago.

Memorials of a Tour in Scotland, 1803, ix. The Solitary Reaper
WILLIAM WORDSWORTH, 1770-1850

Peter Young has also written:

BEDOUIN COMMAND

STORM FROM THE SEA

THE GREAT CIVIL WAR, with the late Lt. Col. A. H. Burne, DSO., FRHist.S

CROMWELL

WORLD WAR 1939-1945

THE BRITISH ARMY 1642-1970

THE ISRAELI CAMPAIGN 1967

EDGEHILL 1642: THE CAMPAIGN AND THE BATTLE

DECISIVE BATTLES OF THE SECOND WORLD WAR (ed.)

CHARGE! with Lt. Col. J. P. Lawford, MC. MA.

CIVIL WAR: Richard Atkyns and John Gwyn (jt. ed. with the late Norman Tucker FRHist.S) Military Memoirs Series

CROMWELL (International Profiles)

COMMANDO

MARSTON MOOR 1644: THE CAMPAIGN AND THE BATTLE

CROPREDY BRIDGE 1644: THE CAMPAIGN AND THE BATTLE, with Dr. Margaret Toynbee, Ph.D., MA, FSA., FRHist.S

THE BRITISH ARMY, with Lt. Col. James Lawford

CHASSEURS OF THE GUARD Men at Arms Series

THE ARAB LEGION Men at Arms Series

John Adair has also written:

TRAINING FOR LEADERSHIP

ROUNDHEAD GENERAL: THE LIFE OF SIR WILLIAM WALLER

TRAINING FOR DECISIONS

CHERITON 1644: THE CAMPAIGN AND BATTLE

TRAINING FOR COMMUNICATIONS

ACTION-CENTRED LEADERSHIP

THE LIFE OF JOHN HAMPDEN

THE BECOMING CHURCH

THE PILGRIMS' WAY

CONTENTS

ERRATA

Dustjacket, back flap. Professor John Adair ... was for seven years Senior Lecturer in Military History at The Royal Military Academy, Sandhurst.

page 43, line 32. As Robert Brune wrote...

LIST OF ILLUSTRATIONS

ACKNOWLEDGEMENTS

THE AUTHORS WISH to express their gratitude to some of those who have helped them in the preparation of this book.

To Miss Thelma Graves Cooper, whose local knowledge was invaluable in studying St. Albans; to their colleague William McElwee who was on the staff of 165 O.C.T.U. in 1940–1941 and has fought the battle of Dunbar almost as often as his own campaigns in N.W. Europe. To another colleague, D. G. Chandler whose expert knowledge of the Sedgemoor campaign was particularly helpful; to the late Charles Grant, whose wide knowledge of the Highland Army in the '45 was placed at their disposal; and to David Smith for his work on the Battles of The Standard, Shrewsbury, Pinkie Cleugh and on the campaigns of Montrose.

For their translations of mediaeval Latin texts the authors wish to thank Henry Kendall, David Lewis and James Money.

The chapter on the Lostwithiel Campaign first appeared in 'The Great Civil War' (*Burne and Young*).

In the compilation of the maps, never an easy task, they have received much assistance from Miss Mary Adair, P. C. R. Davis, and Neil Gordon.

The task of deciphering and typing the MS was bravely borne by Miss Joyce Skilling and Joan Young, who deserve every tribute the authors can pay them.

The Authors and Publishers acknowledge with gratitude the assistance they have received from the following for their help in locating illustrations; The National Army Museum, The National Portrait Gallery and the Monumental Brass Society; and to John Wright Photography Ltd. and A. C. Cooper Ltd.

PREFACE

BATTLES HAVE A fascination for most people, whether they are military historians or not. This is hardly strange when one considers that they are crises in human affairs which bring out the characters of the participants and reveal their true natures.

In this book we have attempted to describe the most important of the battles that have taken place on British soil. We have restricted ourselves to the post-Conquest period simply because in many cases the very location of earlier battles are in doubt and for all of them the authorities are excessively meagre. We have made no attempt to describe all the battles that have been fought in this country. We are conscious that many important ones, such as Neville's Cross, do not figure in these pages, nevertheless, we have dealt with those that have had most influence on the course of our history.

In every case we have worked from the original sources, preferring a fresh look at the old authorities, rather than reliance upon modern work. The opinions and controversies of other historians who have described these fights find but little room in our pages. Our views, for example, on Bosworth and First Newbury bear little resemblance to those of other modern writers ; and anyone acquainted, for instance, with the work of the Lt.-Colonel A. H. Burne, will observe that we are far from being in agreement with even our most distinguished predecessors. When we venture to differ from authorities such as Burne and the late Sir Charles Firth, as we do over First Newbury and Dunbar, respectively, it is not without a careful reassessment of the authorities. In the second case, we consider that Sir Charles placed altogether too much reliance on Payne Fisher's picture map of the battle. As to First Newbury, a class of officer cadets at Sandhurst who visited the field declined to accept the traditional view as to how the battle was fought, compelling us to reconsider the whole engagement. The solution here offered depends on what may be called the Parliamentarian Official Account.[1] From this, their order of battle can be reconstructed and with the exception of the Orange

Regiment of the London Trained Bands, we can account for every Roundhead unit. Earlier historians have depended too much on the assertion of Sergeant Foster that his Regiment was on the Roundhead Right, whereas the Sergeant, whose view of the battle was necessarily limited, was really on the right of Skippon's wing, which itself formed the left of the army. Thus the Red Regiment of the Trained Bands found itself opposite the main Royalist battery in their centre.

We trust that anyone can visit the battlefields described and find his way about with the aid of the maps and the chapter at the end of the book 'Seeing the Battlefields'. It was, indeed, the complaint of an American diplomat visiting Naseby, with its misleading monument, which inspired this approach to the problem.

We have concerned ourselves as little as possible with the causes of the wars described, but we have attempted to show the state of the Art of War in the various periods, and the resources at the disposal of the generals of those days.

Lastly, it is our conviction that one cannot really understand any battle without visiting the ground, and it is in the hope that the reader will be tempted to enjoy this pursuit that we have written this book.

P.Y.
J.A.

[1]See Select Bibliography, the first entry under 'First Newbury'.

It is not too much to say that our Navy has been 'a going concern' at least since the reign of King John, and it is to this that we have owed our immunity from invasion. King Henry VIII's castles and Pitt's martello towers were never put to the test.

MOUNTAINS AND RIVERS

Marshes and forests have had some influence on warfare in England. One thinks of Alfred taking refuge in Athelney and of Hereward the Wake defying the Normans from his stronghold in the Isle of Ely. But it is the rivers and mountains that have most influenced warfare in Britain, largely because they tend to restrict movement. It is not an accident that the majority of the big battles in this country were fought in the English Midlands, rather than in the mountainous areas.

The influence of geography on the Welsh wars was most marked. The fertile Severn valley was the natural frontier; the barren mountains, where an invading army could not easily subsist, served as a bulwark. The *massif* of Snowdonia stood between the English and the cornlands of Anglesey and Caernarvon, until King Edward I turned the flank by seaborne invasion.

In the Scots wars the line of the Forth was always a formidable strategic barrier. For centuries Stirling commanded the only bridge, and its castle, was, therefore, the key to the Highlands.

Further south the Pennine Range dictated the invasion routes between England and Scotland. There was the choice of the eastern route which Edward II followed in 1314, Surrey in 1513 and Cromwell in 1650, or the western route taken by Hamilton in 1648, Charles II in 1650 and Prince Charles Edward in 1745. For a formed army – horse, foot and guns – there is only the choice of these two routes. In England itself the hills seldom present a formidable barrier, though the Chilterns, steep to the west, afforded some protection to London during the Civil War.

Most of the mountainous and hilly country lies in the North and the West, the areas furthest from the capital. It is no accident that these regions were the least populous, the most backward economically and, in those days, the most conservative politically.

2

The Strategic Geography of Britain

THE TACTICS OF a battle are conditioned, broadly speaking, by the ground where it is fought, by the various weapons available and by the military ideas of the antagonists. The strategy of a campaign depends to a great extent on the geography of the Theatre of War. For this reason it may be worthwhile to mention at the outset some of the main geographical features that have influenced warfare in Britain.

THE ISLAND

The most important, if the most obvious, has been our insularity – 'This precious stone set in the silver sea.' The battles recorded in these pages, with the notable exception of the first, Hastings, were either fought by the English against the Scots, or in a time of civil strife. The Welsh wars do not seem to have led to pitched battles. Had it not been for the sea this book must have included battles with Napoleon's Grande Armée, or with Hitler's Panzer divisions. Had the Germans been able to motor into England in June 1940 who can say that our remarkable road system and the removal of the sign-posts would have sufficed to prevent their penetrating inland? And yet there are still Englishmen who want a Channel Tunnel. . . .

In the period before the rise of the British Navy – 'the floating bulwark of our island' – the invasion of this country was far from being impossible, for the coasts most exposed to Spain, Holland, France and Germany are also the weakest from a military point of view. The chalk cliffs of Kent and Sussex are a wall with many breaches. Even so the only notable example of an opposed landing on our shores appears to have taken place in 54 B.C., and there has been no seaborne landing of any kind since General Tate's ill-conceived descent on Fishguard in 1797.

The traditional view that King Charles I derived much of his support from the North and the West is confirmed rather than refuted by modern research.

The rivers of England rather than her hills have influenced the strategy of her campaigns.

The Thames for example has played its part as a barrier, for it cuts southern England practically in two, hence the importance as fortresses of London, Windsor, Reading, Wallingford, Abingdon and Oxford. All these were refortified during the 1642-1646 period. The Parliamentarian defences of London, hingeing on a great battery at Hyde Park Corner, never had to stand siege. Windsor, though summoned by Rupert in November 1642, remained in Parliamentarian hands, as fortress and prison, throughout the First Civil War. The Norman castle of Wallingford, a royalist garrison throughout the war, was not surrendered until Oxford fell, while the abandonment of Abingdon in June 1644 was soon recognised by the Cavaliers as a major blunder.

The Severn Valley has a strategic importance every bit as great as that of the Thames, and is rich in battles – Shrewsbury (1403), Tewkesbury, the Evesham campaign ; Prince Maurice's dashing victory over Waller at Ripple Field (1643) and Worcester. Gloucester, cutting the shortest route between the Royalist capital and their recruiting area in South Wales, was the scene of one of the most important sieges of the Civil War.

The Trent plays a similar part ; Newark, the scene of one of Prince Rupert's greatest victories (1644), being the rallying point of the Royalists of Nottinghamshire and Lincolnshire, besides being the place where the Great North Road crossed the Trent. It was, moreover, the nearest point to the sea at which the river was bridged.

From a tactical point of view there was little to restrict the movement of troops in the days before Enclosure Acts and barbed wire. From a strategical point of view the lack of good roads was the chief limiting factor.

COMMUNICATIONS

All the wars discussed in this book were fought before the

days of Macadam and Telford. Armies depended for their roads on the legacy of Rome. Second St. Albans, Tewkesbury and Bosworth were all fought on the Roman roads.

The navigable rivers were used to some extent, but seldom for the movement of troops. In 1643 the Parliamentarian garrison of Gloucester went up the Severn in trows and took Tewkesbury; the Royalists used to send provisions from Oxford to Reading by barge; but on the whole the rivers seem to have been used as obstacles rather than lines of communication.

Sea transport was sometimes employed. Edward I's invasion of Wales has already been mentioned. Earlier the baronial party had tried to use it to cross the Severn in 1265, only to be foiled by Prince Edward. The Royalists shipped a small army from Minehead to Swansea in coal boats in 1642, but Warwick's navy was unable to save Essex's army hemmed in by King Charles at Lostwithiel in 1644.

TOWNS AND FORTRESSES

The position of a town, itself based upon geographical factors, is an example of the indirect way in which geography influenced warfare.

The special position of London requires consideration. Not only because it was the seat of government, but because of its wealth and manpower, it was an incalculable asset. As a port, a fortress, and a centre of communications, it was a valuable objective. In any civil war the possession of London was bound to be the chief aim of the two sides.

Bristol, too, was a desirable objective, the second city of the Kingdom in the days of which we write. Tactically it was not particularly strong, being somewhat overlooked, but strategically its control of the lower Severn was very significant, Its port, its wealth, its population added to its value and account for the two sieges of 1643 and 1645.

The possession of ports was particularly important in the Civil Wars. Newcastle, Portsmouth, Chester, Hull and Plymouth, to name but a few, all suffered at least one siege, though the last two, being provisioned and reinforced from time to time by the Navy, were able to hold out.

Inland towns, like Reading, at the junction of Thames and Kennet, and controlling the gap south of the Chilterns, derived a strategical importance from their position. Gloucester and Newark, at vital passages of Severn and Trent, were continually being besieged during the Civil Wars.

Lesser fortresses, castles and converted country houses, usually had some strategic purpose beyond the desire to hold down a particular district. Pontefract, for example, controlled the line of the Aire between the Pennines and the Humber. Basing, though no more than a converted sixteenth-century mansion, guarded the road from London to Salisbury and Winchester (A 30).

But despite its many walled towns, its castles and its rivers, England was a comparatively open country with few military obstacles. Moreover, in most districts an army a few thousand strong could live off the land.

The battlefields of England are to be found scattered wide across the whole country. No doubt the comparative ease with which armies could traverse the Kingdom is the explanation of this pattern.

The Battle of Hastings

THE CAMPAIGN

1066

5 January	*Death of Edward the Confessor.*
6 January	*Harold crowned King of England.*
May	*Tostig raids Kent and the Isle of Wight.*
8 September	*Harold's fleet leaves the Isle of Wight for London in order to revictual.*
20 September	*Battle of Fulford. Hardrada defeats Edwin and Morcar.*
25 September	*Harold wins the battle of Stamford Bridge. Hardrada and Tostig slain.*
28 September	*William of Normandy lands unopposed at Pevensey*
2 October	*Harold, at York, hears of William's landing.*
7-11 October	*Harold in London.*
13 October	*Harold camps on Caldbec Hill.*
14 October	*The Battle of Hastings.*
25 December	*William I crowned at Westminster.*

THE BATTLE

14 October, 1066

'Hic Harold: Rex: Interfectus: Est.'
THE BAYEUX TAPESTRY

ON THURSDAY 5 JANUARY, 1066, King Edward the Confessor lay dying in his palace of Westminster. Around him as his life ebbed slowly, the great officers of Church and State pondered the question of the succession, for their monk-like sovereign left no son, and his nearest heir, Edgar the Atheling, was a minor.

Among the watchers, confident of his own claim to the throne, stood the Confessor's brother-in-law Harold, son of Godwin, Earl of Wessex and the greatest subject in the Kingdom. He could trace descent through his Danish mother to the Scandinavian kings of England. He was head of a family which controlled almost the entire southern half of the country. Now about 44 years old, in his Welsh campaigns he had established a reputation for swift and audacious generalship. Surely he was the obvious successor. But he had the misfortune to have as his rivals two of the most formidable warriors in Europe, William, Duke of Normandy and Harold Hardrada, King of Norway.

According to Norman chroniclers, Edward the Confessor had formally promised the crown to William as early as 1051. Unlikely as this seems, it is true that the Confessor, who had been protected by William's family during the invasion of England by Canute of Denmark, had for many years appointed Normans to high office in the Church and in his household – much to the wrath of Harold's father Godwin. In 1064 Harold was shipwrecked on the coast of Ponthieu and fell into the hands of William. Though treated as a guest the Englishman was not permitted to return to England until, whether under duress or no, he had sworn an oath to further the Norman's interest so that he might one day wear the English crown.

Hardrada's claim, though he was a kinsman of the family of King Canute, and was supported by Harold's exiled brother Tostig, was only as good as his wild Vikings could make it.

Harold had one advantage over his rivals – he was the man 'on the spot'. The King died on 5 January, and at high mass on the following day, the Feast of the Epiphany, Harold was proclaimed by the Witan and crowned in Westminster Abbey.

Harold's reign of nine months was overshadowed by the double threat of Norwegian and Norman invasions. As soon as William heard the news of the coronation he gathered his nobles together at the castle of Lillebonne, on the Seine, and told them of his resolve to invade England before the end of the year. In return for 'knight service' the Duke promised any who would follow him a share of broad English acres. The project was greeted with enthusiasm for, although they refused in Council to commit the Duchy officially to what was in fact a predatory raid, most of the barons volunteered privately. William Fitz Osborn, who had already pledged 60 ships and their normal complement of soldiers, spoke on behalf of the barons. He declared that all present would follow William, bringing with them twice the numbers which they were bound by Norman feudal law to provide. The Duke's half-brothers, Odo, Bishop of Bayeux and Robert, Count of Mortain, promised 120 ships ; Robert of Montgomery and Roger of Beaumont each offered 60 ships. Many others, such as Remigius, Almoner of Fécamp Abbey, who was to become the first Bishop of Lincoln, said that they would prepare one ship for the great expedition. Blessed by the Pope, who sent a consecrated banner, practically the whole of Norman society was going to war ; not so much as a feudal levy but as a sort of mediaeval joint stock company, on a profit-sharing basis.

Through the spring and early summer shipwrights and sailmakers laboured to build the invasion fleet. Messengers rode far and wide in search of seamen and oarsmen to man the ships. Meanwhile many volunteers, the landless younger sons of the Norman and French nobility, enlisted in the Duke's army. Some of these adventurers had come from as far afield as southern Italy where Robert Guiscard and a small band of Normans were carving a kingdom for themselves. By September the armada was ready. The winds, however, were contrary, and the best that the fleet could do was to beat up the Channel from Dives, as far as St. Valéry-en-Caux, in the mouth of the Somme. There Duke William waited impatiently for a fair wind.

Against this array Harold could put into the field a very different army. In England land was not held for knight service but every thegn had an obligation to support his king in time of war. He did not have to bring an agreed number of correctly equipped and trained knights. He came himself mounted and well-armed, and he could be used either to fight with a body of thegns or as a commander of the fyrd. The fyrd, which was of Saxon origin, consisted of all able-bodied freemen, whose duty it was to muster in times of national crisis under the sheriff of their county.

The limitations of this force were numerous. The fyrd men were enthusiastic and effective enough when called on to protect their farms and fields against Viking raids, but they were reluctant to march far from home, especially at harvest time. Harold, there-fore, had come to rely upon the thegns who held land from the crown and also upon his house-carls. These were a body of profess-ional soldiers, never more than 2,000 in number, who were the 'mobile striking force' of the Kingdom. Each man went to war on his horse or pony, hence Harold's extraordinary mobility in this campaign, but, like the dragoons of later days, they dismounted to fight, forming the shield-ring and keeping the enemy out with their long Danish battle-axes. They were formidable foot soldiers in their old-fashioned way, but they fought without the support of archers or cavalry.

With the mixed forces at his disposal, it is not surprising that King Harold sought to avoid a pitched battle with the Normans. His plan was to defeat them where they were unable to use their mailed cavalry – at sea. He therefore gathered a fleet of perhaps 100 warships off the Isle of Wight and waited through the long summer weeks of 1066 for the first sight of Norman sails. He devised his own early warning system, sending spies into Nor-mandy to observe Duke William's preparations and to estimate his date of departure. English ships patrolled the Channel, while on high points in the south of England, such as Beachy Head and Bexhill, great beacons were prepared. Relays of messengers were posted so that the fyrd in the south and in London could be swiftly called together at prearranged rendezvous. If the Normans did land King Harold intended to defeat them on the beaches, perhaps before they could get their horses ashore.

Over-eagerness, a characteristic which had been manifested some years earlier in the swift impulsive marches of his Welsh winter campaigns, now marred Harold's preparations. He had mobilised too soon, and by 8 September his men had finished their provisions. His fleet set sail for London, and arrived a few days later, battered and damaged by the North winds that penned William in St. Valéry – though that prudent warrior had not run out of supplies. Convinced that the equinoctial gales had broken and that there would be no invasion that year Harold ordered his hungry fyrdmen to disperse and rode to London.

Twelve days later the winds that had battered Harold's fleet and delayed Duke William wafted Hardrada's 300 ships to the shores of Northumbria. The Norsemen cannot have numbered less than 6,000 men. Their commander, formed in the heroic mould, was six foot six inches tall, cunning and valiant, who had commanded the renowned Varangian Guard of Byzantium, had fought before the walls of Novgorod, and had won the sister of the King of Russia for his wife. After ravaging Cleveland and seizing Scarborough the Vikings defeated the northern fyrd under Edwin, Earl of Northumbria, and Morcar, Earl of Mercia, at Fulford outside York (20 September).

Harold reacted promptly. Riding up the Roman road at the head of his house-carls, perhaps 2,000 strong, and gathering the Midland levies as he went, he reached York at dawn on the 25th, and, pushing on with his usual eagerness, surprised the Norwegians in their camp seven miles away at Stamford Bridge. Hardrada's men knew nothing of his approach until through the morning mist they saw the English armour, 'like glistening ice'. Hastily they retreated across the Derwent and on the high ground beyond formed their shield-ring, a hollow circle of tightly packed men behind interlocked shields. To gain time one berserk Viking, however, defended the bridge, laying about him with his war axe. He held his own until one of Harold's men jumped into an old tub under the bridge, pushed himself out into the stream until he came directly beneath the Viking and slew him with one swift upward thrust of his stabbing spear. The English rushed across the bridge and hurled themselves on to the shield-ring. The fierce hand-to-hand struggle lasted for several hours and finished only when King Harold Hardrada had been killed under his famous banner the World Ravager. Tostig too was slain and 24 ships sufficed to carry away the survivors of the Norwegian army.

There was little time for those Saxon drinking bouts which usually followed a victory. On the second day of October King Harold learned that the winds in the Channel had changed and that during the night of 27 September the Norman fleet had crossed to England. 'Had I been there', he cried, 'they never had made good their landing.' Then bidding his house-carls and thegns to follow him, he rode furiously for London, covering 190 miles in six days and arriving on 6 October. In answer to his urgent summons the southern fyrd began to muster once more. The young Earl Waltheof marched into London at the head of the Huntingdon-shire, Nottinghamshire and Bedfordshire levies. Sheriff Godric rode in with the men of the Chiltern counties and the Thames Valley. Aelfwig, Abbot of Winchester, came himself with 12 monks to fight for his royal nephew, as did many a humbler subject.

Meanwhile Duke William had not moved far from his ships. His Norman caution had led him to spend his first fourteen days on English soil securing his bridgehead. He knew that one battle would decide the fate of the kingdom and preferred to fight it near his ships. After his first line of archers had waded ashore, bows at the ready, watching warily the silent woods beyond the pebble beaches, William had speedily disembarked his whole army. Workmen made strong entrenchments which were strengthened with pre-fabricated materials brought over in the invasion fleet. The ships were then dragged up on to the shore under the cover of these defensive works and their masts unstepped. These were pre-cautions against a surprise attack from the English fleet which had sailed from the Thames to harass Norman supply lines and perhaps cut off any attempted retreat. His ships secure, Duke William then moved his headquarters and army to Hastings. There a wooden motte-and-bailey castle was erected in the place of the fortifications which Harold had dismantled the previous year.

Such passive strategy did not appeal to King Harold. On 11

October he led his army out of London on the road to Hastings, some 60 miles away. He was joined by more shire levies, angered by the Norman raids into Sussex and Kent. By the evening of 13 October King Harold and his army had arrived six miles northwest of the Norman camp outside Hastings. Here they camped for the night within a few hundred yards of a ridge across the road where the great oak forest of Andredsweald broke into more open country.

This camp was not chosen at random; it effectively barred the way to London. It is true that there was a Roman road from Hastings to London by way of Bodiam and Maidstone. This route, however, was impracticable for an army unless the Brede estuary could be circumvented, and this could only be done by taking the prehistoric trackway to Caldbec Hill (where Harold was camped), crossing the Brede at Whatlington, and then regaining the Roman road. If this road was defended, for example, at Whatlington an army could still reach London from Caldbec Hill by way of Lewes. If Harold was to make certain of opposing a Norman march on London it could only be done by confronting them at this particular fork in the road. King Harold also chose Caldbec hill because it was the centre of a number of ancient paths and tracks. The Anglo-Saxon chronicle records that Harold met the Normans at 'the hoar apple tree'. This suggests that on this slight hill there was a well known landmark, a tree standing conspicuously in the open perhaps at the junction of several tracks of which some local record still survives. It was probably a time-honoured assembly point for the Sussex fyrdmen, like the blackthorn tree that had been Alfred's rendezvous before the battle of Ashdown (871).

King Harold also decided to camp on Caldbec Hill because it stood close to a good defensive position. A valley divides the forest plateau of Andredsweald and Caldbec Hill from the downs north of Hastings. The London road is carried across this shallow depression by a narrow neck of land, which falls sharply away on either side. Just south of what is now the site of Battle Abbey (275 ft) this dips to a height of 213 ft. On either side of the Abbey a cross ridge stretches for some 400 yards. Several streams flowed from this ridge, making the surrounding valleys marshy. The slopes were sufficiently short and steep to hinder cavalry charges.

12

To the rear several ravines and the dense forest made a mounted encirclement impossible. From every point of view this ridge astride the London road made an excellent position for Harold's foot soldiers.

Warned by his scouts of the arrival of the Saxons and fearing a night attack, William ordered his men to stand to their arms through the night. Soon after dawn on the 14th he led out his columns towards Harold's position, reaching Telham Hill at the head of his main body at about 7 o'clock. A knight named Vital, a vassal of Bishop Odo of Bayeux, rode back from the advanced guard and reported that he had sighted the Saxon army a mile away. Almost simultaneously, as the Bayeux Tapestry records, Harold's scouts also reported that the enemy were at hand. William halted his troops, and donned his coat of chain mail. It chanced that his servants almost pulled it on back to front, an ill omen to the superstitious, but the Duke passed off the incident with a jest, saying it signified that he would be changed that day from Duke to King.

THE NORMAN ARMY

It did not take long for William to array his army, which probably numbered no more than 8,000 or 9,000 men. Of these perhaps 3,000 were mailed knights and men-at-arms, mounted on heavy horses. The rest were foot, armed with bows, slings, javelins, short spears and swords. The archers had a short bow, which was drawn to the chest, not the ear. Still they could pierce a hauberk at 50 yards. The spearmen wore helmets, and mailed shirts.

The army was deployed in 'national' divisions. On the right Eustace of Boulogne and Robert of Montgomery commanded the French, Flemings and Picards.

The Duke himself commanded the centre: his Normans. There floated the papal gonfalon and the Leopard banner of Normandy. The leaders included the warlike Bishop Odo and Count William of Mortain, while the troop commanders numbered among them men like Roger le Bigod and William Malet, whose surnames were to be notable in English history.

On the left were drawn up the men of Brittany under Count Alan Fergeant. They were to receive many lands in Kent and south-east England for their work that day. Among them were the men of Coutances, under Neal of Saint-Saviour, whose rocky peninsula had been devastated by King Aethelred's sailors not many years before.

Although these men came from different parts of the Latin world they were familiar with the same ideas of warfare. The central feature of these tactics, whether fighting among themselves or later against the Saracens, was the shock charge of bodies of mailed cavalry. Foot soldiers were often used to make gaps in the enemy ranks prior to the decisive charge. William adhered to this well-tried tactical device at Hastings. He drew up each division in three lines – archers and slingers, spearmen and bodies of mounted knights and men-at-arms. The latter varied no doubt in size from squadrons of 150 to troops of 30, each grouped under the banneret of some greater or lesser lord. Duke William, astride the spirited stallion that King Alphonso of Spain had given him and armed with a heavy iron mace, stationed himself in the centre of the Norman cavalry, beneath his two banners. His main task as general was to unleash the cavalry at the right time. After this had been done he could only influence the outcome of the battle by building up some sort of reserve from troops who had already been committed.

THE SAXON ARMY

The Saxon array was much simpler, a wall, 1,000 yards long, of brightly painted yellow and red shields with the house-carls in the centre and the shire levies on the flanks. The great majority of Harold's men, who were probably rather more numerous than William's, were armed with axes, though there were a few bow-men, and some of the levies no doubt were armed with spears and scythes, or even clubs. A Norse poet tells us that King Harold was 'a little man' and 'sat proudly in his stirrups'. Now he fought like his men, dismounted, stationing himself in the centre of the shield

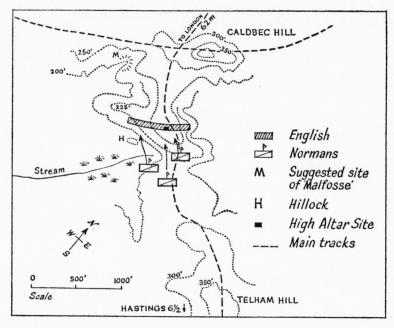

THE BATTLE OF HASTINGS, 1066

wall beneath the Golden Dragon of Wessex and his own banner, the Fighting Man. A few of his followers' names survive : Aefric of Gelling, a thegn of Huntingdon, and Bremea, a freeman who came in the retinue of Earl Gurth.

When the Normans were ready their columns began to march down Telham Hill, fanning out as soon as the ground permitted, and forming into battle array within about 500 yards of Harold's position. According to Wace, a late chronicler, the centre came up last and filled in the gap between the two wings. There was a halt ; and the two armies gazed upon each other and fell silent.

This silence was suddenly shattered by trumpets, horns and the hoarse shouts of the leaders. Then the invaders advanced. William's archers ran forward and sent their arrows uphill at the English. Some of the thegns and house-carls, who lined the front of the fyrd, took five or six arrows on their tough limewood shields. Most of the arrows hissed harmlessly over the heads of the rear ranks. As their quivers emptied the archers fell back to the safety of their own ranks. No breach appeared in the solid Saxon wall.

The fact that the English array still retained its order was not lost upon Duke William. No cavalry charge could be effective against that dense mass of men. The English casualties had been replaced from the rear ranks. William therefore ordered his spearmen to attack. They marched up towards the English until, at a range of 40 yards, they were suddenly met with a hail of ill-assorted missiles, ranging from arrows and axes to stones tied on throwing handles. At close quarters the angry Normans cut and thrust against the house-carls, who resisted valiantly 'each man according to his own strength'. The shouts of both sides were drowned by the clash and ring of weapons, like some mad blacksmith's shop, and the pitiful cries of the maimed and dying.

Immediately after the infantry attack many of the knights charged on to the ridge eager to close with the enemy. Disdaining to fight at long range they hurled their lances like javelins, and drew their swords. The uphill slope and the presence of their own infantry seriously reduced the impact of their charge, and their formations disintegrated as individual horsemen hacked and slashed at the Saxon line. Their mail shirts and conical helms gave them little protection against the keenly honed axe blades of the house-carls, which could kill man and horse at a single blow. The Bayeux Tapestry represents these axemen sheering off Norman limbs with their mighty strokes.

How long this hand-to-hand conflict lasted cannot be told, but after a hard struggle the Breton soldiers on the left, who had confidently advanced up the relatively gentle slope before them, began to waver. The ferocious violence and demeanour of the house-carls struck terror into their hearts, and panic blew like a wind through their ranks. As the Bretons ran away they scattered some of the cavalry which had been supporting them. The horses backed and reared, carrying their riders in confusion to the marshy bottom of the valley. Not a few Saxons, their blood up, charged out and hewed down the knights who were thrown from their horses.

And now the Norman infantry in the centre, realising that their left flank was exposed, began to fall back. The French and Flemings on the right hesitated. The cry 'The Duke is dead', was heard and men began to flee. In this crisis William spurred forward into the crowd. He pulled off his helmet and stood up in his stirrups so that all within hail could recognise him. In his harsh voice he shouted at them : 'Look at me well. I am still alive and by the grace of God I shall yet prove victor.' Threatening them with his mace William rode at his men. Fearing their terrible Duke more than the English the Normans turned and with a shout fell on the enemy once more. William, with Bishop Odo and Eustace of Boulogne, then led a squadron of cavalry against the Saxons who had rashly followed the retreating Bretons. Some of these heavily moustached English axemen are shown in the Bayeux Tapestry making a desperate stand on a small hillock which may still be identified with some probability (see Map). The Normans soon overcame their resistance. King Harold, in the centre of his unbroken 'shield-wall', looked on as the Duke's men struck down those who failed to regain the ridge. In disarray the thegns and fyrdmen were easy prey for the horsemen.

No doubt after this unnerving spectacle Harold shouted to his earls and sheriffs to keep their men closer together. Had he been able to ride up and down the line he might have been able to encourage his men, but in order to underline his resolve he had sent his horse to the rear with the rest. The Londoners, under Esegar the Staller, closed their ranks, and the whole English force prepared for the next bout.

William, his cavalry heartened by their easy and fortunate success, now signalled forward the main body of his host. Troop after troop, in close order, pounded up the corpse strewn slope and crashed into the English line. The English, so massed that the dead were held up by the living, received the charges without giving ground or allowing any fatal breach to open in their ranks. Once again the terrible din of battle echoed over the downs. But the aimed blow of the massed cavalry had failed to break the spine of the grim phalanx on the ridge. With cries of 'God help us !' the Normans pressed their way forward, to be met with roars of 'Out ! Out !' as knights leant from their saddles and hacked with their swords at the handles of the Saxon axes. Slowly the pressure of the horses forced gaps in the line of house-carls. The few remaining cavalry troops were hurled in to widen them. On the right wing Robert, son of Roger of Beaumont, in action for the first time, led up his troop with the utmost courage. But still, despite heavy casualties, the English presented an unbroken if irregular front.

On several occasions the Normans fell back, much to the encouragement of Harold's men, who, despite their earlier and bloody lesson, followed them with derisive shouts and insults. Some Norman chroniclers declared that these withdrawals were in fact feigned to draw the English from their position. More likely they were undertaken to allow the cavalry squadrons to rally under the pennons of their leaders. It is true that the strategem of a feigned flight was not unknown to the Normans, but it is hard to believe that in so desperate a battle Duke William, skilful though he was, could have controlled such a manoeuvre, particularly as many of his men had only been prevented with difficulty from fleeing in real earnest! One suspects that the Norman chroniclers invented the stratagem story to conceal the misconduct of some of their host. The few English who pursued were swiftly slain. Time after time, throughout the grey October afternoon, the Norman nobility urged their tired horses to renew the onslaught. As William of Poitiers wrote, 'This was a battle of a new type : one side vigorously attacking ; the other resisting as if rooted to the ground,' and 'The only movement was the dropping of the dead ; the living stood motionless.'

At last the severe emotional and physical strain of the day told upon the English. As twilight made faces indistinct and the cold of evening sapped their strength many of the fyrdmen slipped away into the forest. Almost imperceptibly the English shield-wall began to contract into a hollow ring around the royal standards. There was less shouting from the weary thegns. As one chronicler recorded, the movements of those who were severely wounded on the ground appeared greater than those who were still standing. King Harold, roaring his own battle cry 'Holy Rood, Holy Rood', fought on with his dwindling army. The Norman horsemen attacked inwards from the east and west ends of the ridge. They were now fighting not only against men but against time, for nightfall would cover a Saxon withdrawal. Then Harold, with fresh levies from Northumbria and Mercia, could fight another day.

Duke William bent every effort to break the house-carls and thegns who stood, loyal and immovable, beneath the Dragon of

Wessex. He himself had two horses killed under him. The Norman archers, who had replenished their quivers from supply waggons, once again appeared on the scene. Some began shooting high into the air ; others on a flat trajectory. The house-carls, preoccupied with hand-to-hand combat, could not adequately protect either themselves or the remaining fyrdmen by holding their shields aloft, and many fell. With shouts of 'God Almighty !' the Norman knights pressed home their attack, and Harold himself was slain, as the Bayeux Tapestry shows, by a sword cut. The tradition that he was struck in the eye by an arrow is strong, but is mentioned by no contemporary. The King's brothers, Gurth and Leofwine, had already been killed. The death of these leaders caused many more thegns to scatter. Those who remained fought on doggedly against those who had come to rob them of their manors and estates.

Most of the fugitives reached the safety of the forest. A handful, rallied by some nameless hero unwilling to admit defeat, made a stand behind a steep valley, intersected with ditches, which was known henceforth as the Malfosse. Many of the Norman knights, ignorant of the ground, and on tired horses came crashing to the ground. Eustace of Boulogne turned back with his troop of 50 knights. Seeing Duke William riding towards the ravine, he came up to him and begged him to withdraw. Hardly had Eustace spoken when he was dashed from his saddle by a blow in the back, so that blood gushed from his mouth and nose. William, however, attacked with such troops as had come so far, and in spite of the terrain, routed this improvised Saxon rearguard.

William then cantered back to the battlefield. Here, around the broken banners of King Harold, a scene of dismal carnage greeted him. Apart from the dying and the dead there were no Saxons left on the ridge. The Norman foot-soldiers were busy by the light of torches stripping and robbing the fallen. Next morning they were joined by relatives of the dead, who were allowed to bury the corpses before wolves of the Weald forest should devour them. The two brothers of the King were found, and then, near them, Harold himself who could only be identified by certain tattoo marks on his throat and right wrist. With crude humour the Normans buried him by the seashore which he had failed to defend.

Of the Saxon nobility only two are recorded as surviving : the sick and wounded Leofric, Abbot of Bourne, and Esegar the Staller, Sheriff of the Middle Saxons. Many thegns and house-carls, however, escaped abroad and took service as mercenaries in the Varangian Guard where they were destined to fight once more with their axes against Norman cavalry at the Battle of Dyrrachium (1081).

William of Poitiers would have us believe that the Norman victory at Hastings was due to the 'soldier-craft' of Duke William. There is little doubt that the Duke fulfilled most of the requirements of a successful mediaeval general : he had drawn up his army in divisions, and unleashed his cavalry at what he considered to be the right time. But King Harold's generalship had not been inferior. He had formed up his men on carefully selected ground, and inspired them to heroic resistance. Lacking cavalry and bowmen his tactics were severely limited.

The only English source which mentions the battle, the Anglo-Saxon Chronicle, states that Harold's army stood in disorder when the Normans attacked. This is the only hint at an English explanation for the disaster. From the Norman accounts it would appear that it was the tactical combination of archers, spearmen and cavalry which wore down the English shield wall. Above all the Norman bowmen eventually paved the way for their cavalry to break through.

Although London made some resistance Hastings was the end of all serious fighting. One stroke had decided the fate of the Kingdom. Harold, the impetuous strategist, had risked his crown and his obsolete army at one throw, and had lost. William, the skilful organiser and tactician, was still only 40 when on Christmas Day 1066 he was crowned, as perhaps the Confessor would have wished, in the new abbey at Westminster. This fierce, efficient, unfriendly man was to rule England for 21 years, planting his Normans everywhere in great place, and in the long run changing the whole course of English history.

A 'shield-ring' was formed by infantry standing almost shoulder to shoulder behind a wall of shields. By levelling their spears the foot soldiers could keep at bay even the most determined cavalry charges, provided that their close formation was not broken. It was introduced into England by the Danes and Vikings, and among its direct descendants in British military history are the Scots spear phalanxes at Bannockburn and the redcoat infantry squares of Waterloo.

The warriors armed with the long, two-handed axes, shown in the Bayeux Tapestry and figuring so largely in Norman accounts were not the whole of the English infantry. They were supported by a number of spearmen and a small proportion of slingers and archers. The front of the English shield-wall was probably formed of axemen and spearmen in more or less equal numbers. The fact is that the axemen seemed to have impressed the Normans, perhaps because they were a novelty!

1066-1264

The civil wars of the reigns of Stephen and John, the Welsh wars of Henry II and Prince Edward (1255-1257), and the Scots invasion of 1173-1174, when William the Lion became Henry II's prisoner, offer us no major battles, although the Battle of the Standard (1138) described below certainly merits our attention.

MILITARY ORGANISATION

The Norman conquest supplemented the old fyrd with the feudal levy. The former was still employed in times of national emergency. Scutage, (from the Latin *scutum*, a shield) the practice of compounding for military service by money payments, steadily grew, and was favoured by the Plantagenets, who used the money to hire mercenaries. By feudal law a man only had to serve for 40 days, but a mercenary would serve as long as the pay lasted. Since a campaign might be expected to last much more than 40 days, the advantages of scutage are obvious.

In the field, armies were usually divided into three divisions or 'battles': the vaward, centre and rearward.

CAVALRY

Cavalry dominated the battlefield. Throughout the period their arms and armour were becoming heavier. A great helmet now covered the whole face (Plate 2 (a)). They carried a longer, stouter lance.

INFANTRY

The Danish axe was still used, but spears were more common. Archery was gaining ground; the crossbow was used by mercenaries, townsmen and castle guards, and the long bow, which seems to have originated in Wales, was employed early in the twelfth century.

CASTLES

The rapid improvements in castle-building had a great influence on strategy; sieges became as important as battles and far more frequent. A demand for skilled pioneers was created.

Not all the developments outlined above made their appearance felt on every field of battle, for sometimes local circumstances dictated otherwise. At the Battle of the Standard, for example, where the task of resisting a Scottish invasion fell chiefly to the Yorkshire fyrd, most of the available mailed knights had to be deployed on foot to stiffen the line—tactics reminiscent of Hastings. In order to understand the battle it is necessary to review briefly the events which led up to it.

The reign of King David of Scotland (1124-53) was spent in attempting to unite his country under one strong head. But in addition to Scotland he was able to lay claims to Northumbria through his wife's father Waltheof, Cumbria through her grandfather Siward, and also the Earldom of Northampton and Huntingdon granted to her first husband Simon de Senlis.

The Scottish King took advantage of the chaos in England during the reign of Stephen to further his English claims, first siding with Matilda's party, but eventually signing an agreement with Stephen in 1136 that David's son Prince Henry (who died in 1152) should be recognised as the Earl of Huntingdon ; that he should take possession of the castles of Doncaster and Carlisle ; and that Henry's claim to Northumberland should be preferred to that of Simon de Senlis's son.

This mere 'preference' soon appeared an insufficient guarantee to the Scottish King, and to force the English into making the arrangement more certain he invaded England in 1138. As his army moved south it harried the countryside of Northumberland and Durham, but the civil turmoil in England prevented a royal army from being sent against it.

As a result the force which eventually took the field consisted mainly of the Yorkshire feudal levy under the command of Walter L'Espec, Sheriff of Yorkshire and William of Albemarle, together with a few mailed knights from the south, Derbyshire and Nottinghamshire. With them came the Bishop of Orkney, sent by Thurstan, Archbishop of York, who had been preaching a Holy War against the invading Scots.

The Scottish army consisted of Highlanders and Galloway men organised by clan, English-speaking men from the Eastern lowlands, and a small contingent of knights from exiled English families now living in Scotland.

The armies met on 22 August on a small ridge some three miles to the north of Northallerton in North Yorkshire. The English were arrayed in one deep line with the knights, all dismounted, forming an armoured front line behind which the half-armed men of the shire levy gathered. With them was a small body of archers who appear to have been mingled with the levy, and not formed into a unit of their own. In the centre of this line stood the English standard, symbol of the Holy War, a huge pole fixed onto a four-wheeled cart, with a pyx and consecrated wafer at its top. From four cross-pieces high on this mast hung the banners of the Yorkshire saints – St. Peter of York, St. John of Beverley, and St. Wilfred of Ripon – together with the banner of St. Cuthbert of Durham.

At first the Scots were ordered to form a similar deep line with the knights and archers in the front line and the foot massed behind them ready to pour through any breaches made in the English line. However this plan had to be altered because of the martial pride of the clansmen : the Highlanders refused to go into battle behind the English knights, and the Galloway men asserted their ancient right to lead the army into battle. After a bitter argument between Alan Percy, one of the knights, and the Earl of Strathearn, the King was forced to alter the Scottish formation.

At the front came the Galloway men with, a little behind and to their left, Lothian and the English knights with the men of Lorn, Argyle and the Hebrides. Prince Henry with the mounted knights, the Eastern Lowlanders and the men of Strathclyde formed the right wing behind Galloway while in the rear stood King David with a small bodyguard of mailed knights and the men of Moray and the East Highlands.

As was usual, offers of peace were made, and Robert Bruce, a Yorkshire baron, was sent to the Scottish line to ask David if he would consent to terms. He was sent back with the cries of 'traitor' in his ears, for he also held the Earldom of Annandale in Scotland.

The battle began with a furious foot charge by the Galloway

men, yelling their war cry 'Albanach!' as they threw their light spears and rushed to the English line. With their claymores they beat against the Yorkshire shield wall which reeled and was shaken under the onslaught but held firm and slowly pushed back the clansmen. As they retired to re-form the English archers fired at them over the heads of the fyrd-men. A second and third charge brought similar results, and the first phase of the battle became a frantic hand to hand fight along the English line until Prince Henry on the Scottish right made his move.

He had scarcely more than sixty horsemen, the rest of his wing being on foot, but with these he charged the English left, cutting a passage right through the English line until he could see the grooms in the rear holding the English horses. Thinking that the rest of his men would exploit the breach he had made, he led the cavalry to capture the horses, but behind him the shire levy had managed to close up the hole in their line in the face of the Strathclyde men, and the bitter mêlée continued.

The Strathclyde soldiers were gradually pushed back and, seeing this, and with their leaders Donald and Ulgerich dead, the Galloway men began to disperse. On the Scottish left Lothian and Lorn, who might have yet rallied the Scots centre, made one half-hearted charge, but after their repulse drifted from the field. David was forced to commit his Highland reserve in a final attempt to break the English line. All along the Scottish line men were slipping away from the battle, and seeing this the reserve melted away during the advance, leaving the King with only his body-guard of mailed knights. To continue the attack would have been futile, so David withdrew to a nearby hill where the remnants of his army eventually gathered around him before withdrawing.

Prince Henry, now cut off from the rest of the army and still in the English rear, had realised that the Scottish attacks had been beaten off. Ordering his men to throw off their distinguishing badges, his horsemen moved forward with the English who had begun to advance.

The re-forming Scots were too large in number to be attacked by the English, who merely followed them as they retreated, killing or taking prisoner any stragglers they found. With them went the unrecognised Scottish knights. Drawing away from them under the pretext of harrassing the Scots, Prince Henry and his men eventually escaped and rejoined the main body by a circuitous route three days later.

This defeat was also the end of the campaign, but despite this complete failure in battle David still managed to come to a settlement with Stephen (perhaps as an assurance of no further Scottish invasions) whereby Henry's claim to the Earldom of Northumbria was recognised. In effect, Scotland's boundary in the south east now came to the Tees, as by the 1136 agreement its south western border had been fixed at Carlisle and the River Eden.

These gains, however, were only temporary. In 1157 during the reign of Henry II much of the land was recovered. The Scottish King Malcolm IV was left only with the Earldom of Huntingdon while his brother William was granted the Liberty of Tynedale.

The Battle of Lewes

THE CAMPAIGN

1264

23 *January*   *The Mise of Amiens.*

5 *April*   *The capture of Northampton. Leicester and Nottingham surrender to Prince Edward shortly afterwards.*

18-26 *April*   *Siege of Rochester Castle.*

1 *May*   *Capture of Tonbridge Castle.*

14 *May*   *The Battle of Lewes.*

THE BATTLE

14 May, 1264

A BROKEN LEG prevented Simon de Montfort, Earl of Leicester, from attending the Mise of Amiens in January 1264. Had he been there he would have heard King Louis IX of France annul the Provisions of Oxford, the system of baronial control saddled on King Henry III in 1258. Even the royalist chronicler, Thomas Wykes, thought that the French King had 'acted with less wisdom and foresight than was necessary', for he gave the Earl the choice of either breaking his oath to maintain the Provisions or fighting to enforce them. Simon chose to fight.

By 1264 traditional loyalty to the crown and respect for legality had already induced certain barons and knights to desert Earl Simon's party, though it has been calculated that six earls and 59 barons still supported him. The King, on the other hand, could rely upon six earls and some 50 of the remaining 102 barons.

It is thought that there were as many as 12,000 knights in the country, though the names of only some 400 survive, of whom only a quarter are known to have been royalist. It is likely that Simon drew much of his backing from the lesser gentry. The citizens of London, alienated by King Henry's misrule, also favoured the baronial cause, but their military value was not remarkable. Indeed deliberate efforts had been made to prevent their training, and on one occasion Henry's courtiers had dispersed a drill session, saying the practice of arms was 'not fit for bran dealers, soap-boilers and clowns'. Nevertheless in 1264 Earl Simon controlled rather more of the military resources of England than did the King.

Both leaders spent the spring preparing for war. On 12 March, some Scots barons who held lands in England rode into the royal camp at Woodstock near Oxford. The King had taken the precaution of dispersing the students of the University in order that they might be out of the great danger of meeting the chieftains – many of whom were fierce and untame. On Passion Sunday, 5 April, the King's eldest son, Prince Edward, struck the first blow by capturing Northampton from the barons. The prisoners included Earl Simon's son, known as Simon the Younger, a kinsman Peter de Montfort, 15 barons and bannerets. A gallant band of Oxford scholars, who had fought with bows, slings and crossbows under their own banner, also became prisoners. It is said probably with truth, that their missiles did more damage to Prince Edward's men than all the rest of the baronial garrison put together. Leicester and Nottingham, which lacked such learned reinforcements, now surrendered without a blow.

What of Simon de Montfort? In April he had concentrated his forces at St. Albans, intending to support his strongholds in the Midlands. After the fall of Nottingham the Earl decided to retaliate by taking Rochester, the one royal castle near London. Before the walls of the Medway town he met Gilbert de Clare, the 21 year old Earl of Gloucester, and together they began the siege.

On Good Friday, 18 April, baronial men-at-arms burnt down a fortified bridge, using a fireboat loaded with blazing pitch, coals, sulphur and pork fat. They fought their way into the streets of the town and began plundering. For instance, some stole gold and silver plate from St. Andrew's Church while others stabled their war horses in the nave. The two Earls reassembled their men and by the evening of 19 April the outer bailey of the Norman castle had been occupied, but both sides abstained from fighting on Easter Sunday. John de Warenne, Earl of Surrey, and the royalist garrison defeated each assault upon the massive masonry of the Norman keep. Hearing that King Henry threatened London from the north, Earl Simon raised the siege on 26 April, and fell back towards the capital.

In fact the King had only sent forward a squadron of cavalry under Prince Edward to reconnoitre the city walls. Meanwhile he out-flanked London and came to Rochester. His soldiers easily drove off Earl Simon's blockading forces, and cruelly maimed those unfortunate enough to be taken prisoner. Instead of occupying London the King then moved to the West, capturing Gloucester's castle at Tonbridge on 1 May. Leaving behind a strong garrison of 20 bannerets and some foreign mercenaries, the King moved to Winchelsea and Romney. The royalists may have intended sailing up the Thames to London in the fleet of the Cinque ports. They found, however, that on the Earl's orders every ship had put to sea.

King Henry therefore continued his march westwards. As the royalists straggled out on the trackways of the Weald, they were harried by Welsh archers in the service of Earl Simon who shot at them from the cover of woods and copses. The King's army at length halted at Lewes, a town belonging to John de Warenne. Simon de Montfort, who had marched from London in pursuit of the royalist field army, camped at Fletching, a village in the Weald forest eight miles north of Lewes. From here he sent three bishops with his peace terms to the King. With the King's angry reply Prince Edward and his uncle, Richard, Earl of Cornwall, sent their own accusations to the 'perfidious traitors'. A battle had become almost unavoidable.

The town of Lewes stands in the South Downs on the west bank of the River Ouse. The stout walls of the Cluniac priory of St. Pancras and tidal mudflats protected the southern end of the town. Warenne's castle, built on two mounds and enclosed in a strong curtain wall, stood sentinel on the northern approaches. The downs, a mile or more away, yielded to open grazing fields on the west side of the town. On this side the town lay exposed and vulnerable.

On the evening of 13 May Earl Simon knighted Gilbert, Earl of Gloucester, surnamed *Rufus*, Robert de Vere, the 23 year old Earl of Oxford, and many of his young barons and knights. Long before dawn the next day, after absolution from the Bishop of Worcester, the baronial army began its march towards Lewes, nine miles away. At Offham (see Map) Earl Simon turned off the road and led his army up a steep track on the side of the Combe valley. Soon he arrived on the broad heights of Offham Hill. Among the gorse bushes a solitary royalist scout lay asleep, wrapped up in his cloak against the morning dew, deserted by his fellows, who had endured 48 hours without food or wine. Simon's men prodded him awake and listened to his pleas for quarter, but John of Oxenede, who tells the tale, does not relate whether he obtained it or not.

THE BARONIAL ARMY

The army resumed its march in high spirits until the Bell Tower of the priory came into view. On a suitably level stretch of ground the army halted, and the baronial leaders formed their divisions. No accurate estimate of numbers survives, but it is unlikely that there were more than 5,000 with Earl Simon, including perhaps 600 mailed horsemen. The paucity of cavalry can be explained by the fact that many of the Earl's most trusted commanders and their retainers had been taken prisoner. Besides those surprised at Northampton, William Bardolf had surrendered at Nottingham and the Earl of Derby had been captured in his castle of Tutbury.

Earl Simon divided his army into four divisions, three in line and one in reserve. Considering the smallness of his forces, this creation of a reserve deserves special notice. The names of the leading men in the other three divisions can be given.

Left	Centre	Right
Sir Henry de Hastings	Gilbert, Earl of	Henry de Montfort (Simon's
Sir John Giffard	Gloucester	eldest son)
Sir Henry de Borham	Lord John Fitzjohn	Guy de Montfort (Simon's
Sir Nicholas de	Lord William de	third son)
Segrave	Montchensey	Humphrey de Bohun (eldest
		son of Earl of Hereford)
		John de Burgh

Legend has it that Simon had so few commanders with him that he had to array the soldiers himself. The above list hardly supports this tale. Many of the nobles were experienced soldiers. Sir Nicholas de Segrave, who commanded the main body of Londoners, had escaped from Northampton and fought at the siege of Rochester. Henry de Hastings had served in two Welsh campaigns. The Montfort brothers were seasoned warriors. For troop commanders Earl Simon could rely upon many veterans of the Gascony wars, such as John de Vescie. Both Robert de Ros and John Giffard had fought in Wales. Other bannerets had returned from the Crusades. Hugh Neville, the chief forester, who commanded a troop at Lewes, had soldiered in the Holy Land, as indeed had Earl Simon himself with distinction in 1245.

In his reserve Simon de Montfort placed a force of Londoners, under the command of an alderman of the city, Thomas de Pevelsdon. He also appointed Sir William le Blound and a handful of soldiers to stand guard over the baggage waggons, which were probably left near Offham village. The carriage which Earl Simon had used while his leg mended stood among the waggons. In it three recalcitrant Londoners, Augustine de Hadestock, Richard Pycard and Stephen de Chelmaresford, were locked for safe keeping.

THE ROYALIST ARMY

His preparations completed, Simon resumed his advance towards Lewes, which was now less than two miles away. Some grooms, who had taken their masters' horses out early into the fields to graze, had already sighted the Earl's columns and raised the alarm in Lewes. Royalist soldiers rushed out of their lodgings into the streets, buckling on their armour. Each man already knew which division he would serve in during the battle, and this, to some extent, lessened the confusion. The whole army, perhaps 9,000 strong, put itself into array in the fields west of Lewes facing the baronial forces. The right wing stood near the castle, and the other two divisions took up positions in line with it. The King's main commanders were men of high rank:

Left	Centre	Right
Richard, Earl of Cornwall and King of the Romans	King Henry III	Prince Edward
	Robert de Bruce, Lord of Annandale	William de Valence
		John de Warenne, Earl of Surrey
Edmund of Almain, his son	John Baliol, Lord of Galloway	Hugh Bigod, the Justiciar
Humphrey de Bohun, Earl of Hereford	John Comyn	Henry of Almain, son of Richard of Cornwall
	John Fitzalan	
	Henry de Percy	

The King had detached many troops for garrison duties at captured castles such as Tonbridge. Even so he had enough men to form a reserve had he wished for one. His army included 1,500 mailed knights. The Bishop of Durham alone had sent 83 mounted tenants to the royal host. Henry also had with him a select band of Picardian crossbowmen, his personal bodyguard, numbering perhaps 20 men in all.

There were no preliminary skirmishes. The royalists had advanced no more than 300 yards from Lewes when Earl Simon ordered his front three divisions to charge. As it would have been fatal to receive a shock cavalry charge standing still, the royalist leaders shouted at their own men to gallop. Both sides met with a mighty crash. At once the carefully arrayed lines of knights, riding stirrup to stirrup, splintered, and the battle developed into a multitude of noisy duels.

The baronial left contained fewer cavalry and the lightly armed London infantry offered little resistance to Prince Edward's charge. Some of their leaders fought hard. John Giffard was taken prisoner, but Henry de Hastings turned his rein too soon for the good of his reputation. Meanwhile the Londoners scattered. Some headed northwards and attempted to cross the river, others scrambled up the slopes of the downs, seeking refuge in steep and

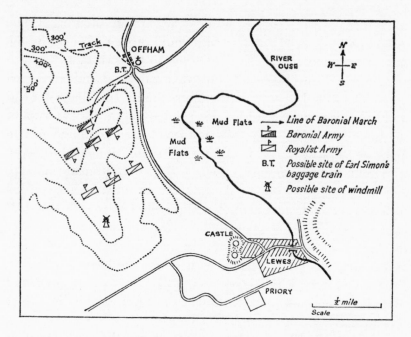

THE BATTLE OF LEWES, 1264

wooded places where no cavalry could follow. But Prince Edward pressed the pursuit. Had not the Londoners recently insulted his mother the Queen, pelting her barge with mud and stones as she passed under the city bridges on her way to Windsor? No wonder Prince Edward, as one chronicler recorded, 'thirsted after their blood as the hart pants for cooling streams'. Death to the Londoners!

The Prince's lieutenants included his unpopular Poitevin relatives, Guy de Lusignan and William de Valence. Young Henry of Almain had changed sides some months before the battle, and no doubt Earl Simon's contemptuous words to him lingered in his mind: 'Go and return home with your arms, I do not fear them.' Now Henry's sword flashed among the fleeing Londoners of Earl Simon's left wing. Sixty Londoners drowned in the Ouse, and William de Say cut down others as far afield as Croydon.

Seeing a carriage in the waggon park and believing Simon de Montfort to be in it, Prince Edward led his knights towards it in the hope of taking or killing the Earl. Sir William le Blound lost his life defending the baggage train. After his men had been overcome men-at-arms crowded around the carriage shouting 'Come out, Simon you devil!' Before they could prove their identity the three Londoners in the coach were put to the sword.

While Prince Edward hunted down the Londoners Earl Simon had won the battle. In the centre the Earl of Gloucester had fought his way to the great Dragon standard of the King, no doubt the same which the royal goldsmith had been commissioned to make in 1244, with the dragon 'of red samit, to be embroidered with gold, and his tongue to appear as though continually moving, and his eyes of sapphire'. Around the banner knights battled furiously, often against their own kinsmen. 'Oh, wretched sight!' lamented William of Rishanger, 'when the son strives to overpower the father and the father the son: kinsman against kinsman, fellow citizen against fellow citizen, with their swords brandished on either side, drunk with the gore of the slain, felling, maiming, and trampling their foes under the horses' feet or binding their prisoners alive in straightest bonds.'

Eventually Bruce, Comyn and Baliol threw down their swords. King Henry, who had two chargers killed under him, retired to St. Pancras priory, escorted by his household knights. The last to leave the field, although gashed with twenty wounds, was Philip Basset.

On the royalist left Richard of Cornwall, who on account of his exalted continental titles was regarded with some amusement by the barons, had taken refuge in a windmill with a few of his followers. 'Come out, you bad miller,' mocked Simon's men as they hacked at the thick timbers. 'You forsooth to turn a wretched mill master – you who defied us so proudly and would have no meaner title than "King of the Romans" and always "August".' At length Richard surrendered to a squire, John Beavs, who was later made a knight by Earl Simon for his services that day.

Most of the King's men fled into the houses and streets of Lewes or found shelter in the castle or priory. From the left division, however, some rode south across the brown mud near the Ouse. Next day, the ebbing tide revealed scores of corpses, stuck fast in the slime, many still astride their horses.

When at last Prince Edward and his cavalry returned to the field, they were in time to witness the rout of the main royalist forces. The 24 year old Prince attempted in vain to prepare his men for a charge against the baronial infantry who were trying to batter down the gates of Lewes Castle. To his right he could also see some of the enemy shooting blazing arrows, 'spryngelles of fyre', against the wooden outhouses of the priory. Before he could attack, however, Earl Simon sallied out of the town with a force of cavalry, presumably from his reserve division. Although Prince Edward wished to renew the fight, the other commanders had no stomach for it. The Poitevins, Surrey and Bigod, with 500 men, turned their reins and rode off. The Prince with his personal following fought his way through to the priory and joined his father. As a long defence of the priory was impossible the King sued for peace. The next day he sealed a treaty with Earl Simon which is known to history as 'The Mise of Lewes'.

The Abbot of St. Pancras estimated the dead at 2,700 and there is no need to question this figure. One seldom meets with such precision in mediaeval authorities. In 1810, three burial pits near the modern prison were opened, and 1,500 skeletons unearthed. Yet very few of the leaders were slain. The royalists lost only William de Wilton in the battle and Fulk Fitzwarren drowned in the marshes. On the baronial side only the Kentish banneret Ralf Heringot and Sir William le Blound died. Financially a dead noble had no value but a prisoner could earn his captor a large ransom. The profit motive and the high quality of plate helmets and mail armour at this time accounts for the lack of bloodshed.

In the months after Lewes bitter quarrels broke out among Earl Simon's leading supporters over the question of ransoms. For example, on the baronial left flank at the battle John Giffard and William de Maltravers had captured the royalists, Reginald Fitzpiers and Alain de la Zouch. Giffard himself had then fallen prisoner after the collapse of the Londoners, and his two prisoners escaped. Fitzpiers fought for the rest of the day with his own sword before yielding it a second time, and de la Zouch, in a monk's cowl, was taken in the priory. When unknown knights received these two royalists' ransoms Giffard and Maltravers deserted Earl Simon's cause.

The factors which led to Earl Simon's victory on the field are not hard to identify. He showed himself to be a competent general by mediaeval standards : he divided his army into divisions and made good use of the ground ; he launched his mailed cavalry like a well-flung lance when a suitable target presented itself. Two unusual elements which Earl Simon introduced into the campaign – a night march to surprise the enemy and the formation of a reserve – may have derived from the Earl's crusading experience in Palestine. Lastly Simon fulfilled the central requirement of a mediaeval military leader by fighting personally in the battle with great valour.

On the royalist side the main cause of defeat may have been divided command. Prince Edward's relations with his father had not been good, and his impetuous charge might indicate a failure to understand or agree with the King's plan. The King had a reputation for simplicity of mind, and if he had insisted upon commanding the army such prominent English earls as Surrey and Hereford may have decided to go their own way. The problem of controlling in council or on the battlefield such headstrong adventurers as the Poitevin half-brothers or the Scottish chieftains may well have been beyond King Henry, who was placed by Dante among the inactive in his Purgatory. Possibly Prince Edward, his advice ignored in council, attempted to vindicate himself by reckless gallantry. This, however, is only conjecture.

The Battle of Evesham

THE CAMPAIGN

1265

January	Simon de Montfort summons shire knights and burgesses to Parliament. Pevensey Castle held successfully by royalists. Gilbert de Clare, Earl of Gloucester, abandons Simon's cause.
28 May	Prince Edward escapes from Hereford. Prince Edward and Gloucester meet at Ludlow to plan campaign.
June	Royalist troops march down Severn Valley, burning bridges and dredging fords, intending to prevent Earl Simon marching from Hereford to join forces with his sons at Kenilworth. Gloucester, the last crossing over the Severn, falls to Prince Edward.
9 June	Prince Llewellyn of Wales promises Earl Simon 5,000 spearmen in exchange for grants of border lands. Earl Simon's attempt to cross Wye at Monmouth repulsed by John Giffard. Earl Simon marches south to Newport. Three royalist war galleys destroy eleven transport ships in Newport harbour. Prince Edward's army besieges Newport. Earl Simon returns to Hereford.
14-30 July	Earl Simon attempts to cross Severn unsuccessfully.
1 August	Prince Edward's raid on Kenilworth.
4 August	Battle of Evesham.

THE BATTLE

4 August, 1265

'Such was the murder of Evesham, for battle it was none'

ADVERSITY IS OFTEN kind to the defeated. In the year following Lewes King Henry's supporters drew closer together. While Earl Simon, in an attempt to consolidate his position in the country, summoned for the first time shire knights and burgesses to parliament (January 1265), royalists in France under Queen Eleanor prepared for an invasion. The castle of Pevensey, constructed within old Roman walls, resisted all Earl Simon's siege operations. In the west a friend of the King, Roger Mortimer, kept the Welsh Marches in disorder. In December, a young Marcher lord named Warin de Bassingbourn stormed Wallingford Castle in a vain attempt to rescue Prince Edward who was held there as hostage by Earl Simon. Early in 1265 far worse news reached de Montfort. Ransom quarrels and the overwhelming pride of Earl Simon's four sons had gradually alienated one of the chief supporters of the baronial party. Gilbert de Clare, the young Earl of Gloucester, had changed sides.

Events now began to move swiftly. On 28 May Prince Edward, who had been taken to Hereford, escaped by a stratagem and rode hard to Mortimer's castle at Wigmore, twenty miles away. Soon afterwards he met Gilbert de Clare at Ludlow, and they agreed to restore the King to his sovereign power. The gentry of Shropshire and Cheshire at once responded to their call to arms. Prince Edward, 26 years of age, took command of the new army, and demonstrated for the first time his skill as a strategist.

Earl Simon remained at Hereford, and so Prince Edward resolved to cut him off from his great castle of Kenilworth and the forces of Simon the Younger. He marched along the east bank of the Severn burning bridges and boats, dredging fords deeper. Simon de Montfort sent Robert de Ros with 300 men to hold Gloucester, the last crossing over the Severn before the estuary, but at the end of June the town had fallen to Prince Edward.

On 10 June Earl Simon left Hereford in order to meet an ally, Prince Llewellyn of Wales. At Pipton, near Hay, the Prince promised Earl Simon 5,000 Welsh spearmen and he undertook to raid the estates of Mortimer and de Clare. In return it was agreed that he should receive lands and castles from the royalist lords of the Welsh March. De Montfort then attempted to ferry his army over the Wye at Monmouth but the traitor John Giffard and his men-at-arms repulsed him. The Earl marched south to Newport in order to ship his army across the Bristol Channel. Unfortunately for him Prince Edward sent three war galleys from Gloucester which sailed boldly into Newport harbour and captured or sank eleven of the merchant ships which Bristol had supplied to de Montfort. Almost simultaneously Prince Edward's army arrived at Newport and drove Simon's troops within the town walls. Simon returned to Hereford, keeping the river Usk between him and the pursuing royalist army. His soldiers complained bitterly of the milk and mutton rations, the only provender which the desolate Welsh countryside could offer. Twice in the last week in July de Montfort tried to cross the Severn. On both occasions Prince Edward, who had marched swiftly back to Worcester, opposed the passage.

On 31 July Prince Edward decided upon a hazardous night march. Perhaps he had learned the value of surprise from Earl Simon at Lewes. He planned to ride with his cavalry to Kenilworth and fall upon the reinforcements which Simon's sons had gathered outside the castle walls. A woman spy called Margot, disguised in a man's clothes, had reported the arrival of Simon the Younger at the castle. His march from Pevensey, where he had been in command of the siege, had been delayed by a massacre of Jews in Winchester. Young Simon's army now threatened to encircle the Prince at Worcester.

The risks of such a night march made Prince Edward hesitate. The results of the rash pursuit at Lewes no doubt haunted him. The royalist chronicler, Thomas Wykes, records that the Prince spent a 'sleepless night' before agreeing to withdraw his soldiers from the river line and concentrate them against Kenilworth. Some years later Sir William de Vesci told Sir John Fitz-Thomas that

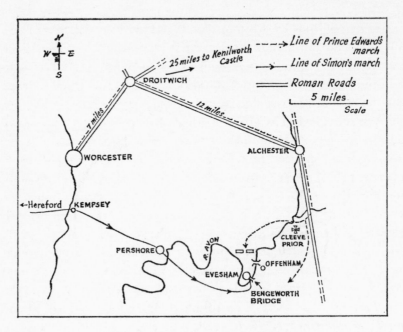

THE CAMPAIGN OF EVESHAM

late in the evening of 31 July Prince Edward expressed his concern that he would take all the blame if the raid miscarried. Sir Roger de Clifford remonstrated with him for holding back. "Indeed," said Sir Roger, "you will reap more shame and blame for this matter and this business than the rest of England." And then said Sir Roger, "However it be, we will go on," and he said, "Banners forward!" And he rode ahead, and the King (Prince Edward) could not but go on for shame, and they carried it out well.'

The dawn attack not only proved an outstanding tactical success, it also decided the outcome of the Civil War. Many baronial soldiers were killed in their night shirts, and although Simon the Younger saved himself by rowing across the moat to the castle he took little further part in the Evesham campaign. Riding captured horses the royalists returned to Worcester on 2 August, having covered 68 miles and fought a sharp engagement in two days.

On that day, unaware of the disaster which had overtaken his son, Earl Simon ferried his army over the Severn at Kempsey, four miles south of Worcester. Apparently he planned to join his son

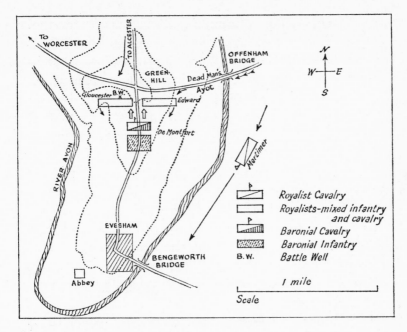

Royalist Cavalry
Royalists-mixed infantry and cavalry
Baronial Cavalry
Baronial Infantry
B.W.   Battle Well

1 mile

Scale

THE BATTLE OF EVESHAM, 1265

at Kenilworth going by way of Pershore. On 3 August he finished the day's march at the small town of Evesham, which lay almost enclosed in a loop of the River Avon. From there the Earl had a choice of two roads from Evesham to Kenilworth. That night Simon and King Henry, who had been compelled to accompany the army for political reasons, slept in the guest rooms of Evesham Abbey.

On the evening of 3 August Prince Edward led his army out of Worcester along the Roman road to Droitwich seven miles away. At the town he turned south-east and reached Alcester some time during the night. He then marched south on the Roman road for five miles before crossing the River Avon with his main forces west of Cleeve Prior. This brought him to the Evesham-Alcester track which Earl Simon could have followed to Kenilworth. The Prince and Gloucester marched with their men towards Green Hill while Mortimer, who had been detached at Cleeve Prior, rode with a cavalry force to cut off Earl Simon's escape route over Bengeworth Bridge. The baronial army had been caught in a trap.

The first enemy which Earl Simon's scouts reported were

Mortimer's troops. For some minutes the baronial leaders thought that Simon the Younger had arrived at last, for the royalist army carried at their head some thirteen standards captured at Kenilworth. According to tradition Simon's keen-sighted barber ascended the Abbey tower and detected the blue and white banner of Mortimer. 'We are all dead men,' he shouted down to the Earl, 'for it is not your son who comes as you thought, but the King's son, the Earl of Gloucester and Roger Mortimer.' Earl Simon at once realised his plight. 'Let us commend our souls to God,' he said, 'because our bodies are theirs.'

As Mortimer completed his flank march, Earl Simon formed his small army into a single column, shaped like a battering ram. For a steel tip he arrayed a line of 100 mailed knights on heavy chargers; the wooden beam consisted mainly of Prince Llewellyn's Welsh spearmen. In all he had perhaps 350 cavalry and 5,000 foot soldiers.

The Prince and Gloucester had already assembled their columns on Green Hill into two long divisions facing Evesham. The royalist army consisted predominantly of cavalry. The Prince had with him over 1,000 mailed horsemen, and perhaps 7,000 infantry. The Chronicle of Mailros gives the royalist superiority as seven to two. This probably refers to mailed horsemen. Neither side employed longbowmen, although the Assize of Arms (1252) had recognised the bow as a national weapon. Slingers and crossbowmen had fought at Lewes, however, and no doubt many were present at Evesham. 'By the arm of St. James,' Earl Simon said, as he watched the royalist divisions advance, 'they approach wisely, and they have not learnt this manner themselves but from me.'

It was about ten o'clock in the morning. The sky had become overcast with grey storm clouds; in the still air a few large drops of rain splashed on the mail hauberks and great helms of the knights. Trumpets blared, standard bearers drove their spurs into their horses and Simon de Montfort's army moved forward. Faces hidden behind iron masks and lances couched, the baronial cavalry hurled themselves against the two enemy divisions, aiming their blow at the weak point in the centre, where the Prince's and Gloucester's divisions joined.

At first the impact of Montfort's charge compelled the royalists to give ground. Warin de Bassingbourn, however, is said to have rallied the centre with jibes about Lewes, although he had not been present at that battle. Other troop leaders steadied their men, shouting above the tumult of battle cries and the shrill scream of wounded horses. The line held. The royalist cavalry upon the extreme wings, finding that they had nothing to do, charged home against the flanks of the baronial column. The Welsh foot broke ranks and ran to the river Avon, where many drowned. The shaft of the battering ram was gone.

For several hours the unequal struggle raged. No quarter was asked or given. Everywhere the Prince's knights, with red crosses on their white surcoats, pressed towards the Earl's White Lion standard. Beneath this fought the Earl and his sons, surrounded by their household knights. In spite of his 58 years, Simon de Montfort battled bravely until Gloucester's soldiers killed his son, Henry. 'Is my son slain?' he cried, 'then indeed it is time for me to die.' He was last seen alive in a confused mêlée, wielding his sword with both hands.

The vindictive slaughter continued for some time. The aged and captive King Henry, who had been dragged into the battle, only saved himself by shouting repeatedly 'I am Henry of Winchester your King! Do not harm me!' At length the baronial survivors scattered. Many headed for Offenham bridge, and were cut down in the fields near it in a place now known as Dead Man's Ayot.

The Prince's soldiers scoured the field, stripping and robbing the slain. They found among the dead some baronial leaders still alive and spared them in hope of ransoms. In this way Humphrey de Bohun, John FitzJohn, Henry de Hastings and Guy de Montfort fell into royalist hands. Around Earl Simon lay the corpses of Peter de Montfort, Despenser the Justiciar, John de Beauchamp, William de Mandeville, Robert de Tregoz, Roger de Rivle and many more. As Robert Bruce wrote:

'Sir Rauf the gode Basset did ther his ending,
Sir Guy Baliel died there, a yong knight and hardy,
He was pleyned more than other twenty'.[3]

Prince Edward ordered his men to bury the dead. It was found that the body of Sir Guy Baliol, who had carried Earl

43

Simon's standard, had been so mangled that it could not be stripped for burial. Prince Edward wept at the funeral of his boyhood friend, Henry de Montfort, but would have no mercy shown to the corpse of Earl Simon. A rider carried its severed head upon a lance point to Roger Mortimer's wife at Wigmore Castle. 'May the precursor of the Lord, whose head was served up at a banquet by a dancer, help the sender's soul,' commented William Rishanger.

The chronicler of Lanercost listed the baronial losses as 180 knights, 220 squires, 2,000 English and 5,000 Welsh infantry. The last figure, however, probably includes the numbers of Welshmen who escaped in the early stages of the battle. Otherwise these figures are probably correct. Prince Edward lost only two knights. One chronicler states that 2,000 royalist soldiers were killed. This suggests that Prince Edward used his spearmen as a breakwater against Simon de Montfort's cavalry charge, and kept his own cavalry largely in reserve.

Within four days Prince Edward's army had marched 85 miles and defeated two armies – a worthy prelude to a great military career. The approach march to Evesham revealed strategic insight of an unusual order. At 26 years of age, the Prince had equipped himself for a lifetime of soldiering in Wales, Scotland and France. To the tactics which he had learnt from Earl Simon he would add his own innovations. In his reign he laid the foundations of those English armies which conquered at Crécy, Poitiers and Agincourt.

Under dark thunderclouds at Evesham Prince Edward had broken the field army of the barons. But the 'Disinherited', as the remnant of the baronial party were called, still held their forfeited castles against all comers. In Ireland Simon the Younger prepared to carry on the war. Only slowly did baronial resistance crumble. In December 1267 Prince Edward captured Kenilworth Castle after a two year siege. But even then John FitzJohn and others still fought on. Many more, however, followed William de Montchensey's example, and made their peace with the King. Montchensey died later in Prince Edward's service, when the wall of a Welsh castle he was besieging fell and crushed him. Still more barons were reconciled when the best of the reforms advocated in the Provisions of Oxford were incorporated in the Statute of Westminster by King Edward's first Parliament in 1275.

Bitter feelings die hard. In March 1271, Simon and Guy de Montfort, exiles in Italy, shocked Europe with an act of barbarity. Henry de Almain had arrived in Viterbo to reconcile the two brothers with the King. The Montforts, however, could not forget that this Henry de Almain had deserted their father before Lewes. In full armour they attacked the King's nephew as he heard mass in San Silvestro Church. Four fingers of Henry's left hand were slashed as he struggled to hold on to the altar. 'I have had my revenge,' Guy de Montfort declared, as his victim lay dying from dagger wounds. 'How was your father dragged about?' cried his servants. And so they pulled Henry of Almain by his hair into the bright Italian sunshine to die. Neither brother outlived the disgrace of this deed. Simon died soon afterwards, but Guy de Montfort finished his days in the darkness of a Sicilian dungeon many years later.

GENERAL

Although there was no great battle during this period there was almost continual warfare against the Welsh and the Scots. In Wales King Edward's policy was to consolidate his conquests by building at key points: Beaumaris, Conway, Caernarvon and Harlech castles all date from his reign.

In Scotland the only important battles were Stirling (11 September, 1297), where Wallace defeated de Warenne, who had fought with Edward at Evesham 32 years before; and Falkirk (22 July, 1298), where the English king defeated Wallace.

MILITARY ORGANISATION

Under Edward I the vague power of the sheriff of summoning the county levies, the successors of the fyrdmen, was supplemented by more definite Commissions of Array, addressed to the prominent men in the county and giving them authority to muster and train all men able to bear arms. The feudal system of land tenure by military service still produced short service armies. But the indenture method of raising armies developed as Edward I preferred to employ long-term professional soldiers.

CAVALRY

There was little change in the armament of heavy cavalry, mounted on 'dextrarii', the powerful heavy ancestors of shire horses. A new class of light horsemen, known as 'hobelars', emerged on the borders.

INFANTRY

The most important single development in warfare during this period was the growing number of skilled longbowmen. They were especially useful for breaking up the tight phalanxes of spearmen into which the Scots and Welsh formed themselves when confronted with the mailed English cavalry in the few pitched battles of the late thirteenth century.

The Battle of Bannockburn

THE CAMPAIGN

1313	*The Scots lay siege to Stirling Castle.*
23 December	*King Edward II summons his tenants in chief, and issues Commissions of Array.*
1314	
10 June	*The English army assembles at Berwick.*
12 June	*The English march north.*
21 June	*Edward reaches Edinburgh.*
22 June	*The English reach Falkirk.*
24 June	*The Battle of Bannockburn.*

THE BATTLE

24 June, 1314

BY DECEMBER 1 3 1 3 Robert Bruce, King of Scotland, had captured all the English castles in his realm except Berwick, Dunbar and Stirling. In that month his brother, Sir Edward Bruce, besieged Stirling Castle. The English seneschal, Sir Philip Mowbray, agreed to surrender the castle if no relieving army reached him before Midsummer's Day, 24 June, 1314.

King Edward II could scarcely countenance the loss of Stirling, the strategic key to the Lowlands of Scotland. On 23 December, 1313, he ordered 93 tenants in chief to muster their tenants. By Commissions of Array he summoned 21,540 foot soldiers from the northern counties. The Welsh Marches supplied archers. Royal requests for soldiers to serve under Richard de Burgh, Earl of Ulster, reached Eth O'Connor, Prince of Connaught, and 23 other Irish Chieftains. The King ordered all these forces to muster at Berwick on 10 June, 1314.

By the appointed day not less than 3,000 cavalry and 20,000 infantry had assembled. The relatively large number of foot soldiers demonstrates how even a mediaeval army could be tailored for a particular task. Edward had reliable information as to the ground around Stirling. In the preamble to his Commissions he let the country sheriffs know that Robert Bruce would resist him in a 'strong and marshy place' and that 'a great part of the exploit will come to footmen'.

On 12 June the King marched northwards, accompanied by the Earls of Gloucester, Pembroke and Hereford. Behind his army trundled 110 supply waggons, each drawn by eight oxen, and 106 four-horse carts. The English entered Edinburgh on 21 June, and replenished their waggons with provisions unloaded from the fleet. Resuming his march the King reached Falkirk, 10 miles from Stirling Castle, on the evening of 22 June.

Meanwhile Bruce had raised his standard at Torwood, a few miles north west of Falkirk. With an army of 14,000 men he marched to a wooded plateau two miles south of Stirling, and prepared to fight a defensive battle on ground of his own choice, with the Bannock burn covering his front. The Roman road forded it opposite the centre of the Scots position, and in order to strengthen this area Bruce ordered 'pottes', knee deep holes covered with bracken, to be dug on each side of the road north of the burn. These field defences passed Bruce's inspection on 22 June. Having seen the English cavalry in action at Falkirk in 1298, when he had fought on the English side, Bruce had no wish to see his infantry shattered by the shock of their cavalry.

King Robert divided his army into four 'battles' of spearmen, placing his handful of cavalry under the command of Sir Robert Keith, the Marshal of Scotland. The vaward he committed to Randolph, Earl of Moray. His experienced brother, Sir Edward Bruce, led the centre, the Earl of Douglas and Walter the Steward the rearward. The 40 year old Scottish King may have remembered his grandfather's tales of de Montfort's victory at Lewes. At any rate he kept a strong reserve under his own hand.

48

On Sunday afternoon, 23 June, the English army advanced towards the Bannock burn, and halted a mile south of it. These movements were carefully observed by Scottish scouts. Meanwhile Sir Philip Mowbray made a long detour from Stirling Castle to come to the King's tent where he declared that the army need advance no further for technically Stirling Castle had been relieved. He also added that large bodies of Scottish infantry had been seen moving in New Park. The King ordered two cavalry squadrons to reconnoitre the Scots position. Sir Humphrey de Bohun, Hereford's nephew, led the first straight up the Roman road. Splashing over the Bannock burn ford, Bohun reined his horse and found himself face to face with the Scottish King, sitting his grey palfrey. Bohun recognised him by the simple gold crown which encircled his leather-covered bascinet. Couching his lance he spurred his charger towards the King. Bruce calmly deflected the point of the lance, then standing in his stirrups, crushed Bohun's skull with one mighty blow. As Scottish cavalry cantered out of the wood, the English turned and fled. 'I have broke my guid battle axe', said the King.

The second cavalry detachment fared no better. Sir Robert de Clifford with his own troop of 50 border horsemen and Henry de Beaumont's rather larger contingent rode to the east. They crossed the Bannock burn lower down, and outflanked the Scottish army. When they had drawn parallel with St. Ninian's Kirk they sighted the Earl of Moray's division advancing towards them from the woods. Both sides halted and looked at each other.

Although Moray could not hear the words a violent argument raged among the leaders of the English squadron. Instead of charging the Scots before they could array themselves into a hedgehog-like 'schiltron' of pikes, Beaumont insisted that more Scotsmen would be killed if they were allowed to venture further into the open. 'Let us wait a little and let them come on. Give them room !' Sir Thomas Gray, a Yorkshire knight, disagreed vigorously. 'Sir, I doubt not that whatever you give them now they will have all too soon.' Beaumont turned on him angrily. 'Very well, if you are afraid you can leave.'

Without a word Sir Thomas rushed his horse against the Scots who had a formed a hollow square. His charger fell to the

49

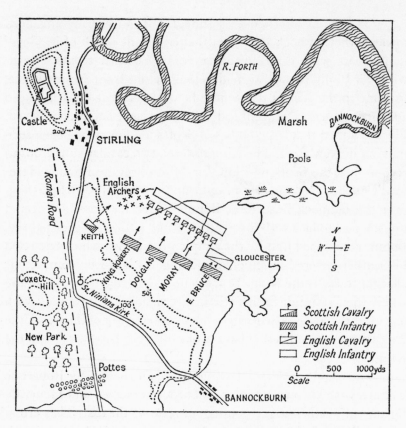

THE BATTLE OF BANNOCKBURN, 1314

ground, pierced by twelve-foot spears and Sir William Deyncourt threw his life away in an attempt to support him. Without bowmen the English men-at-arms could not break the Scots formation. They hurled their lances like javelins, but to no avail. As the Scots advanced the English cavalry rode off in disorder, some to Stirling Castle and the rest to King Edward's camp. Moray's division, who had lost only one yeoman, marched back to their position, removing their helmets to cool themselves in the heat of the afternoon.

The English leaders wisely resolved to avoid a frontal assault. That night they conducted the army to the right and forded the Bannock burn below the village. The soldiers used doors and thatch from cottages to spread over the marshy ground on the banks of the burn. The army then halted in an 'evil deep wet marsh' and waited for dawn, their horses standing bridled beside them. 'The gret stratnes of the plase' crowded the troops of cavalry and foot soldiers uncomfortably together, and the grey light of dawn revealed a scene of confusion.

Meanwhile Bruce had swung his four divisions round to face the English. But now the division of Douglas and Walter the Steward stood on its right with those of Moray and Sir Edward Bruce. The King brought his reserve into the line on the left, and stationed his cavalry somewhat to the north. In the early morning King Robert knighted Walter the Steward, James Douglas and other young men in his army. The Abbot of Inchaffray sealed the Scottish preparations with an absolution, as the soldiers waited in silence or muttered a Pater Noster. Bruce then ordered his 14,000 men to advance in echelon upon the English.

The English King had also completed his dispositions. Nine cavalry squadrons, each perhaps 250 strong, composed the front line. A larger cavalry division, usually known as the 'vanguard', massed on the left of them. The King had crammed his infantry behind the nine bodies of horse. To the Scots the English appeared as one mass, except the 'vanguard', who were arrayed by themselves.

Another dispute arose in this 'vanguard'. First the Earl of Gloucester challenged the Earl of Hereford's right to command it as Constable of England. Then he rode up to King Edward and advised him to delay the battle for a day until more favourable ground could be selected – dubious counsel indeed, for the Scots were already within two bow shots, and Edward angrily accused his nephew of cowardice and treachery. In a fury the 24 year old Earl, who may have misjudged the situation but was certainly no traitor, rejoined his own tenants and without waiting even to don his emblazoned surcoat, charged at the nearest Scottish 'schiltron'. His horse struck the pikes of Sir Edward Bruce's division and fell dead. Soon the young man himself was killed, and his banner of red chevrons upon a gold field could be seen no more. Afterwards it was said that, had but 20 of his 500 men supported him properly they could have rescued him.

Meanwhile the other four Scottish 'battles' converged on each other as they came within bowshot of the English. Against this solid front the mailed cavalry of England hurled itself, squadron after squadron. 'The two hosts came together, and the great steeds of the knights dashed into the Scottish pikes as into a thick wood; there arose a great and horrible noise from rending lances and dying horses, and they stood locked together for a space,' wrote the Lanercost chronicler. The Scots, in buckskin leather coats and iron caps, aimed at the horses; once a knight had been dismounted he fell an easy prey to their short stabbing swords and dirks.

Behind this interlocked host the English foot soldiers stood idle. The majority were armed with some sort of staff weapon, usually a spear. At least 200 of them never drew sword throughout the battle. The archers had bent their long white bows once or twice in an effort to shoot on low trajectory just over the heads of their own cavalry. One chronicler laconically reported that 'they hit some few Scots in the breast, but struck many more English in the back.' Others ran to the English right and gathered on the flank. From here, having successfully driven off some skirmishing enemy bowmen, they began to let fly with grey goose feathered arrows. They shot so fast and had their shooting lasted it would have gone ill with Robert Bruce. The Scottish King knew the danger, and had ordered his cavalry to disperse any large group of archers. Sir Robert Keith with 500 light horsemen soon scattered them for they had no spearmen with them as protection against a cavalry charge.

In the centre the English horsemen fought against a tide of spears. 'On them! On them, they fail!' roared the Scots. King Edward himself had to strike hard with his studded mace as they grasped at his horse's trappings. The struggle lasted for an hour until the English, catching sight of a body of men with banners on a hill in New Park, suddenly lost their nerve. Thus it was that these grooms and sutlers, who may only have been spectators, panicked the chivalry of England into flight.

The Scots found that English backs made good targets. 'Slay! Slay!' they shouted. But not all ran away. Sir Giles D'Argentine hacked his way to the King, and led him by the horse's bridle from the field. Then the old crusader turned back to the fight saying 'I have never been accustomed to fly'. His battle cry 'D'Argentine! D'Argentine!' sounded as he charged the Scots once more. His body was later buried in St. Cuthbert's Church, near Edinburgh.

The rout lasted until darkness put an end to it. They found the corpse of Sir Edward Manley, Steward of England, trodden into the mire near the Bannock burn. Bridges formed of dead bodies stretched across the stream. The waters of the Forth drowned many a fugitive. Some 100 English horsemen were slain, including many barons, knights and squires. Twenty-two barons and 68 knights yielded to the Scots. On their part the Scots lost many spearmen but only two knights – Sir William de Vepont and Sir Walter de Ross.

Those who escaped from the battlefield faced other hazards. The governor of Stirling Castle, short of provisions, begged King Edward and his large party to go on elsewhere and eventually a Lowland knight guided the King to Dunbar, where he took ship for England. The Earl of Hereford and Sir Ingram de Umfraville, with 600 men-at-arms and 1,000 foot soldiers, reached Bothwell Castle in safety. But Sir Walter Gilbertson, the castellan, only gave refuge to the barons and knights. A party of Scottish horsemen appeared and attacked the leaderless English soldiers killing over a thousand of them. Sir Walter completed an ill day's work by handing over his 'guests' to the Scottish commander. The prisoners included Robert Northburgh, Keeper of the Privy Seal, and all his clerks, and the seal itself.

Contemporary chroniclers offered many reasons for the English disaster at Bannockburn – the worst they ever suffered at the hands of the Scots. One monk attributed it to divine retribution for the spoliation of a monastery during the march northwards. Yet the reasons were straightforward tactical ones. Beyond question Robert the Bruce was a better general than King Edward II, and, although out-numbered and very short of cavalry, marshalled his army to better advantage. The night march which left the English crowded together in the chilly dawn in boggy ground totally unsuitable for their cavalry, was probably too ambitious an operation for their new-levied host. The failure to afford the bowmen the support of cavalry or men-at-arms was a rudimentary blunder. It was typical of the lethargic and unfortunate Edward that the most spectacular episode of his whole reign should have been an unparalleled catastrophe.

The lessons of Bannockburn were not lost on the English, and a generation later we find them combining their chivalry and their archers to good effect, not only at Crécy and Poitiers, but at Neville's Cross. Indeed, their whole military system came in for a thorough reorganisation. The shortcomings of the feudal levy had been ruthlessly exposed. The great French wars were to be fought by professional armies, raised by a contract, or indenture, system.

Bannockburn set the seal on the work of Sir William Wallace and Robert the Bruce. If the chronicles of mediaeval Scotland are a long tale of treachery and violence, that does not diminish the importance of the event that won Scotland four centuries of independence. Bannockburn must be regarded as a decisive event in the history of these islands.

1314-1455

THE PERIOD OF the Hundred Years War with France (1337-1453) saw but little fighting on British soil. The English found it more profitable to pluck the Lily than the Thistle. Defeated at Halidon Hill (1333) and Neville's Cross (1346), the Scots were content to allow the English to pursue their continental ambitions undisturbed. The battle of Shrewsbury (1403), described below, was the most important battle on English soil during this period, and was probably the biggest since Hastings. The defeat of the Percies and the Mortimers with thier Scots and Welsh allies cost some 7,000 lives.

This was the great age of the English longbowman. The archer with his high 'rate of fire', and his accuracy, was as successful, in his way, as the Swiss pikemen in combat against the armoured chivalry of France. English commanders often made their foot mobile by mounting them. Billmen and bowmen alike usually wore some body armour and a steel helmet or salet. Some preferred a quilted 'jack' with steel discs sewn into it.

The cavalry in order to protect themselves from arrows and crossbows quarrels, eventually equipped themselves with full plate armour. During the period the English armoured knights and men-at-arms usually fought on foot, with the exception of a small cavalry force reserved for the pursuit of fugitives once the battle was won. These tactics were favoured mainly because the skill of the longbowmen caused great loss, in particular among horses which could never be as well protected by heavy armour as their riders. Moreover, it was found that the English foot soldiers fought better when backed by strong forces of fully armoured men. They were also less inclined to fear betrayal if they could see their leaders standing with them.

These changes, especially the growing importance of the English archers, are illustrated by the battle of Shrewsbury, the first major encounter where longbowmen were employed on both sides. The political events leading up to the battle also reveal how far the Hundred Years War served to divert the energies of the English nobility, for peace in France usually led to outbreaks of rebellion in England. In 1396 Richard II made a peace treaty with Charles VI of France which ensured such a cessation of nearly twenty years.

In 1399, only three years after concluding the treaty, Richard was deposed by Henry Bolingbroke who ascended the throne as Henry IV, helped by several of the leading baronial families, and not least the Percies, Earls of Northumberland. Thereafter Henry's reign was beset by baronial dissensions and even outright rebellion.

Nor was the principality of Wales quiet and submissive under its new ruler. A petty land dispute between one of its natural leaders Owain Glyndwr and his neighbour, Lord Grey of Ruthin, escalated into a series of raids on Shropshire, which resulted in the confiscation of Glyndwr's land. The redoubtable Welshman then stirred up a rebellion in Wales. In the spring of 1402 he had captured Edward Mortimer, uncle of Richard II's heir who entered into an alliance with his Welsh captor against the usurper Henry.

Henry's offensive against Glyndwr was to be continued in the following year, but on 11 July 1403, as the King was marching north to repel a Scottish raid, the Earl of Northumberland's son Harry 'Hotspur', declared against him at Chester. Ostensibly Hotspur was angered both at Henry's broken promise at Ravenspur (that he had returned to England only to claim his baronial rights), and also by the fact that he had not been paid for his military service against the Welsh and Scots. It is perhaps more likely that Hotspur saw more hope of advancement with a Mortimer protegé on the throne, for he was married to Edward Mortimer's sister.

Hotspur came to Chester with about eighty horsemen,

including the Earl of Douglas who had been captured at the battle of Homildon the previous year, and who had been promised his freedom if the King was defeated. He began raising an army, and was joined by his uncle Thomas Percy, Earl of Worcester.

The King, who had been moving north, marched to Lichfield on 16 July where he sent out his warrants for levies before continuing to Stafford on his way to meet the rebels at Chester. Here further news reached him that Hotspur was marching on Shrewsbury, occupied by Prince Henry (the future Henry V) with a small band of men employed to police the Welsh border. Hotspur probably intended to capture Shrewsbury and the Prince, afterwards using the fortified town as a safe base until a northern army, being raised by his father the Earl, could augment his own soldiers from the northern Welsh marches and Cheshire. It may be that Glyndwr, delayed by floods in Carmarthen, was to have joined Hotspur, but though there must have been some understanding between them there is no evidence that they planned to unite their forces.

The King left Stafford early on 20 July and reached Shrewsbury later the same day. Hotspur, marching south through Whitchurch and Wem, reached the town only to find the gates barred against him, and withdrew some three miles north-west to the village of Berwick.

On the following day, 21 July, Hotspur heard that the Royalist forces were moving to meet him and he moved his army into position on a small ridge called Hayteley Field, three hundred yards to the north of the present church at Hurlescott. Between three and five hundred yards away, facing him across the fields and narrow lanes, King Henry had drawn up his own force.

Both armies were arrayed in a similar way – a deep line with men-at-arms in the centre, bowmen in the front rank, and bodies of archers on each wing. The rebels were in one line eight hundred yards long, but in the King's army there was a gap between Prince Henry's body on the left wing and the main force under the King.

The Abbot of Shrewsbury rode out and attempted to make a peace between the leaders, but with no result. After his departure there was a long pause of one or two hours. In the tense silence Hotspur's soldiers began plaiting together pea plants from the fields before them to make a rudimentary barrier against the King's men.

Then the King's division of the line began to advance, and as they struggled up through the crops and up the ridge they received in their faces flight after flight of arrows from the rebel archers. Although not directly involved in this advance Prince Henry received an arrow wound in the face, but steadfastly he refused his surgeon's advice to leave the field. By the time the King's forces had gained the brow of the ridge they had suffered so many casualties that after only a brief struggle they fled back down the slope.

Immediately Hotspur sent his men-at-arms after them and at the foot of the ridge, where the King began to rally and reform his men, a murderous and confused hand to hand combat took place. Hotspur, accompanied by Earl Douglas and thirty men, hacked their way to the Royal Standard, hoping to settle the matter by killing the King, who had to fall back out of danger. Henry, perhaps foreseeing such a tactic, had robed several of his household guard in the royal surcoat to confuse the rebel leaders.

At this time – the crux of the battle – Prince Henry began to move his men forward. Through not being in the initial advance his men had suffered less from the rebel archers, and they now began to envelop Hotspur's right until they were able to attack the rebels in the flank and rear. The superior numbers of the King's army began to tell, and in the furious fighting which followed Hotspur was killed by an arrow when he raised his vizor to wipe his face.

The news spread rapidly throughout the rebel army, causing a panic, and the line broke. Henry's victory was complete and the subsequent pursuit was carried on for more than three miles.

Hotspur, who had been buried at Whitchurch, was subsequently disinterred and his head placed on Micklegate Bar in York. His uncle, the Earl of Worcester was executed after the battle, and his head displayed on London Bridge. His father, the Earl of Northumberland, who had been too ill to attend the battle, hastened to make his peace and, perhaps inexplicably, was forgiven by the King.

In 1415 Prince Henry, now King Henry V, renewed the war with France, and added Agincourt to Sluys, Crécy and Poitiers on the list of great English victories. Besides occupying the barons and developing still further the latent patriotism of the English as a nation, the Hundred Years War saw further changes in the organisation of war. Armies were now raised by contracts called indentures; companies served under professional captains; and the royal household took on the aspect of a permanent military staff.

On the field of battle an important change associated with the Hundred Year's War was the use of gunpowder and cannon. Artillery seems to have been used at Crécy (1346), and was certainly employed in the siege of Calais (1347). The last great French victory, Castillon (1453) was due in great measure to their artillery.

The virtual extinction of England's military power in France was followed only two years later by civil war, the Wars of the Roses. In 1444 King Henry VI and Suffolk, his chief minister, had negotiated the Treaty of Tours, by which Henry married Margaret, 'the she-wolf of Anjou', and by which Calais was to be ceded to France. Gloucester and Richard of York, both of whom wished to continue the war, were bitterly opposed to this truce.

The final defeat in France was soon followed by the first of King Henry's periods of insanity. The prospect of a long regency by the vindictive French queen was unattractive to the Yorkists. The end of the French wars had left every baron with a private army of restless retainers, eager to be back at their old trade. The Duke of Norfolk, for instance, could put 3,000 men in the field, with cannon, when he went to besiege Caister Castle in 1469 – and that was a private fight.

The war between York and Lancaster was fought with great ferocity. But though the aristocracy bled itself almost to death, the struggle scarcely touched the bulk of the population. This final breakdown of feudalism turned out to be a blessing in disguise, paving the way for the great age of the Tudors.

The First Battle of St. Albans

22 May, 1455

IN THE NEW YEAR 1455, King Henry VI recovered from one of his periodical spells of insanity, and in consequence Richard, Duke of York, lost his position as Protector. One of the King's first acts was to release the Duke of Somerset from the Tower where York had lodged him for countenancing a private war between the Percys and the Nevilles. Moreover, on 4 March he dismissed York from his place as Captain of Calais and bestowed it upon Somerset instead. Three days later the Earl of Salisbury, head of the Neville family and Chancellor of England, reluctantly yielded the Great Seal to Thomas Bourchier, Archbishop of Canterbury.

The Duke of York resolved to fight rather than submit to the rule of Somerset and his friends. With the help of the Nevilles he quickly raised an army in the North and by the third week of May he had reached Ware, in Hertfordshire.

The Lancastrians evidently believed that talk rather than arrows would settle the quarrel, and it was not until 18 May that the King summoned his array. That day, for example, he wrote to the citizens of Coventry, asking them to send 100 soldiers 'to be with us wheresoever we be in all hast possibull'. The letter did not reach Coventry until four days later, and by that time the fighting was already over. Other contingents also, notably the Duke of Norfolk's men, were unable to join the Royal army in time.

The King summoned a council to meet at Leicester and he decided, despite the Yorkist threat, to attend it. The royal party slept the night of 21 May at Watford, less than eight miles from St. Albans. Meanwhile the Duke of York had written to him on 20 May from Ware, protesting loyalty and claiming that he had only assembled his retainers becuase he feared molestation on his way to Leicester. Some say that neither this manifesto nor York's letter to Archbishop Bourchier, ever reached the King.

Early next morning Henry heard that York had arrived near

St. Albans and immediately held a council of war. A few nobles advised the King to remain in Watford. The Duke of Buckingham, however, who as Constable of England had been given command of the royal forces, favoured marching on to St. Albans. Apparently he believed that York would open negotiations. At dawn the army, which consisted mainly of royal and baronial household retainers, dressed in their masters' liveries, set out. Besides Somerset and Buckingham, and their two heirs, the Earls of Devon and Stafford, three other earls and six barons accompanied the King.

At 4 a.m. the royal column entered the town. The Duke of York's men had pitched their tents in Key Field, which lay on the east side of the gardens behind the houses of St. Peter's and Holywell streets. When the King halted in St. Peter's Street and entered the house of Edmund Westby he had actually come within crossbow shot of the Yorkist camp.

At once the Lancastrian leaders sent out detachments to secure the town, which stood upon a hill some 100 feet above the surrounding plain. The river Ver flowed around the southern foot of the ridge, and a ditch ran round the houses and the buildings of the great abbey of St. Alban. The ditch and rampart which had been dug in the wars of Simon de Montfort, had fallen into disrepair, and only near St. Peter's Church were the town defences formidable. The main roads, however, had been barricaded by moving heavy beams or 'bars' across them. The Lancastrians did this immediately, posting their most experienced soldiers to guard these points. At St. Peter's Church Sir Richard Harrington, Sir John Hanford and Sir Bartin Entwistle – all veterans of the French wars – stood ready to resist any attack.

For over an hour negotiations dragged on. For the royalists the aged Duke of Buckingham conferred with Mowbray Herald, York's plenipotentiary, who entered the town past Sir Richard Harrington's men. York's demand that Somerset should be handed over to him finally put an end to comings and goings. The King would not give up any lord with him. 'By the feith that I owe to Seynt Edward and to the Corone of England I shal destrye them every moder sone and they be hanged and drawen and quartered that may be taken afterward of them to have ensample to alle such traytours to be war to make only such rysing of peple withinne my

61

londe and so traytorly to abyde her Kyng . . .' one chronicler makes
him declare. Probably skirmishes had already broken out at the
'bars' as both sides made their final preparations. When Mowbray
Herald returned from his last interview he met York's forces
advancing in array, their banners flying.

The Yorkist army probably numbered 3,000, mostly
northern archers. The Lancastrians may have been as few as 2,000.
Many of these were levies from the East Anglian counties, armed
with staff weapons. The main strength of their army was the nobles
and their retainers, encased in plate armour and equipped with
poleaxe and sword. Most of the leaders, on both sides, had served
in the French wars. Somerset had been taken prisoner at Beaugé
in 1421, and under his generalship the English had lost Nor-
mandy. Forty-five years old, York had soldiered with more distinction. In 1436 he had advanced almost to the gates of Paris.
Buckingham's military experience had been comparatively slight.

The King raised his standard at Goslawe, in St. Peter's
Street – a symbolic act of great significance. All who fought when
the royal banner had been displayed were *ipso facto* traitors. The
first serious clash took place at the 'bars' in Sopwell Lane and
Buttes Lane. Here Lord Clifford and his men fought valiantly for
almost one hour, resisting every attack. Richard Neville, the 27
year old Earl of Warwick, broke the Yorkist 'impasse' by leading
his archers to the right, through the gardens behind St. Peter's
Street and up to the line of timbered houses. There 'they and theyr
peple brake downe vyolently houses and pales on the este side of
the towne and entred seynt Petres strete'. Sir William Stonor,
Steward of St. Alban's, probably an eye witness, gives a more precise account. According to him Warwick 'ferociously broke in by
the garden sides between the Sign of the Key and the Sign of the
Chequer in Holywell Street, and immediately they were within
the town, suddenly they blew up trumpets, and set a cry with a
shout and a great voice "A Warwick! A Warwick!" '

It is hardly surprising that the next phase of the battle was
confused. Apparently Warwick's small band ran down Holywell
Street and fell upon Lord Clifford's men from the rear. The Yorkist leaders rushed on foot as swiftly as plate armour would allow
to the market place in the broad waist of St. Peter's Street. Sir

Robert Ogle of the Scottish March, with 600 archers in salets and 'jacks' arrived first, and found that the Lancastrians who had remained with the King, probably the nobility and their immediate retainers, had not even armed themselves. Then the alarm bell was rung and every man got into harness, for at that time every man was out of their way, and they joined the battle immediately. Many of the Lancastrians, however, seem to have fought without their gorgets or salets. Buckingham was hit 'in the vysage' with an arrow. Another shaft grazed the King's neck; Stafford, who had presumably forgotten to put on his gauntlets, received an arrow wound in his hand.

The mêlée soon broke up. Yorkist soldiers cast down the royal standard, which had been left unattended. In a letter the Duke of Norfolk subsequently blamed Sir Philip Wentworth for deserting his post beside the banner. Other Lancastrians, such as Henry Filongley, fought stoutly. No doubt most of the household retainers listed as dead fell at this time. The Abbot, who evidently saw this last stand, wrote afterwards 'Here you saw one fall with his brains dashed out, there another with a broken arm, and a fourth with a pierced chest, and the whole street was full of dead corpses.' Somerset, who had no illusions about the fate which awaited him if he was captured, defended himself with his sword. The 'Davies Chronicle' related how a soothsayer had warned Somerset that he would die under the shadow of a castle. Consequently, Somerset avoided going to Windsor, although he had been made constable. Surrounded by Yorkists, Somerset fell mortally wounded at the door of the Castle Inn. Some writers dismiss this tale, made famous by Shakespeare, but it is not unlikely for there was a Castle Inn in St. Peter's Street in 1455.

With Somerset's fall the fight was as good as over. York hastened to the King, who had taken refuge in a tanner's house. Kneeling down he besought the royal forgiveness, and congratulated him on the Duke's death, which he said would be a source of joy to all people. He then accompanied the monarch to St. Alban's Abbey for a thanksgiving service.

While the soldiers of the Welsh Marches sacked the town the servants of the wounded Lancastrians carried some of their masters home in carts. Thus the Earl of Dorset, Sir John Wenlock and

Henry Filongley survived. Lord Ros became a prisoner of the Yorkists. Lord Clinton and Sir Robert Ogle died that day. But of the 5,000 men present only about 120 men were killed, mainly Lancastrians.

The political results of the battle proved to be ephemeral. York did not retain his supremacy in the government for more than a few months. Warwick, however, succeeded Somerset as Captain of Calais. The possession of Calais and control of the garrison, the largest professional force of soldiers at the disposal of the English crown, gave the Yorkists a base for their future operations.

The Second Battle of St. Albans

THE CAMPAIGNS OF 1459-1461

1459

| 23 September | Battle of Bloreheath. Yorkist victory. |
| 12 October | Collapse of Yorkist army at Ludlow. |

1460

15 January	First Sandwich raid.
25-6 June	Second Sandwich raid. Warwick marches on London.
10 July	Battle of Northampton. Yorkist victory.
21 December	Battle of Wakefield. Lancastrian victory.

1461

January	Queen Margaret marches south.
2 February	Battle of Mortimer's Cross. Yorkist victory.
17 February	Second Battle of St. Albans. Lancastrian victory. Queen Margaret retires northwards.
26 February	The Earl of March enters London.
March	Yorkists gather their forces and march north.
26-7 March	Skirmish at Ferrybridge.
29 March	Battle of Towton.

THE BATTLE

17 February, 1461

IN 1456 QUEEN MARGARET wrested the control of her husband, King Henry VI, from the Duke of York. The Yorkist leaders either retired to their strongholds or took part in empty reconciliations with their opponents. Both sides began to recruit armies for a renewal of the conflict.

In the summer of 1459 Queen Margaret's forces assembled at Coventry and marched on Ludlow, where the Duke of York owned the castle. The Earl of Salisbury and his men set out towards Ludlow, but a Lancastrian army under Lord Audley met him at Bloreheath, near Market Drayton. Salisbury's archers, using the tactics of Agincourt, arrayed themselves behind sharpened wooden stakes and repulsed three attacks. Treachery among the Lancastrians then gave the victory to the Earl (23 September).

On his arrival at Ludlow, Salisbury found a concentration of Yorkist forces. York had mustered his retainers there, and soon the Earl of Warwick rode into the town with 200 men-at-arms and 400 archers in red jackets, each with the Bear and Ragged Staff badge on his shoulder. Most of these men belonged to the Calais garrison, and were therefore trained soldiers.

The Yorkists had constructed a fortified camp outside the town. The River Teme formed one side of the defences, and a moat flooded from the river marked out the rest of the perimeter. Behind this ditch the Yorkists erected an earthwork, mounting several big guns and bristling with stakes.

Meanwhile the main Lancastrian army had pitched camp on the opposite side of the river. On 12 October Queen Margaret's men shouted across the river an offer of free pardon to all who would abandon the Duke of York. The soldiers of the Calais garrison, who had all served under the dead Duke of Somerset before Warwick had become their Captain, were the first to weaken. That night Andrew Trollope deserted to the Queen with many followers. The Duke of York lost his nerve and ordered his army to disperse. He himself fled to Ireland, while Warwick, Salisbury

66

and Sir John Wenlock made their way to Calais, and their Yorkist supporters scattered to their homes.

Queen Margaret and the Lancastrians could not rest while York or Warwick lived in freedom abroad. In Ireland, where he had been Lord Lieutenant, York reigned like a king, and those Irish chieftains, who had been bribed by the Lancastrians to cause trouble, did not earn their pay.

Queen Margaret entertained higher hopes of dislodging Warwick. Many of her soldiers, such as the traitor Andrew Trollope, had firsthand knowledge of the fortifications and canals around the city. In all Warwick had some 20 square miles to defend. Yet although the garrison had been under Lancastrian influence and could not be wholly relied upon, like most professional soldiers they were primarily interested in pay. Warwick could depend upon the English wool merchants, who traded with the Low Countries at Calais, to pay his men well in order to keep the town open. The issue would be how far Lancastrian sympathies would triumph over avarice.

With political astuteness Queen Margaret had appointed her own Captain of Calais – the second Duke of Somerset. In November 1459, with Andrew Trollope at his side, the young Duke landed in France. Trollope soon persuaded the garrison of Guines, one of the main outlying forts of Calais, to surrender. With tongues and not swords the Lancastrians hoped to win Calais itself.

Contrary winds, however, carried many ships of the Lancastrian fleet into Calais roads. Their anchors splashed into a stretch of water commanded by Warwick's great guns. In panic Somerset's soldiers and sailors sent the master of *The Trinity* ashore to speak on their behalf to the Earl of Warwick. They offered their services, all Somerset's military stores and his horses in exchange for their lives. Warwick drove a harder bargain. On Calais pier his lieutenants divided the sheep from the goats. Those who had deserted him at Ludlow were put to the sword ; the rest donned the Bear and Ragged Staff livery. After this spectacle, watched no doubt by a silent garrison, Warwick suffered no more from treachery amongst his own troops.

Against stiffer opposition in the swamps around Calais the Duke of Somerset's soldiers made little headway. The Duke asked for reinforcements. In January 1460 Richard Woodville, Lord Rivers, began to assemble a relief expedition at Sandwich. The Earl of Warwick, however, kept a ship in Sandwich harbour and he heard of these preparations. On 15 January, Sir John Wenlock and Sir John Denham, two trusted Yorkists, disguised as wool merchants, sailed into Sandwich harbour. With 300 men they landed and sought out Queen Margaret's startled men in the houses of the town. They captured Lord Rivers in his bed; his son, Sir Antony Woodville, rushed out of his quarters with his breastplate under his arm and was knocked on the head. The jubilant Yorkists then returned to Calais with their prisoners.

Queen Margaret replied to this affront by hanging Richard Neville, a lawyer of the Temple, and eight London merchants who had been stopped on their way to Calais with bowstrings and arrowheads in their purses. The Lancastrian council also ordered Osbert Mountford, a professional soldier, to take 500 men to Somerset's army. For some reason this force mustered again at Sandwich. Once more Wenlock and Denham descended on the town and took a substantial number of prisoners. At Calais, Osbert Mountford, who had served under Warwick, paid for his betrayal with his head.

This time, however, a small Yorkist force remained behind in Sandwich. On 26 June, the day after Mountford's execution, Warwick landed there himself. Scores of Kentishmen, weary of Lancastrian misrule, turned up with their weapons to welcome him. He entered London a few days later with the loss of only a handful of men, who had been pressed to death as the ill-disciplined Yorkist host hurried across Southwark bridge. The London Lancastrians retreated behind the white walls of the Tower.

On 3 July Warwick and the Mayor of the City made plans for a siege. Salisbury, Lord Cobham, and Sir John Wenlock were left to organise the details of the siege, while Warwick with the bulk of the army marched north on the following day. The Londoners under Wenlock and John Harow, a mercer, set up two batteries of heavy guns which pounded the Tower walls. Lord Scales, commander of the garrison, replied with a bombardment

68

of his own. No doubt, when his gunners missed, their stone shot would plunge through the houses of the citizens which must have caused some ill-feeling. A Yorkist knight, captured while examining the curtain walls from a boat, had all his limbs broken in the Tower torture chamber.

Meanwhile Warwick's army trudged over muddy roads to St. Albans, where he found 400 Lancashire archers waiting to join him. On 10 July Warwick and his men assaulted King Henry's earthwork camp near Northampton. Through the treachery of Lord Grey he won a resounding victory. One chronicler related the sorry tale of Sir William Lucy, who heard the opening cannon shots of the battle and 'came into the field to help the King, but the field was done before he came; and one John Stafford, a Yorkist, was aware of his coming, and loved the knight's wife and hated him, and anon caused his death'.

Warwick returned to London with the King as a captive. York arrived at last from Ireland in October and had himself appointed heir to the King. Queen Margaret, however, who had escaped after Northampton, assembled a Lancastrian army in the north, determined to preserve at all costs her son's birthright. This army she placed under the command of the Duke of Somerset, with Andrew Trollope as his lieutenant.

On 21 December Somerset's cavalry ambushed a party of foragers from the Duke of York's army, which had been quartered outside Sandal Castle, two miles from Wakefield. The Duke of York led a sortie, and after a brief fight was killed. Lancastrian troopers placed his head over a York city gate, with a paper crown on it.

Warwick, whose father (the Earl of Salisbury) had been executed at Wakefield, began recruiting a Yorkist army. London contributed 2,000 silver marks to his war chest and released many of his soldiers from their jails. The Duke of Norfolk and Viscount Bourchier sent him their 'fellowships'. Eighty Burgundian handgunners, with their strange weapons, landed in the city. The smaller followings of Lord Bonville, Sir Thomas Kyriel and Sir John Neville answered Warwick's urgent summons.

In January 1461 Queen Margaret and Somerset marched

southwards from York, burning and pillaging on a 30 mile front. The Bishop of Ely hired 35 Burgundian crossbowmen to protect his cathedral. After Peterborough the Queen's border soldiers sacked Huntingdon, Royston and Melbourne. 'Blessed be God who did not give us for a prey unto their teeth,' wrote one thankful monk of Croyland Abbey.

At Shrewsbury the Earl of March (York's heir) received news of his father's death at Wakefield and marched into the midlands. Near Mortimer's Cross, in Herefordshire, he defeated a Lancastrian army on 2 February. Owen Tudor, grandfather of the future King Henry VII, stood among the prisoners. The old man, sentenced to the block, 'trusted in pardon and grace until the collar of his red velvet doublet was ripped off. Then he said, "that head shall be on the block that was wont to lie on Queen Katherine's lap" '. Thus died the man who had married the French widow of King Henry V.

The Earl of March hastened to London. While he marched, preparations for a great battle were being made at St. Albans. On 12 February Warwick occupied that town and blocked the possible roads that Queen Margaret could have followed to London.

Two of these routes, the Baldock and Sandridge roads, converged on Barnard's Heath, north of the town. Warwick expected the main Lancastrian army to march down the Baldock road and he arrayed his forces in two divisions to meet them on the heath, one commanded by himself assisted by his brother, Lord Montague, and the other by the Duke of Norfolk.

The chronicler Gregory describes the preparations of the Yorkist soldiers. 'They (the handgunners) had such instruments that would shoot both pellets of lead and arrows of an ell in length with six feathers, three in the middle and three at the other end, with a great long iron head, and wildfire withal. Also they had made great nets of cord, 24 feet in length and 4 feet broad, and at every second knot there was a nail standing upright, that no man could pass over it without the likelihood of being wounded. Also they had pavises and loops with shutting windows to shoot out of, they standing behind the pavis, and the pavis as full of 3d. nails as they might stand. And when their shot was spent and done they cast the pavis before them ; then might no man come over the pavis

70

at them for the nails that stood upright unless he would do mischief to himself. Also they had a thing made like a lattice full of nails as the net was, but it would be moved as a man would ; and that served to lie at gaps where horsemen would enter in, and many a caltrap. . . .'

Warwick also stationed a company of archers by the Great Cross in St. Peter's Street to guard against a surprise attack from Watling Street. No doubt he also sent a lookout to the top of the Abbey tower. Eleven miles up Watling Street, at Dunstable, Warwick posted a further 200 mounted archers.

These careful dispositions, however, formed the substance of a message which a traitor called Lovelace, 'captain of Kent', despatched to the Lancastrians on 14 February. Two days later Lancastrian horsemen surrounded the Yorkist outpost at Dunstable and accounted for every archer. That night the Lancastrian army marched down Watling Street. Warwick's scouts 'came not home to bring no tidings how nigh that the Queen was, save one who came and said she was nine mile off'.

Apparently someone listened to the voice of this solitary 'pricker'. When Andrew Trollope led the Lancastrians up Romeland Street at dawn next day he met with a brisk reception. At short range the shaft arrows of the Yorkists inflicted terrible wounds. Trollope retired down the steep hill to the vicinity of St. Michael's Church. After a hasty council of war, Trollope renewed his attack, ordering some of his captains to lead their men through lanes north of Romeland Street. When a few of the enemy appeared behind them in St. Peter's Street the gallant band of Yorkist archers made their way back to Barnard's Heath.

This street fighting gave the Earl of Warwick time to change his front, so that his soldiers awaited the Lancastrians about half a mile beyond St. Peter's Church. His army, composed mostly of East Anglian followers of the Duke of Norfolk, the Earl of Arundel and Viscount Bourchier, numbered perhaps 6,000 men. A strong Kent contingent and the remnants of his archers, perhaps the most dependable soldiers in the army, made up Warwick's forces. Besides his handgunners and moveable field defences the Yorkist leader had several cannon with him.

The Duke of Somerset mustered at least 9,000 men for an

71

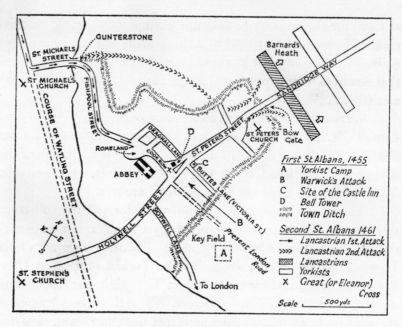

Legend on the map:

First St.Albans, 1455
A Yorkist Camp
B Warwick's Attack
C Site of the Castle Inn
D Bell Tower
Town Ditch

Second St. Albans 1461
→ Lancastrian 1st.Attack
»»» Lancastrian 2nd.Attack
Lancastrians
Yorkists
X Great (or Eleanor) Cross

Scale 500 yds

THE FIRST AND SECOND BATTLES OF ST. ALBANS

attack upon Warwick's main army. His tough northerners varied in quality from the accomplished bowmen of the Marches to ill-armed border levies. As many as 5,000 of his men, however, probably had some skill with a bow. Moreover, the Duke had several veterans of the French wars as advisers, notably Trollope, and in the skirmish at Dunstable these officers had demonstrated their professional ability. Unfortunately no details of the Lancastrian divisions are known. Trollope continued to command the vaward. Somerset himself led the centre, and there may have been a small rearward. The Lancastrians made a colourful sight, for each man wore the livery of his lord and also the 'white ostrich feather on crimson and black' badge of the Queen's son, Edward, who accompanied the army.

The Lancastrian divisions probably advanced towards the Yorkists in column, with the vanguard in extended order leading. Warwick's guns thundered as the first line came within range. Then his archers loosed a cloud of arrows. The wind, which blew snowflakes into their eyes, reduced the distance of their shot and played havoc with the spluttering matches of Warwick's hand-

72

gunners. Some of the pieces blew up, sending jagged metal among the Yorkist ranks. Eighteen gunners were burnt to death when the flames, presumably from the 'wildfire' which they tried to shoot on their heavy arrows, blew back into their faces.

With a shout the Lancastrians threw themselves upon Warwick's men-at-arms. Glaive and halberd crashed down upon plate armour, and swords slashed the emblazoned tabards. The archers shifted for themselves; their padded leather 'jakkes' gave them good protection against poleaxe blades. The Kentishmen, however, had an 'undysposycion' for serious fighting, and many followed Lovelace when he changed sides in the middle of the battle.

This treachery weakened the morale of Warwick's soldiers. The Earl encouraged his men with the hope of reinforcements, countering a bad rumour with a good one. Whether he expected succour from the Earl of March's army or from a detachment at Sandridge is not known, but no one appeared. During the desultory fighting in the afternoon Warwick's men 'huddled together' and would not be 'guided and governed by their captains'. Quite suddenly they turned and fled.

Lancastrian cavalry, perhaps from the rearguard, who had been waiting for this moment, spurred after them, hunting down the fugitives over the heath. Hedgerows and ditches aided the Yorkists. Thomas Denys, a friend of the Pastons, lost horse, armour and money to the value of £20 in this rout, but lived to tell the tale. Sir John Grey, who had been knighted by the King that morning, did not survive the pursuit. Some of the cavalry found King Henry sitting under a tree with the Yorkists Sir Thomas Kyriel and Lord Bonville still guarding him. Apparently he had promised them their lives if they would stay and protect him. Later they were executed, some say at the command of eight year old Prince Edward. Lord Montague, Lord Berners and Sir Thomas Carleton were given quarter, perhaps because Somerset's brother was held a prisoner in Calais.

Before the assembled Lancastrian captains King Henry knighted his son, Prince Edward and thirty others. As Sir Andrew Trollope rose to his feet he declared 'My Lord, I have not deserved it, for I slew but 15 men, for I stood still in one place and they came unto me, but they bode still with me.'

73

One chronicler recorded that 1,916 men lost their lives on both sides, and there is no reason to question this figure. Whethamstead thought that the Yorkists had lost the battle because the sun had dried up their blood, making them softer and gentler than the Lancastrians from the North. He quoted Vegetius as an authority for this psychological observation.

There may have been truth in his remark. The men of Kent and East Anglia had not been exposed to the rigours of border life, and the constant opportunities which it offered for warfare. Norfolk's 6,000 men had arrived too late for the first battle of St. Albans, and they had never fought against the men from the borders. They may have lacked experience with the longbow. This fact, combined with Somerset's bold strategy in marching down Watling Street and the treachery of Lovelace, accounts for the Lancastrian victory at St. Albans.

The Battle of Towton

29 March, 1461

'On Palme Sonday he wan the palme of glorye
And put hys enemys to endelez languor.'
YORKIST POLITICAL BALLAD (1462 or 1463)

AFTER HER VICTORY at St. Albans Queen Margaret did not
enter London, as she dared not risk open hostilities with the citizens. An angry crowd at Cripplegate stopped one Lancastrian
foraging party and shouted that they would not victual those who
had come to rob them. Later some Londoners killed three Lancastrians outside the city gates. After this incident the Mayor sent
the Duchess of Bedford, Lady Scales and 'divers sad fathers of the
spiritualitie' to soothe the Queen while commissioners from the
army and city met on Barnet heath to discuss the problem of food
supplies.

Tidings of the Yorkist victory at Mortimer's Cross interrupt-
ed these uneasy negotiations. In late February, as the triumphant
Earl of March drew near to London, the Queen and Somerset led
their army north to York. Their nine day delay in St. Albans after
the battle had cost them London and the chance of a decision in
their favour. The contemporary William of Worcester wrote of
the Lancastrian withdrawal that 'this was the ruin of King Henry
and his Queen'.

On 26 February the Earl of March and Warwick entered
London with much pomp at the head of 8,000 soldiers. The
chronicler Gregory lyrically described their reception : 'Then all
the city were fain and thanked God . . . and said "Let us walk in a
new vineyard, and let us make a gay garden in the month of March
with this fair white rose and herb, the Earl of March".' On the
following Sunday a great crowd of Londoners in Moorfields heard
the heralds proclaim Edward as King of England.

75

This London idyll in the spring did not last long. Queen Margaret and a large Lancastrian army threatened like a dark cloud in the north, and the new king made preparations to march to Yorkshire. On 5 March, the Duke of Norfolk, who had changed his allegiance since first St. Albans, summoned his indentured retainers in East Anglia, and Warwick went to the West Midlands to enlist men, accompanied by Seigneur de la Barde and his Burgundian handgunners. Forty Coventry men joined Warwick's force under the Elephant and Castle banner of their city and 60 more men made ready to follow them later. Near York Warwick waited for Edward who had left London on 13 March two days after his Welsh and Kentish infantry. When the two forces met one chronicler estimated that the combined Yorkist army numbered 20,000 men, a large army by the standards of the time.

For her part Queen Margaret had assembled a host of perhaps 26,000 Lancastrians. Edward's usurpation of the throne had no doubt rallied many of the undecided gentry to her cause. In the second week of March she established her camp at Tadcaster, eight miles from York.

Meanwhile Edward had reached Pontefract and ordered Lord Fitzwalter to ride forward with the advance guard and seize the passage over the River Aire at Ferrybridge. There they found only broken piles for the Lancastrians had prudently destroyed the bridge. The Yorkists spent Friday, 27 March, building a narrow pontoon bridge to replace it. When night had fallen Lord Clifford charged into the town with a troop of light northern horse and surprised the Yorkists in their beds. Fitzwalter, awoken by the noise and imagining that his men were quarrelling among themselves, rushed out into the street 'unarmed with a poleaxe in his hand', only to be cut down by Clifford's cavalry. With him died one of Warwick's brothers, the Bastard of Salisbury, 'a valiant young gentleman'. The remnants of Fitzwalter's advance guard fled in panic to Pontefract and the whole Yorkist army stood to arms. Warwick, no doubt remembering the dawn attack at St. Albans, expected the entire Lancastrian army to appear. Drawing his sword he killed his horse, a dramatic gesture signifying his willingness to run the same hazards as his followers – 'Let him fly that will,' he said to Edward, 'for surely I will tarry with him that

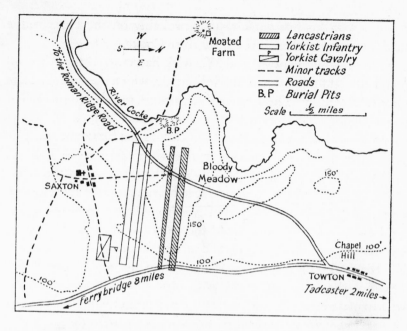

THE BATTLE OF TOWTON, 1461

will tarry with me'. With that he kissed his sword. To steady his soldiers Edward proclaimed that all who were afraid might leave. He also promised rewards to those who killed cowards in battle, and double wages with the chance of loot for those who remained with him.

When Saturday dawned with no further sign of the enemy Edward decided to recapture the abandoned pontoon bridge. The troops which he sent met stout resistance from Lord Clifford's men, who stood on the rafts and defended them vigorously. A Yorkist force under Lord Fauconberg outflanked them by crossing the Aire at Castleford, three miles upstream. Lord Clifford retreated with his men northwards and rode into an ambush of mounted archers which Fauconberg had set for him near Dintingdale. A headless arrow struck Clifford in the neck and killed him. Few of his men reached the Lancastrian army, only two miles away at the village of Towton. Warned of the proximity of the Yorkists Somerset took no chances; he arrayed his army that Saturday evening in 'a fair pleyne field' between Towton and

77

Saxton, with his left flank resting probably on the Ferrybridge road and his right upon the little river Cocke.

Meanwhile Edward and Warwick had crossed the Aire and marched eight miles north to Dintingdale, which they reached late on Saturday night. The army passed through the village and halted just beyond Saxton. Huddled in their cloaks against the sharp frost the Yorkists lay on the ground and waited for daybreak. The grey dawn discovered the two armies within sight of each other.

Owing to the size of his army and the straitness of the place, the 24 year old Duke of Somerset had drawn up his army in two long divisions. The aged Earl of Northumberland, assisted by Sir Andrew Trollope, commanded the front division, composed almost entirely of border archers. The Lancastrian nobility, including the Duke of Exeter, Earl of Devonshire and Lord Dacre, served in the rear corps under Somerset. This consisted of an unwieldy mass of heavily armoured gentry and foot soldiers.

The Yorkists confronted them in the same order, a strong force of archers facing Northumberland's men, with the experienced Lord Fauconberg as their leader. At Northampton Fauconberg had commanded a division, and he had acquitted himself well at Ferrybridge. As he was an uncle of Warwick's he was unlikely to turn traitor. Behind him Edward drew up the bulk of the Yorkist army in one extended phalanx. Over this could be seen the 'Black Bull' banner of Edward and the Bear and Ragged Staff of Warwick. Sir John Wenlock and Sir John Denham waited in the rear with a cavalry squadron both to pursue the Lancastrians when they broke, and to discourage fainthearted Yorkists from flight. Apparently Norfolk, who had been too late for the first battle of St. Albans in 1455, now lingered on the road from Ferrybridge.

In both armies the order 'No Quarter' passed from soldier to soldier. It was Palm Sunday morning, and in the silence the two armies gazed at each other. Across the fields village church bells could be heard tolling in the distance although falling snow blown upon gusts of wind must at times have deadened even that familiar yet ominous sound. One wonders what some of the Lancastrians whose names have survived were thinking. Did Thomas Brampton, late of Guises, and Thomas Crawford of Calais, hardened professional soldiers though they were, experience some misgivings at the sight of Warwick's banner? Did the thought strike John Penycok, 'late of Waybrigge in the counte of Surr' Squier' that he might lose his lands that day? What of 'Lawrence Hille, late of Mocke Wycombe in the counte of Buk' Yomen, Rauff Chernok, late of Thorley in the counte of Lancastr' Gentilman, Richard Cokerell, late of York, Marchaunt' and many others? We shall never know, but they must have been rare warriors indeed if they felt no doubt or fear.

At nine o'clock the armies advanced upon each other and 'rent the air with a mighty shout'. The Lancastrian archers hesitated while their captains assessed the range through the blinding snow. Lord Fauconberg told his captains to order their men to shoot one volley of heavy shaft arrows. These arrows, usually reserved for close quarter work, carried to the Lancastrian lines on the following wind. Believing that the Yorkists had come much closer than they appeared the Lancastrians loosed flight after flight of arrows, which stuck in the hard ground some 40 'taylors yards' short of the Yorkists. Gathering up their opponents' arrows Fauconberg's men shot them back. The two divisions of archers then closed upon each other, hacking and stabbing with axes, swords, mallets, maces and daggers.

After a space the archers became exhausted and retired, leaving many dead. Then the two main bodies of infantry clashed 'with so great slaughter that the very deade carkasses hindered them that fought'. Many who had lost relatives in former fights looked for vengeance. When Lord Dacre took off his helmet to refresh himself during a lull a lad sitting in the branches of an elderberry tree recognised him as the slayer of his father and shot him through the throat with an arrow. Many of the gentry wore distinctive badges or emblazoned tabards and it was not impossible to recognise individuals – with such fateful results.

The battle lasted into the afternoon as front ranks were reinforced by the rear ones. Edward, 19 years old and six foot four inches tall, and the Earl moved about constantly, 'commanding, encouraging and rallying their squadrons like the greatest captains'. At length Norfolk arrived on the field, probably on the Yorkist right, and the appearance of fresh troops proved too much for the weary Lancastrians. One chronicler pictured King Henry

79

watching while 'sodenly his soldiers gave the backe'. In terror some of these men ran to the Cocke, which they found in spate. Many died fighting in Bloody Meadow while others drowned in the river. Most of the broken army fled towards Tadcaster, just over three miles northwards. Those who reached the town found that the bridge had been destroyed at Somerset's orders some days before the battle, presumably to emphasise to his men that there could be no escape in the event of a defeat. The ford near the shattered bridge soon became so choked with dead bodies that men could cross using them as stepping stones. It is said that the Cocke ran red with blood as far as the River Aire.

Few Lancastrians, however, survived the flight to Tadcaster. The Yorkist cavalry under Wenlock and Denham rode among the fugitives spearing and scything them down with their swords. Occasionally small bands of Lancastrian gentry, unable to run in their plate armour, stood like breakwaters against the horsemen, 'such was the obstinacy and boldness of mortal men on the edge of a wretched death'. Many were slain beyond Tadcaster as they struggled on towards York city. So great was the slaughter on this hard-fought day that George Neville could write shortly afterwards that 'quite lately one might have still seen the bodies of these unfortunate men lying unburied over a space of nearly six miles in length and three or four furlongs broad'.

The work of counting and identifying the dead continued into the evening. Among the dead lay the Earl of Shrewsbury, 11 barons and more than 40 knights, including Sir Andrew Trollope. Northumberland died from his wounds in York. The Earl of Devonshire was taken prisoner 'when they were weary of killing', only to be executed later. Somerset and Exeter alone among the Lancastrian leaders escaped death or capture. They found safety in the Percy castles of Northumberland.

The Yorkists buried Lord Dacre in a standing position beside his horse in Saxton Church, but most of the soldiers found nameless graves. Several pits were dug on the banks of the Cocke, and another near Saxton Church. These have yielded scores of bones, odd coins and spurs to local historians. Other bodies were laid in 'certaine deepe trenches overgrown with brushes and briers containinge 19 yards in breadth and 32 yards in length in Towton field, a bowshot on the left hand in the way twixt Saxton and Towton, halfe a mile short of Towton'. Later King Richard III ordered a chantry chapel to be erected 'in token of praier' for the souls of the slain. Sir John Multon's father and other Lancastrians were re-interred near its walls, but owing to the patron's untimely death at Bosworth the building was never completed, and today no vestige remains on Chapel Hill behind Towton Hall.

On Monday, 18 March, Edward marched into York. He took down his father's weather-beaten head from its spike over Micklegate and replaced it with those of Devonshire, Lord Kyme, Sir William Hill and Sir Thomas Fulford. The Yorkists kept Easter with great splendour in York and then moved north to Durham and Northumberland. Early in May Edward had the Earl of Wiltshire beheaded at Newcastle. Returning to London Edward was crowned king on 28 June. George and Richard, the King's brothers, became Dukes of Clarence and Gloucester; faithful Lord Fauconberg was made Earl of Kent and the King recognised the services of many humbler men at Towton. Ralph Vestynden, who had carried Edward's standard on 'Palme sonday field', received an annuity of £10 for life.

The number of fallen on both sides was reckoned by the Yorkist heralds as high as 28,000 men, and one chronicler gives us an exact figure of 26,777. Some contemporaries divided the casualty list between the two sides. John Paston thought that the Yorkists had lost 8,000 men. This number is also given by the correspondent of a Milanese merchant in Bruges in 14 April. Nicholas O'Flanagan, Bishop of Elphin, sent the lowest estimate of Yorkist dead six days earlier to the papal legate. According to him Lord Fitzwalter and 800 men were slain. Even if a Yorkist loss of 8,000 could be accepted this would leave the Lancastrian dead as 20,000, a suspiciously round figure which often means in chronicles 'a great number'. The herald's total probably represents a piece of Yorkist propaganda, and an impartial observer such as Bishop O'Flanagan clearly did not accept it. We may not be far wrong if we calculate the total dead on both sides as between seven and nine thousand. Whatever the exact figure the near contemporary Polydore Vergil summed up in one sentence the significance for many foreigners of the slaughter at Towton – 'that battaile weakened wonderfully the force of Englande, seeing those who were killed had been able, both for number and force, to have enterprised any forreyne ware'.

1461-1471

THE GREAT VICTORY at Towton brought no peace. For two years Queen Margaret organised resistance in the North, and the war developed into sieges of strong Northumberland castles – Bamburgh, Alnwick and Dunstanburgh. In July 1463 the Queen fled to Burgundy where she was received with ceremonious chivalry. Later that year both France and Scotland concluded treaties with King Edward, but these diplomatic successes were balanced by the Duke of Somerset's reversion to the cause of Lancaster after a temporary reconciliation with King Edward after Towton. Lord Montague, however, twice defeated him, at Hedgely Moor near Newcastle on 25 April, 1464, and two months later at Hexham. Shortly afterwards the Yorkists completed their triumph by capturing the feeble-minded King Henry VI at Furness in Yorkshire.

On 29 September, 1464, King Edward told his council that in May he had married Elizabeth Woodville, widow of Sir John Grey. During the next five years the King gradually increased the power of the Woodville family, much to the anger of the Nevilles. In 1469 Warwick, who had also disagreed with the King over foreign policy, withdrew to Calais where he was joined by the Duke of Clarence. Together they plotted against King Edward.

Their first attempt to seize power in England ended in failure. At first, the victory of the northern Lancastrians over a Yorkist army at Edgecote (26 July, 1469) gave them control over King Edward. But the disorder in the country proved too much for Warwick, and after King Edward's captains had crushed a Lincolnshire rising at 'Loose-coat Field' (12 March, 1470) the Earl retired once more to Calais. Apparently he feared that his part in the rebellion would become known, as indeed it did.

The wheel of fortune turned once more for Warwick. On 8 September, 1470, after a *rapprochement* between Queen Margaret and himself, the Earl disembarked again on English soil. Less than a month later, without a fight, the King fled to Holland, and Warwick found himself Lieutenant of England. It was a brief reign,

83

however, for Edward landed at Ravenspur on 15 March, 1471, and marched to York, claiming at first only his rights as Duke of York. More nobles declared for him as he rode south, and by the time he reached London on 11 April he had perhaps 12,000 men with him.

Warwick meanwhile had gathered every available supporter, and moved towards London. The King marched out to meet him from St. John's Wood, and the armies met a mile north of Barnet, after a Lancastrian cannonade which sounded throughout the night of 13-14 April. Warwick's right wing under John de Vere, Earl of Oxford, drove the Yorkist left from the field, but Richard, Duke of Gloucester, led the Yorkist right against the Duke of Exeter with success. Meanwhile Oxford's men 'fell to ryfling', which prevented him from bringing aid to the hard-pressed Warwick. He brought some of his followers back to the misty field, but their silver five-pointed star badges were mistaken for Edward's Sun 'with stremys', and their comrades shot arrows at them. Oxford clapped his spurs to his horse and rode off crying 'Treason! Treason!' The Lancastrians in the centre gave way, and 'everyman shyftyd for himselfe, some one way, some another'. Some nameless Yorkist cut down Warwick in a near-by wood.

Four days after the battle one of the Earl of Oxford's soldiers, Sir John Paston, wrote to his mother. As perhaps the earliest document of this kind in English that has survived the letter deserves full quotation.

'Moodre, I recomande me to you, letyng you wette that, blyssed be God, my brother John is a lyffe and farethe well, and in no perell off dethe. Never the lesse he is hurt with an arrow in hys ryght arme, be nethe the elbow, and I have sent hym a serjon, whyche hathe dressid hym, and he tellyth me that he trustythe that he schall be all holl with in a ryght schort tyme. It is so that John Mylsent is ded, God have mercy on hys sowle!'

The Battle of Tewkesbury

THE CAMPAIGN

1471

15 March	*King Edward lands at Ravenspur.*
14 April	*Battle of Barnet.* *Queen Margaret lands at Weymouth.*
19 April	*Edward arrives at Windsor.*
29 April	*Edward at Cirencester; Queen Margaret in Bristol.*
2 May	*The Sudbury Hill stratagem.*
3 May	*Queen Margaret, refused admittance at Gloucester, marches on to Tewkesbury. Edward's army marches towards Tewkesbury by way of Stroud and Cheltenham.*
4 May	*Battle of Tewkesbury.*

THE BATTLE

4 May, 1471

ON THE VERY day of the Battle of Barnet Queen Margaret, her young son and a small force of mercenaries, landed from 17 ships at Weymouth. The news of the defeat, which reached her the following day, almost caused her to despair. The Earl of Pembroke, however, promised to bring a Welsh army to her standard and the Duke of Somerset offered to raise the West Country in her name. These nobles, who met her soon after her arrival, counselled an early battle. Heartened by this loyalty Queen Margaret moved to Exeter to await there the Lancastrian contingents.

King Edward received a report of the Queen's landing on 16 April, and at once he began to make preparations for a second campaign He sent scouts to find out the movements of the Lancastrian army and commanded his household officers to collect victuals and military stores. On Friday, 19 April, the King rode to Windsor, where he kept the great feast of St. George four days later. He planned to intercept the Queen before her supporters mustered a large army. At Windsor he poised his own forces until he could be certain where the Queen intended to go. Either the Lancastrians could march on London by way of Salisbury or they could move northwards into Lancashire and Cheshire. If the Queen chose the latter course he could attack her at Gloucester, Tewkesbury or Worcester before the northern Lancastrians could join her.

In fact Queen Margaret, advised by her council of war, had resolved upon the latter plan. It was in her interest, however, to make King Edward believe that she had resolved to march on London. Somerset therefore sent 'forarders' to Salisbury, Yeovil and Bruton with orders to requisition quarters and provisions as if the whole army would march along that route. But King Edward's scouts saw through this stratagem. The King set out for Cirencester, which he reached on Monday, 29 April. There he learnt that on the following day the Lancastrian army would arrive at Bath, only 27 miles away, along a straight Roman road, and that they planned to attack him on Wednesday. That night the King camped his army in the fields three miles beyond the town.

On Tuesday, 30 April, the King resumed his march hoping to take the enemy by surprise, but at Malmesbury he heard that they had entered Bristol, where the citizens had supplied the Queen with money, men and artillery. From there the Duke of Somerset, the third of that name to act as general for the Lancastrians, sent out horsemen to see whether the Severn could be crossed at Gloucester. To cover their next move the Lancastrian leaders prepared another deception plan. They publicly announced their intention of giving battle to the King's army, and appointed Sudbury Hill, on the southern spur of the Cotswolds nine miles from Bristol, as the field and Thursday, 2 May, as the day.

In consequence Edward arrayed his 'battles' and marched out from Malmesbury. The King intended to sleep that night in

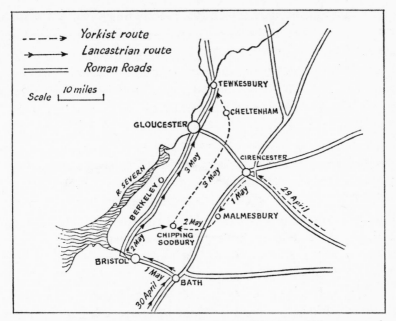

Sudbury, but five or six of his men, who were seeking lodgings for their master in the village, discovered that some enemy 'herbengars' had arrived first. This incident persuaded Edward to pitch his tents some miles short of Sudbury, and he only reached the top of Sudbury Hill after noon on the appointed day of battle. The Lancastrians could not be seen. Nevertheless the King, convinced that they were at hand, ordered his 'scorars' into the countryside to find them. Deprived of the promised battle he lodged his vaward in a valley towards Sudbury while he and the rest of the army camped on the hill.

The night was far spent before he received tidings of his elusive enemy. Scouts told him that the Lancastrians, having made a pretence at moving towards Sudbury, had in fact taken the Roman road to Gloucester, marching throughout Friday night. The King sent his own servants on swift horses to urge Richard Beauchamp, his governor in Gloucester, to hold the town and bridge until he could arrive with his army. Then, with his army divided into three divisions ready for action, 'for ryders and scorars' out on the flanks to guard against ambush, the King advanced his banners towards Gloucester.

Marching on high ground five or six miles east of the main road the vanguard of the Yorkist army soon drew level with some Lancastrian cavalry hastening along the highway to Gloucester. At the end of the morning the King heard that although the Lancastrians had made great 'manasys' against the town and certain merchants favoured them Beauchamp had not only proved faithful to his trust but had succeeded in keeping the garrison to its duty. The Lancastrian leaders had no alternative but to march on towards Tewkesbury where there was a ferry across the Severn a mile south-west of the town, and a bridge across the Avon to the north. After a march of 36 'longe myles' through 'a fowle contry, all in lanes and stonny wayes, betwyxt woodes, without any good refresshyng' the footsore soldiers at last pitched camp late in the afternoon to the south of the town with the Abbey tower standing like a giant sentry behind them.

Meanwhile King Edward had resumed his own march moving by way of Stroud and Cheltenham. Here he learnt of Queen Margaret's presence at Tewkesbury, only eight miles away. His troops had covered 31 miles on a 'right-and-hot day' with no fresh food or water. The men had indeed paused to drink from one small brook, but the waggon wheels of the army had so churned it up that the water had become undrinkable. Beyond Cheltenham the soldiers ate an evening meal from these waggons and set up their tents for the night near Tredington, within three miles of the enemy. Early next morning, Saturday, 4 May, the King prepared to lead his army against the Lancastrians, much against the advice of some captains, who pleaded with him to wait for reinforcements.

On arrival at Tewkesbury the evening before Somerset had chosen the ground upon which he intended to give battle. It is not known exactly where the Lancastrian army stood, but Somerset's position probably stretched across the Roman road facing south-east on the open ground known as the Gastons. Along their front the Lancastrians dug a trench, no doubt backed with sharpened stakes. The Yorkist chronicler hardly exaggerated when he concluded after describing the uneven ground intersected with hedges and ditches, that it was 'a right evill place to approche as cowlde well have been devysed'.

Although the indomitable Queen Margaret certainly rode

88

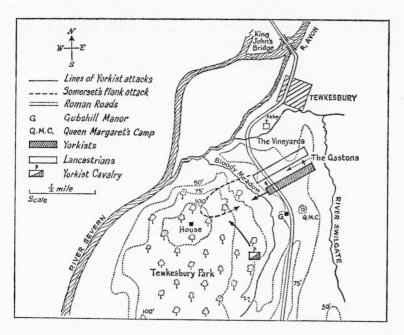

among her troops promising them booty and honours, there is little doubt that Edmund Beaufort, Duke of Somerset, command- ed the army. Previously historians have shown the battle formation he adopted as the traditional three divisions in line with each other. It seems more likely from the evidence that the Lancastrian general deployed his divisions in extended lines, one behind the other. At least one of his divisional commanders, Lord Wenlock, had seen the array used on a similar narrow front at Towton on that fateful Palm Sunday.

The Duke himself took command of the vaward of archers and field gunners; behind him the 17 year old son of Queen Margaret, Prince Edward, and the double-turncoat Lord Wen- lock, who had fought on the winning side at second St. Albans and Towton, led the middleward. The Earl of Devonshire's rearward may have been thin, for the whole army cannot have mustered more than 7,000 men. Indeed many professional captains begged Somerset to wait for Pembroke's Welsh archers.

Somerset, however, had evolved a remarkable tactical plan. After the first artillery broadside and flight of arrows he

89

planned to lead part of the vaward away to his right, using the natural cover of thick hedges and lanes, and then to fall on the flank of the Yorkist army. He told Wenlock that he must charge forward with the main 'battle' as soon as he saw Somerset's men emerging from the woods of Tewkesbury Park. On Friday evening Somerset made a careful reconnaissance of the route which he intended to follow upon this outflanking manoeuvre.

King Edward also arrayed his three divisions behind each other. His army may have numbered as few as 6,000 men. Gloucester commanded the first line and the King the second; Lord Hastings led the rearward which included a proportion of cavalry. In this order the army advanced to within a mile of the Lancastrians and halted out of sight. The very stillness of the surrounding woods menaced the Yorkists. Fearing an ambush party hidden beneath the thick May foliage of Tewkesbury Park the King sent a squadron of two hundred horsemen into a copse somewhat to the left of his line of advance with orders to guard his flank against any Lancastrian ambuscade. Should they detect no attempted surprise from the neck of woods which reached out beyond them they were to employ themselves later in the battle when and where they thought most fitting.

Deployed on both sides of the great white and red banner of St. George the Yorkist army then resumed its march. When Gloucester's vaward came within range the Lancastrian artillery opened fire with their few pieces. The Yorkists replied with some light field guns – one of the earliest occasions in English history that cannon were used in close support of infantry. The Yorkist bowmen followed up the stone balls with a 'right-a-sharpe shwre' of cloth yard shafts. The billmen in the vaward made slow work of coming to hand strokes with the enemy because of the dry ditches and drainage dykes which abounded in the valley at that time.

While this fight developed along the front of the Lancastrian position, Somerset gathered men from his company and 'departed out of the field, passyd a lane and came into a fayre place, or cloos, even afore the King where he was embatteled, and, from the hill that was in that one of the closes, he set right fiercely upon the end of the King's battayle'. This 'cloos' was probably a clearing in the trees of Tewkesbury Park, and Somerset must have relied much more upon the cover afforded by the woodland than the chronicler records.

The King, whose extreme left flank came under severe attack, remained calm. Leading troops presumably from his own household, he drove the Lancastrians across a dyke and hedge and back into the close 'with great violence'. On the high ground towards the site of Tewkesbury Park Golf and Country Club, Somerset's men fought a bitter action against the Yorkists. Some of Gloucester's men from the left files of his long line joined in the fight.

Meanwhile the two hundred Yorkist horsemen in the copse, who had no doubt been straining at the leash, saw their opportunity. Spurring their horses through scattered trees they burst out into the 'cloos' and charged at gallop against the flank of Somerset's force 'asyde-hand unadvysed'. Their lowered lance points pierced many of the Lancastrian foot soldiers as they stood in amazement : the others broke and ran, some further into the park, others into the meadows bordering the Avon.

Somerset, in a blazing temper, mounted a horse and rode back to the main body of the army. He had only one idea in his mind – that Wenlock had failed to attack in the centre as planned. As far as the Duke was concerned this was certain proof that Wenlock had turned traitor once again. There is no evidence that this was true. More likely, Gloucester, 'who lacked no policye', rallied his extended division around his Boar's Head standard, and held the Yorkist centre with a convincing show of force while his brother counter-attacked Somerset on the left. Perhaps it was for this reason rather than because 'his heart served him not' that Wenlock preferred to abide behind his ditch. If this was the truth he never had time to explain it to his irate commander. Riding up to Wenlock the Duke denounced him as a traitor and then, carried away by his wrath, dashed out his brains with his battle axe. History records no more summary dismissal of a divisional commander.

While this grim episode was enacted Gloucester pressed forward over the ditch, closely followed by men of the middleward. After a short hand-to-hand fight, the Queen's soldiers, unnerved perhaps by seeing Wenlock removed, turned and fled. Some ran to Tewkesbury Park, while others rushed towards the towers of the Abbey and the sanctuary of its altars. Many drowned in the struggle to wade across the Mill, the Avon or died in the field now known as Bloody Meadow.

The Earls of Devonshire and Dorset, Wenlock, Lord John of Somerset and ten other Lancastrian leaders were killed in the battle. Those who survived had not long to rejoice. Yorkist soldiers searched the churches and Abbey of Tewkesbury and dragged out the Duke of Somerset, Sir John Langstrother and other Lancastrian knights. A hastily convened court, headed by Gloucester as Constable of England and Norfolk as Earl Marshall, pronounced the inevitable sentence. The executioners beheaded all the notable prisoners in the market place.

Queen Margaret fled in a carriage, overwrought with grief for her son, 'a goodly femenine and well featured yonge gentelman', who had been taken prisoner by Sir Richard Croftes. The King had promised a £100 annuity to his captor, but some overheated Yorkist struck the young prince down with a dagger, no doubt hoping to please the King by ridding him of this potential claimant to his throne.

Hall asserted that some 3,000 Lancastrians died in the battle. This is almost certainly an exaggeration. Perhaps half that number fell, at the cost of only a few hundred Yorkist lives. The King knighted 43 Yorkists after the battle, which suggests that he was well pleased with the valour and tactical skill of his followers, and he was no mean judge.

An interesting comparison between the two seconds-in-command can be drawn. The steadiness of Gloucester gave the King invaluable support in the crisis of the battle, whereas Wenlock, for reasons we shall never know, acted with undue caution – to say the least of it. King Edward, however, deserves all the praise he has received for his strategy before the battle. His ability to recover swiftly from the strategic surprise at Sudbury and the tactical one on the Tewkesbury field qualifies him as one of the most resourceful generals of the fifteenth century.

1471-1483

THE DOUBLE VICTORY of King Edward at Barnet and Tewkesbury effectively silenced the surviving Lancastrians for the last 12 years of his reign. It is true that John de Vere, Earl of Oxford, the commander of the Lancastrian right at Barnet who had escaped to France, made two sorties into the realm. On 28 May, 1473, he landed at St. Osyth's in Essex, but he took to his ships again on the approach of a royal army. In October he tried once more, and captured St. Michael's Mount in Cornwall, but he had only 80 men with him. Within two months the King's soldiers had taken the Mount, and Oxford was imprisoned in Hammes Castle, near Calais.

Free from internal threats the King could turn his attention to the continent, and he decided to take the part of Charles le Téméraire, Duke of Burgundy, in his quarrel with France. By the summer of 1475 an English expeditionary force of 1,200 men-at-arms and 11,000 archers, had been transported to France. Louis XI, however, met the English commanders at Picquigny on 29 August and bought them off with 75,000 golden crowns, with a promise of 50,000 a year more while Edward lived. The King returned to England and disbanded his troops.

One feature of the reign which this expedition revealed was the development of a military staff centred upon the King's household knights. For example, John Elrington, Constable of Windsor Castle in 1474, who acted as treasurer for the invasion of France in the following year, was a 'knight of the body'. Many of these knights served in county administration as crown officers in peace time, building up local influence. In war they were appointed castellans of royal castles or served in command and staff appointments in the field army. One troop guarded the King's person in battle as his 'fellowship'. These were the forerunners of the Gentlemen Pensioners of Tudor and Stuart times, who have a continuous history down to the present day as the Gentlemen at Arms.

During the last years of King Edward's reign, Richard of

Gloucester added to his military reputation by successfully invading Scotland in 1481. On 1 August the following year Edinburgh surrendered to him, but he was unable to bring the Scottish field army to battle. In the peace treaty which followed Berwick, which had been sold to the Scots 20 years earlier by Queen Margaret, became an English town once more.

The Battle of Bosworth

THE CAMPAIGN

1485

7 August	*Henry Tudor lands at Milford Haven.*
15 August	*Henry Tudor reaches Shrewsbury.* *King Richard hears news of the invasion at Nottingham.*
16 August	*Henry, at Newport, is joined by Sir Gilbert Talbot.* *Richard marches to Leicester.*
17 August	*Henry moves from Lichfield to Tamworth.*
20 August	*Henry reaches Atherstone.* *Meeting between Henry Tudor and Lord Stanley.*
22 August	*Battle of Bosworth.*

THE BATTLE

22 August, 1485

'The Cat, the Rat and Lovell our Dog,
Rule all England under the Hog.'[1]

ON 9 APRIL, 1483 King Edward died, and Richard of Gloucester became Protector during the minority of the Prince Edward. Richard soon confined the young prince and his brother in the Tower of London where the two boys 'day by day began to be seen more rarely behind the bars and windows' until these appearances mysteriously ceased altogether. The thorny question of who killed the princes in the Tower remains as one of the baffling problems of history although perhaps it could be said that the weight of circumstantial evidence still points to Richard.

The Protector, however, had to contend with opposition from other relatives of the princes – the Woodville family. With the Duke of Buckingham's assistance he had Earl Rivers, the Queen's father and Sir Richard Grey, son of her first husband, beheaded at Pontefract on charges of treason (25 June, 1483). Sir Edward Woodville, the Queen's brother, still held command of the fleet anchored off the Downs. Gloucester ordered Sir Thomas Fulford[2] and Sir Edward Brampton to seize him. These knights persuaded the captains of the largest Genoese carracks in the fleet to make his English soldiers drunk and then sail to London. The plot worked, although Woodville made his escape to Brittany.

Suspecting that the powerful Lord Hastings, King Edward's staunch friend, sympathised secretly with the Queen's party, Gloucester accused him of treason at a council meeting in the White Tower (13 June). The Protector's guards rushed into the chamber and led Hastings outside to Tower Green where he was promptly beheaded. Lord Stanley, the Lancashire magnate, who had been similarly arraigned at the meeting, was put under house arrest but later released.

This 'coup' paved the way for the coronation of Gloucester as King Richard III at a sumptuous ceremony on 6 July, three months after his brother's death. By October, however, Richard discovered that the man who had arranged the details of his coronation, the Duke of Buckingham, had connived at a Lancastrian plot to unseat him. The Duke of Norfolk and a royal army soon prevented the unco-ordinated rising from becoming serious ; Buckingham fled into Herefordshire, where bad weather and scant signs of support dispersed his soldiers. A servant betrayed him to King Richard, and the Duke was beheaded in Salisbury market place on 2 November, 1483

King Richard was not permitted to live in peace for long. The Lancastrian heir, a youth called Henry Tudor, Earl of Richmond, had already made attempts to land in Dorset and Devon. Therefore the King moved to Exeter and executed or pardoned those who had taken up arms on Henry Tudor's behalf. When all had become quiet again the King returned to London.

Throughout 1484 the King stood on guard against a Lancastrian invasion. He attempted to take the initiative and compel

The Battle of Bannockburn (fifteenth century manuscript). In the background is Stirling Castle: in the middle, Robert Bruce wielding his battle axe against Sir Humphrey de Bohun.
The Master and Fellows of Corpus Christi College, Cambridge

Here shewes howe at the batell of Shrewesbury. betwen kyng Henr the
iiijⁿᵈ & Sir Henr Percy / Erle Richard there beyng on the kynge party ful
notably & manly behaued hym self / to his grete Lawde & Worship / In
which batell was slayne the said Sir Henr Percy and many other wᵗ
hym And on the kynge party there was slayne in the kynge co beanm̄
chief of other . the Erle of Stafford. Erle Richardes Auntes Son wᵗ
many other in grete nombre . on Whos sowles god haue mcy Amē

PLATE 2
The Battle of Shrewsbury, from 'The Pageant of the Birth, Life and Death of Richard
Beauchamp, Earl of Warwick'. The army of Harry Hotspur is fleeing from the King
(left), with Hotspur himself dead.
The Trustees of the British Museum

PLATE 3
Monumental brass of 1491 to Paul Dayrell. An outstanding example of a figure in full plate armour.
Lillingstone Dayrell P.C.C., Bucks.

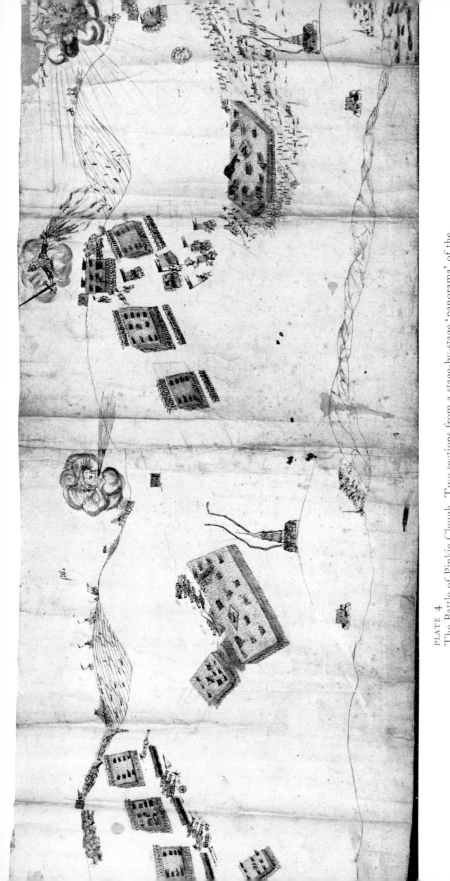

PLATE 4

The Battle of Pinkie Cleugh. Two sections from a stage-by-stage 'panorama' of the battle. On the right the rout of the Scots army is beginning.

The Bodleian Library

the Duke of Brittany by diplomatic pressure to expel Richmond, but without success. At home he placed men whom he could trust in key positions in both the civil and military administration. King Richard made full use of the household as a military staff. For example, Sir Richard Huddleston, a 'knight of the body', was sent to command Beaumaris Castle, an important stronghold seven miles north east of Bangor. Other household knights remained with the King, with Sir Richard Ratcliffe as their unofficial head.

The royal accounts show how diligently the King set about increasing the ordnance in the Tower of London. The legislation in his parliament also reflected military necessities. One act countered the Venetian merchants' habit of charging exorbitant prices for bowstaves by legislating that every barrel of Malmsey and sweet wine imported from Italy should have ten staves with it, and that only the best of these should be put up for sale to Englishmen. In 1478 Parliament had also prohibited football and other games in order to keep up the standard of English archery.

Nevertheless the professional soldiers of Richard's army were hardy and experienced. An Italian visitor named Dominic Mancini who came to Richard III's coronation in 1483, described them :

'There is hardly any without a helmet, and none without bows and arrows; their bows and arrows are thicker and longer than those used by other nations, just as their bodies are stronger than other people's, for they seem to have hands and arms of iron. The range of their bows is no less than our arbalests; there hangs by the side of each a sword no less long than ours, but heavy and thick as well. The sword is always accompanied by an iron shield; it is the particular delight of this race that on holidays their youths should fight up and down the streets clashing on their shields with blunted swords or stout staves in place of swords. When they are older they go out into the fields with bows and arrows and even the women are not inexperienced at hunting with these weapons. They do not wear any metal armour on their breast or any other part of their body, except for the better sort, who have breastplates and suits of armour. Indeed the common soldiery have more comfortable tunics that reach down below the loins and are stuffed with tow or some other soft material. They say that the softer the tunic the better do they withstand the blows of arrows and swords, and besides that in summer they are lighter and in winter more service-able than iron. The soldiers who had been sent for arrived equipped with this sort of armour, and in addition there were horsemen among them. Not that they are accustomed to fighting on horse back, but because they use horses to carry them to the scene of the engagement, so as to arrive fresher . . . therefore they will ride any sort of horse, even pack horses. On reaching the field of battle the horses are abandoned, they all fight under the same conditions so that no one should retain hope of fleeing. . . .'

The spring of 1485 found King Richard at Nottingham Castle – a central headquarters from which he could move rapidly to any part of the country. Horsemen at 20 mile intervals along all the roads to the coast waited to warn him of insurrections or invasions. A trial mobilisation of the Surrey, Middlesex and Hertfordshire forces had already taken place in order to discover how many men could be mustered at six hours' notice. Viscount Lovell and the fleet gathered at Southampton to safeguard the Channel. In Wales, where Henry Tudor would receive much support, Richard placed more of his firm supporters. Richard Williams was sent as castellan of Pembroke, Tenby, Manorbier, Haverfordwest and Ciegerran castles, while the Earl of Huntingdon and Sir James Tyrrell held commands in South Wales. These detachments, however, weakened the central army at the King's disposal.

On 7 August, 1485, Henry Tudor landed with 2,000 men at Milford Haven. He was accompanied by his uncle, the Earl of Pembroke and John de Vere, who had persuaded the Lieutenant of Hammes Castle, James Blount, to change his allegiance. The small force marched to Haverfordwest unmolested by Rhys ap Thomas and Sir Walter Herbert, who were rumoured to be at Carmarthen with royalist soldiers. On his way to Shrewsbury Henry was joined by many North Wales gentry. Rhys, who had been promised the lieutenancy of Wales by Henry Tudor, brought 'a great baulk of soldiers' to his standard, and Sir Walter Herbert also judged it expedient to change sides.

Despite his post system it was not until Henry Tudor had reached Shrewsbury that Richard first heard the news of the landing and march through Wales. At once he put into operation his carefully planned mobilisation scheme. The great men of the counties were summoned to bring their levies and personal retainers to him at Nottingham without delay. Sir John Paston, Sheriff of Norfolk and Suffolk, received orders to ride with the 'tall men' of the counties, in the Duke of Norfolk's livery to Bury St. Edmunds on 16 August. Sir Robert Brackenbury, Constable of the the Tower, was told by letter to come at once with Sir Thomas

Bourchier and Sir Walter Hungerford. The citizens of York, who favoured Richard of Gloucester, sent John Spon, 'sergeant to the Mase' to Nottingham, to find out when and where the King required the city's soldiers. On 19 August after a message from the King, '4000 men, defensibly arrayed, John Hastings gentleman of the mace being captain, were ordered, in all haste possible, to depart towards the King's Grace, for the subduing of his enemies'.[3]

Not all who received the royal command responded so favourably. At Newport, 17 miles east of Shrewsbury on the road to Stafford, Sir Gilbert Talbot, Sheriff of the county of Shropshire and 2,000 levies, joined the Lancastrian army. Lord Stanley, who was the stepfather of Henry Tudor, refused to obey the summons, pleading indisposition. Richard, however, had allowed for this and held Stanley's son, the young Lord Strange, as a hostage. Bourchier and Hungerford deserted to Richmond at Lichfield.

Hearing that Henry had reached Lichfield the King resolved to defeat him before the Lancastrian army grew any larger. Perhaps he also feared that Richmond intended to interpose his army between Nottingham and London, cutting off the King from his capital. On 16 August, Richard mustered his small army in Nottingham market place, and set out for Leicester, covering the 25 miles that day. The army, divided into two divisions, marched four in a rank. Behind the baggage train in the centre a Tudor historian pictured the King 'environed with his satellites and yeomen of the crown, with a frowning countenance and truculent aspect, mounted on a great white courser, followed with his footmen, the wings of horsemen coasting and ranging on every side'. In this array he entered Leicester, welcomed by a salute from the city guns, and lodged for the night at the sign of the Blue Boar. It is said that he had his own bed carried into the inn with 300 gold coins concealed in it.

The next morning Richard led his army over Bow bridge to Elmesthorpe 9 miles away. Afterwards it was rumoured that an old woman who saw the King strike his foot against the side of the bridge prophesied that his head would bump against the same timber.[4] That night many of his household knights slept in the village church, while the bulk of his army camped in some fields

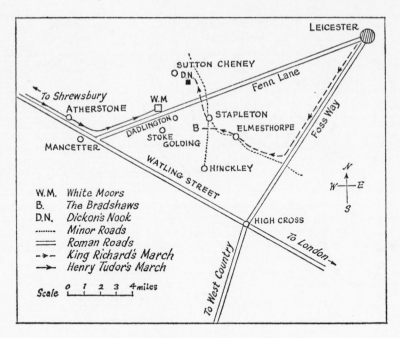

THE CAMPAIGN OF BOSWORTH

called the Bradshaws just outside Stapleton. From here the King was in a good position either to oppose Henry's march along Watling Street or to block a sudden advance on Leicester up Fenn Lane. Later, when it became apparent that Henry might be resolved on the second course, the King moved his camp to the area known as Dickon's Nook, just by Sutton Cheney.

On 17 August Henry had marched from Lichfield to Tamworth, where he had been met by Sir John Savage and his men, in white jackets and hoods. From Tamworth, where he stayed at the sign of the Three Tuns, Henry Tudor moved on to Atherstone and during the night of 20 August he met Lord Stanley and his brother, Sir William Stanley, in secret. Henry Tudor then decided to seek battle at the earliest opportunity. Next day a local Lancastrian, John Hardwick, guided Henry's army along the old trackway known as Fenn Lane, through Fenny Drayton, until the Tweed was reached near Shenton Mill. Here, in an angle of the river known as White Moors, one mile from Ambion Hill, Henry Tudor pitched his camp for the night.

Early on the morning of 22 August, as the grey dawn revealed once more the fields of Leicestershire, both armies made ready for the forthcoming battle. Sir Simon Digby, who deserted from King Richard's camp at dawn, brought details of the royal forces to Henry Tudor. Shakespeare's description of the King's guilt-ridden nightmare has no historical foundation. A more characteristic story relates how the King, coming out of his tent early in the morning, found a sentry dozing. It is said that he stabbed him, commenting 'I found him asleep and I have left him as I found him'. Donning the armour which he wore at Tewkesbury the King ordered his captains to leave the tents standing and to lead their men to Sutton field, on the high ground south of Sutton Cheney.

THE ROYAL ARMY

There the King arranged his army of 9,640 men for battle. The formation he adopted perhaps reflected the influence of the continental tactics evolved by the Swiss. First he arrayed a long screen of 1,240 archers, spread out to give the enemy the appearance of great numbers. Thomas, Earl of Surrey, and Sir Robert Brackenbury commanded the left half of this ward and John, Duke of Norfolk, the right. The flanks were protected by two squadrons, each of 200 cuirassiers. This force was supported by a division of 1,000 men – presumably archers, handgunners and artillerymen – protected by a further 2,000 pikemen, each with a 16 foot spear. Finally came the main ward under the banner of St. George, commanded by the King, consisting of 2,000 foot soldiers, flanked by 1,500 cavalry on each side, 'cast in square maniples'. The Earl of Northumberland probably commanded the horsemen on the right. The Stanley chronicler tells us that the King 'had vii skore sergeants that wer cheyned and lockyd in a row, and as many bumbards, and thousands of morys (moorish) pyks, haggebushes, etc.' It is quite possible that the chronicler, who may have written in the next generation, assumed that the formations and weapons current in his own day were already in use at Bosworth. On the other hand Richard may have studied continental methods of war in 1475 and adapted something of what he then saw. He had certainly developed the artillery arm since that year and there is some archaeological evidence that there were more spearmen present at Bosworth than was usual in a battle of the Wars of the Roses.

These dispositions could not, however, guard against an unseen enemy – treachery. During the night some anonymous well-wisher had pinned a note on Norfolk's tent door, which read :

> 'Jockey of Norfolk, be not too bold,
> For Dickon thy master is bought and sold.'

This encouraging 'thought for the day' no doubt existed as common rumour in the army, and it would be strengthened by Lord Stanley's reluctance to join the King, although he was not far away. The theory that Richard's possession of Lord Strange prevented him from openly declaring for Henry Tudor has little foundation. Stanley himself said that he had other sons. In fact he could not make up his mind who would win and he therefore decided to watch the battle until he could see who would prove victor before committing himself. Therefore, after assurances to both sides, he took up a position on 20 August where he could observe the events of the next day. Exactly where this was remains a matter of conjecture, but the high ground of Ambion Hill suggests itself as the most likely place. Most historians have placed another Stanley force under Sir William opposite, but this rests on slender evidence. The Stanley retainers perhaps numbered 2,000 men.

While the King arrayed his army Henry Tudor made his own preparations. A skirmisher line of Norman mercenary archers under a captain named Barnard interspersed with English and Welsh bowmen were placed in front, with the Lancastrian veteran John de Vere, Earl of Oxford, in command. Behind stood a slender long vaward, consisting mainly of the Shropshire levies on the

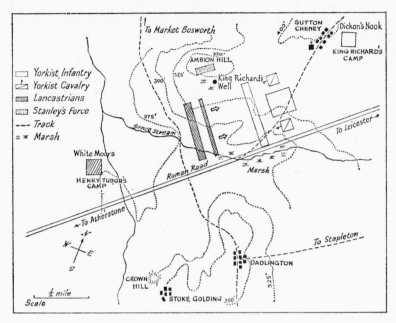

THE BATTLE OF BOSWORTH, 1485

right and Sir John Savage's men on the left. Sir Brian Sanford and Sir Simon Digby acted as captains under Savage. Henry Tudor, mounted on a bay horse, and Pembroke led the main ward, which included the Welsh under the Black Raven standard of Rhys ap Thomas. The great Red Dragon of Cadwaladr banner proclaimed Richmond's claim of descent from the ancient kings of Wales. Henry's captains disposed his few field pieces in the vaward.[5] In all Henry Tudor's army numbered perhaps 8,000 soldiers.

The two main armies approached each other marching north of the line of the Roman road, with the Stanleys looking on, like spectators in a grandstand. When they were in sight of each other, the commanders halted the armies and ordered their men to make their last preparations for battle. Then 'lord how hastely the soldioures buckled their headlines, how quickly the archers bent their bowes and frushed their feathers, how redely ye byllmen shoke there bylles and proved there staves, redy to approche and joyne when the terrible trumpet should sounde the bluddy blast to victorie or death'.

103

In order to face the royal army the Lancastrian leaders had to incline their divisions to the left to avoid a marsh along the banks of the Sence stream. One chronicler, relying perhaps on some soldiers' reminiscences, recorded that when this change of direction had been made the sun no longer shone so directly in the eyes of the Lancastrians.

King Richard, who may have known about the marsh, watched until his opponents had passed it. As soon as the armies confronted each other the ordnance thundered, sending stone cannon balls ploughing into the fields. Then, after the archers had fired at each other, the two front lines clashed :

> 'They encountered together sad and sair,
> Archers let sharp arrows flee,
> They shot guns both fell and fair
> Bows of yew did bended be.
> Then the archers let their shooting by
> And joined weapons in the fight,
> Brands rang on basnets[6] high
> Battleaxes fast on helms did light.'[7]

Fearing that his men would become dispersed Oxford ordered his men to advance no more than 10 feet in front of his Silver Star standard. While some of them fell back to this line, the enemy, suspecting treachery, glanced about them or stood back. Oxford then led his men in a charge and scattered the Yorkist archers. Surrey, however, countered this by presenting a wedge shaped phalanx, pointed in front and thicker at the rear.

A ferocious hand-to-hand struggle followed, with both vawards no doubt reinforced from the rear divisions. Norfolk, a veteran of the French wars who had fought long ago at Castillon in 1453, engaged Oxford in a duel. It is said that he slashed the Earl's hand with his sword, but Oxford's return blow struck away the beaver of his helmet, and a nameless Lancastrian archer shot a deadly arrow at his exposed face. 'A better knight could not die, though he might in a better cause,' Oxford declared.

Sir Gilbert Talbot on the right endeavoured to seize Surrey, but Sir William Conyers and Sir Richard Clarendon rushed to defend him, only to be themselves killed by some of Savage's Cestrians. Surrey meanwhile fought Talbot's men with his sword, striking off the arm of a common soldier who asked him to surrender. At last he handed his sword to Talbot.

It was at this time, when resistance along the King's vaward had slackened, that Lord Stanley chose to lead his men against the right flank of the King's army. While the struggle continued King Richard sat his great white courser watching the ebb and flow of battle with what patience his fiery nature could muster, but when a scout reported that Henry Tudor had ridden within reach, he could restrain himself no more. Spurring his horse along the rear of his own troops he wheeled and charged against Henry Tudor's small party. King Richard, as much man-at-arms as general, pierced Sir William Brandon with his lance. The knight died in his saddle, and the Red Dragon which he carried fell to the earth until Sir Richard Percival picked it up and held it aloft although one of his legs had been almost severed. Pursuing his deadly course, the King struck down Sir John Cheney and Sir Gervaise Clifton with his battle axe. Catesby urged Richard to fly, but it was too late. In the general mêlée Richard's horse stumbled, and the white hooded men of Cheshire closed in on the last of the Plantagenet kings.

Meanwhile more of Stanley's red-coated followers rushed into battle. His 'archers let theyr arrows flye ; they shot of goons ; many a bannar began to show that was on Richard's partye ; with grounde wepons they joyned ; there dyed many a dowghty knight'. The Yorkist army disintegrated and fled, although private duels between the gentry continued such as that between Hungerford and white haired Brackenbury. Meanwhile the men from Cheshire sacked the royal camp. There was no pursuit beyond Dadlington. Lord Stanley found Richard's gold crown in a bush and set it on the head of Henry Tudor.

The Yorkist army lost 900 dead, including Norfolk, Lord Ferrers and Sir Richard Ratcliffe. The Earl of Surrey became a prisoner in the Tower for three years before his restoration to favour, but Sir William Catesby, speaker of King Richard's only parliament, was beheaded at Leicester two days after the battle. Henry, Earl of Northumberland, who had stood still throughout the fighting with an impartiality strange even in that strange war, passed into captivity. Lord Lovell escaped, fought at Stoke two years later, and then disappeared into ignominious exile.

The victorious new King marched to Atherstone, where the townsfolk refused to admit his army, owing to the sweating sickness which the soldiers had brought with them from the continent. A gilt spur found in an earth bank near the town marks the place where some of the Lancastrians fell. But the Lancastrian dead did not number more than 200 men, of whom the most prominent was Sir William Brandon.

From Atherstone Henry marched to Coventry and lodged with the Mayor, a merchant of Smithford Street, next to the Black Bull Inn. The Mayor entertained his guest at a feast costing £23 - 15s. - 11d. and presented him with a cup worth £100. Meanwhile Richard's body, naked and covered with blood and mire, was slung over the back of a horse behind his own herald, Blanch Sanglier, who may have been the 'Richard Watkins, herrauld of armes' listed in the Act of Attainder. The corpse after exposure on Newarke, one of the public gates of Leicester, found temporary rest in Greyfriars until the Dissolution, when it is said that the remains were thrown over Bow Bridge into the River Soar. Whatever he merited as man or king, as a soldier King Richard deserved a better end.

[1] Sir William Catesby, Sir Richard Ratcliffe and Viscount Lovell, the chamberlain, were all members of the Council. Gloucester's badge was a Boar's Head.

[2] Son of the Lancastrian executed after Towton.

[3] Drake, *History of York*, p. 120.

[4] The mediaeval mind loved such prophesies, *cf.* that concerning Somerset's fate at first St. Albans. It was also said that a blind wheelwright declared that if the moon changed twice that day the King would lose the battle. The moon did in fact change, and legend has it that a Yorkist named Moon, or a knight with the moon in his coat-of-arms, changed sides in the fighting. Such stories have to be viewed with suspicion by the historian.

[5] Commines had seen these presented to Henry before he embarked.

[6] The bascinet.

[7] Michael Drayton, 'Ballad of Bosworth Field'.

The Battle of Flodden

THE CAMPAIGN

1513

30 June	*King Henry VIII sails to France.*
1 August	*Surrey sets up his headquarters at Pontefract.*
3 August	*Ambush of Scots raiding party at Millfield.*
22 August	*Scots army crosses border into England.*
29 August	*Surrender of Norham Castle.*
3 September	*Etall Castle falls to the Scots.*
	Surrey reaches Alnwick.
5 September	*English army arrayed outside Bolton.*
9 September	*Battle of Flodden.*

THE BATTLE

9 September, 1513

'Every English archer beareth under his girdle twenty four Scots.'

ROGER ASCHAM

ON 30 JUNE, 1513, King Henry VIII sailed from Dover with a fine army to join the Emperor Maximilian in a war against France. The King left behind him the aged Thomas Howard, Earl of Surrey, as Lord Lieutenant of the North with orders to watch the border, for 'he and his counsaill forgat not the old prankes of the Scottes which is ever to invade England when the King is out'. There had been signs that this royal absence would prove no exception. It was rumoured that ships from the Low Countries daily unloaded cargoes of pikes, armour and gunpowder at Scottish ports. King Francis I offered to finance and equip his Scottish allies if they would open a 'second front' on his behalf. In fact the 34 year old King of Scotland, James IV, needed little persuasion, for he eagerly sought military renown for himself. In 1513 English commitments on the continent and the peaceful state of Scotland created favourable conditions for him to fulfil his ambition. 'My Lord,' King Henry said to Surrey before embarking, 'I trust not the Scots, therefore I pray you be not negligent.'

The fact that Henry left his kingdom in the care of a man who had fought valiantly against his father at Bosworth suggests that Surrey had proved both his loyalty and worth as a soldier. The Earl had served Henry VII well as Lord Lieutenant of the North for many years. When King James besieged Norham Castle in 1497 Surrey had marched to its relief. By 1513 the Earl had established himself as undisputed leader of the northern gentry. Immediately he gathered together a small headquarters staff and lifeguard. The relative importance of these warriors, most of whom would be professional soldiers, is shown by their rates of pay, though unfortunately the table given below is incomplete:

The Earl of Surrey	£5 per day
Lord Berners, the Marshall	6s. 8d. per day
Sir Nicholas Appleyard, Master of Ordnance	6s. 8d. per day
Sir Philip Tylney, Treasurer of the Wars and his staff	
A pursuivant and his staff	
A trumpeter	1s 4d. per day
5 captains	4s. od. each per day
5 petty captains	2s. od. each per day
1 spearman	1s. 6d. per day
43 demi- lances	9d. each per day
446 mounted billmen and archers	8d. each per day
2 surgeons	8d. each per day

Why a spearman was paid as much as two lancers is not clear. The surgeon's skill was evidently not very highly priced.

These men were enrolled for two months, and the royal accounts compiled at Lambeth include an item for 'coats of the King's Livery' of green and white, at 4s. a jacket, to be issued to 500 soldiers and 39 staff.

From Doncaster, Surrey ordered Sir William Bullmer to

patrol the border with 200 mounted archers. Meanwhile he moved to Pontefract, arriving on the first day of August. Some days later he heard that Sir William, gathering together nearly 1,000 border gentlemen and their retainers, had successfully ambushed a Scots raiding party of 7,000 or 8,000 men under the Earl of Home at a place called Millfield. The Scots left behind 500 dead, 400 prisoners, many horses and a standard.

Besides raising the morale of the English, this episode confirmed Surrey's suspicions that the Scots intended to make war, and he intensified his preparations. On 13 August Queen Katherine could write to Wolsey that 'she was horribly busy with making standards, banners and badges'. Surrey summoned the northern gentry to him at Pontefract and swore in 'the mooste wysest and experte gentleman in such causes' as a war council. With them as advisers he conferred with Sir Philip Tylney on how the expenses of a defensive campaign could be borne. Sir Nicholas Appleyard reported that he had already sent his guns to Durham. The council then discussed with him how the ordnance could be moved on to Newcastle and beyond when necessary. Surrey also wrote to all prominent landowners asking them what numbers of tenants they could muster at one hour's notice. He also arranged for a system of horse posts along the main roads as far as the Council of Wales and London so that news could be swiftly given or received. Surrey left as little as possible to chance.

Lord Dacre, Warden of the Middle and West Marches, rode into Pontefract with the first firm information that the Scottish intended to invade England. Rumour said that King James had gathered 100,000 men. Dacre shrewdly advised against an immediate mobilisation lest the Scots should wait until the English forces had been disbanded before attacking. Surrey contented himself with sending a message to John Hainslie, Captain of Norham, telling him to hold the castle at all costs if the Scots came. Norham, the most important of several border castles, could hardly be left untaken by an invading army, and Surrey planned to call out his northern troops only when the Scots had committed their forces there. Hainslie replied that he would defend the castle for so long that King Henry himself would have time to return from France and raise the siege.

The Scots army, which mustered on Borough Moor, outside Edinburgh, during the early summer of 1513, numbered perhaps 30,000 men. The feudal system, which still existed in Scotland, produced these large numbers, but the men lacked training. The King of France had sent two shiploads of weapons, including 400 arquebuses, 600 hand culverins with shot, 6,000 spears, 6,000 pikes and maces. A military mission led by Count D'Aussi, which included, besides his own troop of 50 men-at-arms, some 40 professional captains, arrived to instruct the Scots in the use of these weapons. But it took years rather than months to discipline men in Swiss or German infantry tactics of the day. Many of the Scottish levies from the Highlands and the Hebrides had neither the time nor the patience to practise pike drill – they left that to the Lowland contingents.

When the army set out from Edinburgh it was accompanied by the pride of the Scottish King – his train of artillery. To this the French had only contributed two great cannon and 40 cartloads of powder; the other 15 guns had been made in Scotland, some by Robert Borthwick, the Scottish Master Gunner.

The sizes of these cannon, which were all of brass, can be given, with the English equivalent names beside them :

5 big cannon (demi-curtawts)
2 gros culverins (culverins)
4 culveins pickmoyane (demi-culverins)
6 culveins moyane (sacres and serpentines)

That task of transporting this train of artillery from Edinburgh to Coldstream, a distance of 48 miles, proved to be a major one. Thirty-six oxen drew each of the five larger cannon, attended by 9 teamsters and 20 pioneers. A mobile workshop with a staff of smiths complete with crane, tools, iron, anvil and coals, accompanied the train. The 'gun stonis' were carried in creels or baskets on 28 pack horses, followed by 12 carts of gunpowder. Besides Borthwick's 26 gunners there were over 300 men and as many oxen in the convoy. Near Dalkeith a gun carriage snapped break ropes and rushed down a hill, breaking the neck of an ox; the replacement cost 32 shillings. The men of the train roasted the carcass of the dead beast that night.

The Scottish King, leaving two riders behind to bring some standards which had not yet been finished, joined his army at the border on 22 August. Wark Castle fell to him after a two day siege. He then moved to Norham Castle and watched as his guns thundered against its strong walls. After a lengthy bombardment, the Scots assaulted the fortress on three successive days. After a siege of six days the garrison had run out of ammunition through 'indiscreet spending', and surrendered on 29 August, while a terrible storm raged. Finally on 3 September, the captain of Etall Castle submitted to the King after a brief pounding from the Scots guns.

On 25 August, St. Bartholomew's day, Surrey received news of the invasion. At once he left Pontefract, hastening by way of York to Newcastle along roads so bad that one guide almost drowned in a pot hole. Despite his age the Earl did not spare himself in setting an example to his followers. At Durham, while the storm continued unabated, he heard that Norham had fallen.

After mass in the Norman cathedral next morning, the Earl asked the Prior if he could take with him the ancient banner of St. Cuthbert, which had last been carried at the Battle of the Standard in 1135. Perhaps he felt that the religious symbol would raise the spirits of his superstitious northern levies after the reverse at Norham. With the banner in their midst the English army arrived in Newcastle late that night. At a council meeting, attended by such new members as Lord Dacre, Sir William Bullmer and a veteran of Bosworth, old Sir Marmaduke Constable, it was agreed that the English army should take the field at Bolton in Glendale. On 3 September the town of Alnwick was reached, and here the last large contingent arrived from the fleet under the command of his son, Thomas Howard, Lord Admiral of England.

From the royal accounts the numbers of the English army can be calculated fairly accurately. On 1 September the following received pay :

27 chief captains	4s. per day
12 petty captains	2s. per day
55 demi-lances	9d. per day
11,406 mounted billmen and archers	8d. per day

Sir Edward Stanley, the leader of the Lancashire and Cheshire men, received £4,227 17s. 4d. On calculating the pay at

3s. 4d. conduct money and 8d. a day for two weeks this would represent pay for not less than 6,500 men. James Stanley Bishop of Ely and a kinsman of Sir Edward's father, the Earl of Derby, sent 1,988 men from his lands in Lancashire, but as they do not appear in the accounts they may have been included in Sir Edward's total. To these may be added the Lord Admiral's 928 soldiers, perhaps 300 artillerymen and other small contingents which arrived later. After the battle Surrey claimed to have saved the wages of 18,679 men by disbanding the army promptly on 14 September. This figure possibly included the casualties in the battle, but may have left out some units which the Earl kept in service. In all the English army mustered some 20,000 soldiers.

At Alnwick Surrey divided his army into two main 'battles', each with two wings. Tudor armies favoured this formation, and it may have been used by King Henry in the very same year during his French campaign. The writer of the 'Trewe Encounter' placed 9,000 men in the Admiral's division, 5,000 in Surrey's and 3,000 in each of the smaller wings. Although these figures are on the generous side they indicate the relative sizes of the wards. The Lord Admiral, 'wyse hardy and of greate credence and experience', was given the vaward, and Surrey commanded the rearward. On Monday, 5 September, Surrey arrayed his army outside Bolton, only eight miles from the Scots. Early on Tuesday morning he heard that King James had accepted his offer of a battle on Friday, 9 September. The old Earl of Surrey could ill conceal his joy.

Later that day Surrey led his army to Wooler only three miles from the Scottish position on Flodden Hill. On Wednesday Rouge Croix poursuivant, the English herald, returned from the Scots camp. He had taken Surrey's challenge on Monday to King James but the Scots King had seen fit to detain him, fearing that he would give away details of the Scottish dispositions, and had sent his own herald with his answer. Rouge Croix now told Surrey that owing to a marsh the Scots could only be reached by advancing up a narrow field, at the top of which they had sited their brass guns. After a council meeting Surrey ordered Rouge Croix to request King James to descend on to Millfield, the scene of Bullmer's ambush some weeks before, and fight on equal terms. The King replied haughtily that although it did become an earl to

PLATE 5

The General's tent, guarded by a musketeer, from a portrait (attributed to M. J. van Miereveldt) of Horace Vere, Baron Vere of Tilbury (1565-1635). Although this portrait dates from 1629, the field headquarters of a late sixteenth century or a Civil War commander would have been very similar.

The National Portrait Gallery

PLATE 6
Sir Charles Lucas   *William Dobson*
A portrait of a typical Royalist officer, holding in his left hand a wheel lock pistol, and
in his right a spanner for winding it up. He wears a handkerchief about his neck in
the fashion set by Prince Rupert.
The National Portrait Gallery

PLATE 7
Nathaniel Fiennes c. 1642-3
The colours he wears are those of the Earl of Essex. The buffcoat (which may be seen at Broughton Castle, near Banbury) is worn under armour painted black to prevent rust. The arm guard protects the bridle arm. Although the portrait is inscribed 'MIREVELT. PINXT', Michiel Jansz van Miereveldt died in 1641.
The Lord Saye and Sele

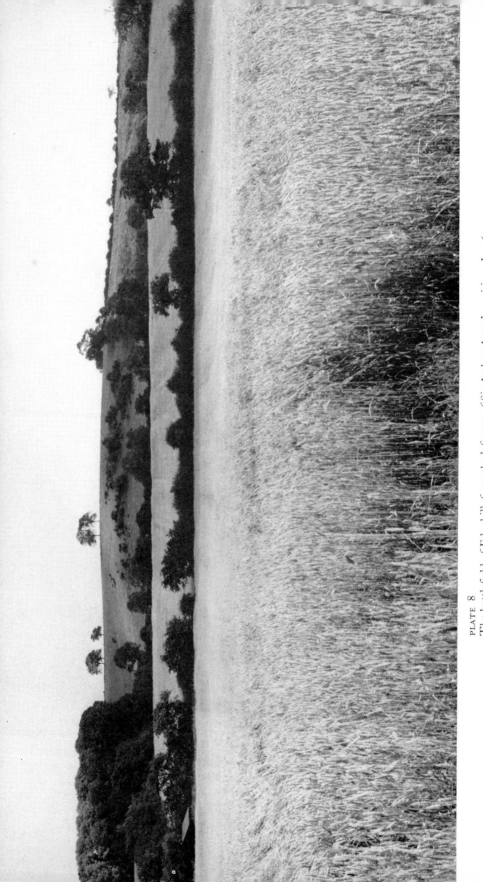

PLATE 8

The battlefield of Edgehill, from the left rear of Sir Arthur Aston's position. In 1642 the whole ridge must have resembled the bare down in the centre of the picture. The

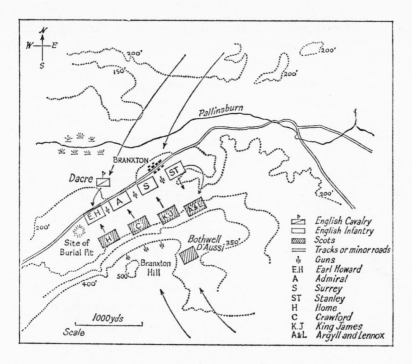

THE BATTLE OF FLODDEN, 1513

address a king in this fashion he would put no trust in either sorcery or the advantage of ground.

On Wednesday evening, while marauding Scots burnt several villages east of Flodden, Surrey's army crossed the Till and camped under the shelter of Barmoor Wood, which at that time probably covered an extensive area on the west bank of the river. The Lord Admiral saw the enemy for the first time from a neighbouring hill. Next day the English generals agreed to draw the Scots from Flodden Edge by marching northwards as if they intended to cut them off from Scotland. Wheeling westwards they could then fight a battle somewhere north of Branxton.

In the early hours of Friday morning the English army set out on its flank march. The rain, which had fallen steadily over the last two weeks, had ceased. Although the soldiers had been without beer or ale for several days the prospect of a battle raised their morale. Soon the vaward reached Twizel Bridge, and began crossing at 11 o'clock. Some distance south the rearward, unencumbered by field guns, waded through the high waters of the Till at Mill-ford. This took more time than had been expected and instead of marching in line with the vaward towards Branxton, Surrey's division followed some way behind on the left. With standards aloft and drums beating the massed bodies of men moved over the open plain.

As soon as the English manoeuvre was reported, the Scots King ordered his army to change front. The army marched north for a mile to the edge of Branxton Hill. Thick clouds of smoke arose as the camp followers burnt the foul straw and litter which the soldiers left behind them.

Some five or six hundred yards short of the ridge and out of sight, the King halted his soldiers in order to check their array. There were five 'grete plumpes', each of 5,000 men, packed tightly together and armed for the most part with pikes or spears. On the left the Earl of Home commanded the men from the Scottish border and the town levies of Aberdeen. Next to Home in the Scottish line came the Earl of Crawford, accompanied by the Fife, Perth and Forfarshire forces. With him under their chieftain the Earl of Huntly, were the Gordon clansmen. King James placed himself at the head of the third division, all chosen men from Stirling, Linlithgow and the Lothians. Over their heads stretched the great standard of St. Andrew, carried by Sir Andrew Forman. On the extreme right the Earl of Argyll marshalled his Campbell followers and the men from the Highlands, armed with broadsword and target, bows and arrows. Three great chieftains, dressed in plaid with white eagle feathers in their bonnets, and the cross of St. Andrew on their shoulders, stood at the head of their clans, the Macleans, Mackenzies and Macdonalds. The Earl of Lennox with the Stuarts, the servants of the Bishop of the Isles, and the Earl of Caithness with 300 followers dressed in green[1] added to the strength and colour of this division. Behind, and somewhat to the right, the Earl of Bothwell commanded a reserve, which included his vassals, some Lothian nobles and the French men-at-arms, in all perhaps 1,500 men. The whole Scots army, although seriously depleted by desertion since crossing the border, still numbered over 25,000 men.

The Scottish change of position and battle preparations consumed the entire morning. At about 2.30 p.m. the King ordered his four divisions to advance. Slowly they breasted the top of Branxton Hill and gazed in silence over the moorland which stretched out before them from Branxton village to the Till. At once the Scottish foot soldiers saw the two great hostile squares with their attendant wings extending, according to one account, like pairs of horns, fairly close to Branxton village.

The Pallinsburn, which lay in marshy ground, did not hold up the English advance. The historian who described it as 'a taylors yard wide', may well have crossed it himself with the vaward. The Lord Admiral, who had almost reached the foot of Branxton Hill when the Scots appeared over the skyline, tore off an Agnus Dei medallion which he wore around his neck and sent a rider with it to his father imploring him to make haste.

When his own soldiers had passed over the Pallinsburn Surrey rode over to his son, and found that the vaward had halted and that English gunners had opened fire upon the Scots at a range of 1,000 yards. The English, in fact, had the preponderance of field artillery. Their 18 falcons and five brass serpentines fired two or three pound iron balls accurately at Borthwick's gunners and killed several before engaging the infantry. In contrast the unwieldy Scottish guns, with a lower rate of fire, but longer range, tended to overshoot the English line. Trunnions, which would have enabled the guns to have been correctly depressed, may not have been introduced. Lord Dacre told the council that during this great artillery duel many of his raw levies from Bamboroughshire and Tynmouth fled from the field, terrified by the noise. No doubt their border ponies proved willing accomplices. They found time to steal horses tethered well behind the rear of the English position. Lord Dacre subsequently recovered 287 of these mounts including 'a grey mare with one eye' and 'a grey trotting nag with a cloudy face'.

Meanwhile Surrey had carried out some last minute re-shuffling of his contingents in order to confront on more or less equal terms the four large Scottish divisions which he could see, as Bothwell's men were out of sight on the reverse slope of Branxton Hill. When he had completed this work the English army stood in four 'battles' with a reserve of light cavalry under Lord Dacre behind them.

The 'battle' on the right, the wing of the vaward much strengthened, was commanded by Sir Edmund Howard, the younger son of Surrey, and consisted in part of 1,000 Lancashire levies under such captains as Sir John Boothe and Sir Thomas Butler. The second strongest contingent of 500 Cheshire men included the band of 17 archers from Middleton, with Richard Assheton as their leader and Henry Taylor as chaplain. The townsfolk of Macclesfield had sent Christopher Savage, their mayor, with a well appointed party of bowmen and billmen. The remainder of the division came from Yorkshire, mustered under the banners of the gentry, such as Sir John Gower ; Richard Cholmely led a contingent formed from the townsmen of Hull and the King's tenants of Hatfield in the West Riding. Whether or not old Sir Marmaduke Constable served with these Yorkshiremen is a matter of conjecture, but his left 'horn' of the vanguard was almost certainly divided up to reinforce the main divisions. In all the English right numbered perhaps 3,000 men.

Next in the line the Lord Admiral commanded the vanguard, composed of the soldiers from the fleet, the men of the Bishopric of Durham under Sir William Bullmer and the indentured followers of many barons, including Conyers, Latymer, Scrope of Upsale, Lumley and Egle. Other small bands mustered under captains of lesser rank.

Immediately on the Lord Admiral's left the Earl of Surrey placed the rearward. Besides his own 500 men he had with him about 3,000 Yorkshiremen, including 500 citizens from York, captained by Sir John Normayle, and the Abbot of Whitby's servants led by Lionel Percy. Lord Scrope of Bolton may have commanded in this division the 300 Craven men whose names have survived.[2] In addition such Yorkshire knights as Sir Christopher Pickering, Sir Brian Stapleton and Sir Ninian Markanyle had brought bands of bowmen and billmen with them. The men of Wensleydale, in milk white coats with red crosses, mustered under Surrey's standard alongside the tenants of the Bishop of Ely's Lancashire lands, commanded by Sir John Stanley. Each man in this last troop had the Stanley badge, an Eagle's Foot, embroidered

116

on his jacket, and a banner with the blue and gold arms of Ely Diocese floated above them. Both centre 'battles' contained over 5,000 men apiece.

On Surrey's flank a trusted soldier, Sir Edward Stanley, commanded a division formed from the remainder of the Lancashire and Cheshire soldiers. These probably included the 1,000 Lancashiremen under Sir William Percy who had originally marched in the 'horn' of the vanguard with Constable. Stanley may have had as many as 3,000 archers and billmen.

Behind the four English divisions Lord Dacre, the Warden of the Middle and West Marches, led the borderers, a motley collection of Cumbrians and Westmorlanders, some on foot, such as the Kendall bowmen, and others mounted. The largest single unit appears to have been the 1,000 border raiders from the Irthing Valley and the moors around Alston and Bewcastle. The preliminary bombardment had already dispersed 400 or 500 men that had been allotted to him from the East March just before the battle. This may have reduced his strength to approximately 2,000 at the most.

Between four and five o'clock the Scottish infantry, galled by the fire of Sir Nicholas Appleyard's guns, lost patience and began to bear down upon the English. With drums beating and trumpets sounding they moved at first 'in good order, after the Almayn's manner, without speaking a word'. The effectiveness of a pike phalanx in the attack depended almost entirely upon the maintenance of formation, and soon the broken slopes of Branxton Hill rendered this difficult. Moreover the English bowmen, loosing flights of arrows, rarely missed their mark. They were shooting into a strong wind, however, and the pavises and body armour of the Scottish gentry, who lined the front ranks, saved the Scots infantry from much slaughter, but probably at the cost of slowing the advance of the lighter armed men behind them. The English guns also scored several direct hits upon the Scots phalanxes, killing perhaps four or five men at a time and breaking up their order.

The Scottish left division, which reached the foot of Branxton Hill first, rushed furiously against young Edmund Howard's billmen. The impact of 5,000 pikemen scattered many of Howard's men but the majority stood and fought as well as they could. Howard himself had been dashed to the ground three times before Lord Dacre charged into the mêlée with 1,000 horsemen and succoured him. Howard slew a Scots knight, Sir Davy Home, and reached the Lord Admiral's 'battle'. Dacre's borderers, by some mutual agreement with the victorious Scots under the Earl of Home, played no further part in the battle. The Scots busied themselves with robbing the dead and stealing horses. The Earl apparently believed that he had done his part. Three years later his inactivity at this stage of the battle was one of the charges on which he was executed.

The Lord Admiral's division, strengthened by the survivors of Edmund Howard's 'battle', met the 6,000 Scots of Crawford and Montrose under equal conditions. The English archers shot down some of the spearmen and this reduced the impetus of the Scots charge and the English yielded no ground. After the battle the Bishop of Durham attributed the firmness of the billmen to the banner of St. Cuthbert, carried beside Sir William Bullmer in this division.

Surrey's men fared equally well against the phalanx led by King James who fought in the first rank armed with a pike. Again Appleyard's guns and the Wensleydale bowmen had opened a few gaps in the Scottish formation before it could cover the 300 yards to the foot of Branxton Hill. In the hand-to-hand struggle the Scots nobility, encased in the most expensive armour the forges of Europe could provide, defended themselves well. Against a background of great noise and confusion the billmen 'disappointed the Scots of their long spears upon which they relied'. Many Scots threw away their pikes and wielded instead 'mells of lead' or 'great and sharp swords'.

The Gaelic speaking Highlanders on the Scottish right had been the last to start down the hill. Stanley had detached a band of his Cheshire archers to take the mass of Highlanders in the flank. They ran to their left until they found a gulley which they could ascend. The 'sudden rain' made the slopes slippery, and the archers often fell on to their hands and knees as they hastened on. Some took off their shoes to get a better footing.

At last they appeared within bowshot of the Highlanders

and subjected them to a volley of arrows. Meanwhile Stanley's main force rushed up the hill and attacked the front of Huntley's division. Soon the Scots, ill protected against bowmen, turned and fled. In pursuit the English stumbled upon Bothwell's reserve force in the hollow ground behind Branxton ridge. Several showers of arrows sent the Scottish horse plunging in all directions, and Bothwell himself fell dead with a grey goose feather arrow in him. Some of his followers stayed their flight long enough to rob their own slain nobility on the slopes beneath them, but these human vultures were driven off by Stanley's enthusiastic archers and bill-men. Mustering his men Stanley then led them down the hill in the wake of the Scots. Thus, after less than two hours the remnants of the two centre Scots divisions found themselves assailed upon all sides.

At close quarters the 16 foot pikes of the Scots proved no equal to the shorter English bills, with their murderous heavy blades, hooks and spikes. In front of the Scots Surrey's men 'did beat and hew them down with some pain and danger to Englishmen', while their foes roared fierce war cries 'without which many would have been saved for pity. These fellows were such large, strong men that they would not fall when 4 or 5 bills struck one of them'. As the evening drew on the English pressed the Scots 'in a round compass' around the blue and white standard of St. Andrew. Eventually, wearied of the slaughter and aware that their king had been killed, the Scottish survivors threw down their pikes and broadswords.

The work of identifying the dead continued by lantern light throughout the night, under the supervision of Rouge Croix and his staff. Without their horses the English could not pursue the fugitives very effectively. Many of the English, however, made their way to the Scots camp, which they looted thoroughly. To their amazement they found 4,000 feather beds and also barrels ale, beer, wine and mutton. The Bishop of Durham wrote some days later that he would not have believed that this Scottish beer was so good had it not been tasted 'by our folks to their great refreshing'. After three days of rain water it was hardly surprising that the English soldiers enjoyed the brew. One Englishman found a great copper pot, which the townsfolk of Louth later melted down and fashioned into a weathercock for their church steeple. Many of the Scots oxen had been stolen, but Sir Philip Tylney succeeded in bringing away 1,000 waggons.[3] The spoil on the field proved equally rich. The complete harness of the Scottish gentry, the 'jackes almayn, rivets, splentes, pavices' of the common soldiers, all had value, and the English had no compunction in stripping the 'well fed and fat' bodies of the Scots. In addition 2,602 pikes worth 5d. each were picked up on the field and left at Alnwick.

Besides their King, who had died near the royal standard, the Scottish slain included the Archbishop of St. Andrews (the King's natural son), the Bishops of Caithness and the Isles, the Abbots of Inchaffray and Killwinning, the Dean of Glasgow, eight earls, 13 barons, three chiefs, four knights. Among the 11,000 to 12,000 dead lay 68 of the lesser gentry, such as Ninian Adair of Kinhilt. Only three names of the 1,200 prisoners survive – Sir Andrew Forman, the standard bearer, Sir William Scot of Balwearie, and James Logan. Home, Murray and Hamilton were virtually the only noble survivors of the battle on the Scottish side. The English lost Sir Richard Harbottle and Maurice Berkely slain, Sir Humphrey Lyle and 'Mr Harry Gray' prisoners to the Scots, Sir John Gower and Sir John Booth missing. Surrey's total casualties numbered 4,000 including 120 captured.

Sir Andrew Forman proved useful because he was the only Scot able to identify the body of King James IV which was covered in bill and arrow wounds. The Durham men had already removed his sword and thigh armour and sent it to be hung up in St. Cuthbert's shrine at Durham with the Scots standard. Surrey, however, despatched the bloodstained royal surcoat, by a messenger named John Glyn, to King Henry who proudly showed it to the Emperor. The King's body was later transported in a lead coffin to Windsor at the cost of £12 9s. 10d.

Throughout the night Sir Edward Stanley and his men stood guard on the 17 guns which the Scots had abandoned. Next day a party of Scottish cavalry appeared on a hill in the distance and reined their horses, obviously intending to recover some of the cannon. Stanley's men, however, swivelled one of the guns round and William Brackenall, master gunner, fired a shot which sent the Scotsmen galloping away. Some months later Lord Dacre wrote to the Bishop of Durham saying that he had been slandered by some lords who were on the field. Surrey had listened more to him than the rest, and he felt that it would be unwise to trust his life to strangers, especially those of the East Marches such as Sir William Gascoyne. The latter had been commanded by Sir Philip Tylney to convey the guns to Etall Castle, but had disobeyed and returned home with seven days' wages. With the help of Stanley's men Lord Dacre brought the guns, which were worth 1,700 gold marks, safely into the castle courtyard.

Many explanations have been offered for the Scottish defeat at Flodden. On 16 January, 1514, the Regency council of Scotland during the minority of King James V wrote to Christian II of Denmark a letter in which they listed the reasons for the late king's defeat. The Scots had not proceeded with sufficient care and the army, already reduced in numbers, included many who were un-used to military service *(laborum et rei militario insuentis)*. King James had also rushed down from a strong position, keeping no order among his men.

Little can be added to this early analysis. The use of the pike phalanx called for drill, and this is where the Scots failed. The English combination of field artillery, archers and billmen proved stronger than pikemen on their own. The Earl of Surrey may have learnt this lesson at Bosworth. It is doubtful whether the superior-ity of the English indenture system compared with the old feudal methods of raising an army practised in Scotland played a decisive role in the campaign, as one recent writer has suggested.[4] The experience and quality of the English generals and their able professional staff officers, contributed to the victory. At least King Henry VIII recognised this when he granted Surrey the dukedom of Norfolk, and gave Sir Edward Stanley the title of Lord Mont-eagle. Lesser captains, such as Sir Edward Norris of Speke, re-ceived letters from the King praising their courage. Superior military leadership and well-tried tactics performed by efficiently paid soldiers were the essential ingredients of the English victory at Flodden. Politically the battle achieved little beyond a temporary check to Scottish raids and forays. The local prophets soon forecast that the Scots would harry England again. The nationalist atmosphere of Tudor England, however, tolerated neither such opinions nor any hint that the Scots may not have lost the battle. On 20 April, 1514, Thomas Graynger, pewterer, laid information before the Mayor of Hereford that John Brown 'the tynkere' and John Gode were at his house on the Wednesday or Thursday before Palm Sunday, and 'there the sayd John Brown talkyd of the Shotyse fylde, and sayde thoughe the Scotes lost their kynge they lost no fylde. Item he sayd that he had seyne and knew the kynges of Scottes ordinance, wyche were as godly ordynances as any was in the worlde, and thoughe they were lost they wolde have as good agayne. Also he sayd that the Scottes wolde come gane into Ynglond unto Hamstone'. Alas, history does not record how the mayor dealt with the honest but indiscreet tinker.

1 Few Caithness men returned after the battle, hence the Scottish saying that it was unlucky to cross the River Ord in green.
2 At Bolton Abbey, in possession of the Duke of Devonshire.
3 Cal. Ven. Papers No. 340. A letter from Lorenzo Pasqualigo to Venice, dated 17 September, 1513.
4 J. D. Mackie, *The English Army at Flodden*. Scottish Historical Miscellany, Vol. 8.

1513—1642

ON 4 SEPTEMBER 1547 the Protector Somerset (c. 1506-1552) crossed the Tweed, and bypassing Dunbar, found the Scots army under the command of the Regent, Arran in superior numbers, in a well-nigh impregnable position on the River Esk, near Musselburgh. On 10 September the Scots quit their position and assailed the English, who fought back skilfully. Panic seized the Scots who were routed and massacred, losing many thousands. The English, it is said, lost but 200. The battle is remarkable as the last fought between England and Scotland as independent Kingdoms, and for the employment by the English of Italian musketeers. The anonymous contemporary drawing serves to illustrate the slaughter suffered by the fleeing Scots.

The armies that fought at Edgehill were vastly different to those of Flodden, for the Art of War had undergone many developments in the interim. Flodden was a mediaeval battle, Edgehill was a modern one. While there is not space here to describe all the changes that had taken place it is worth noting the complete disappearance of the bow, and the revival of cavalry. The bow went not because it was inefficient, but because the archer was no longer prepared to undergo a long and tedious training. In range, 'rate of fire' and accuracy the bow compared very favourably with the early matchlock. The revival of cavalry was due to a combination of several factors : the improvement in the breed of horses ; a reaction against the mediaeval habit of overloading the horse – with the consequent loss of mobility ; the rejection of faulty and indecisive tactics, discussed below.

Since so many changes had taken place it is worth considering the main characteristics of the Civil War armies ; though the causes of the struggle between King and Parliament have no place in these pages.

The Parliamentarians conducted the war through the agency of a Committee of Lords and Commons for the Safety of the Kingdom. This sat in London and governed the strategy of its various armies by remote control. They had a Commander-in-Chief, the Earl of Essex, who held the rank of Captain-General, but, in practice, he merely acted as the commander of their main field army.

The Royalists governed their affairs through a Council of War with a predominantly military flavour. This was a reasonably efficient body, but had practically no control over their Northern Army, that of the Earl (later Marquis) of Newcastle.

A field army on either side had a rather rudimentary staff. That of Essex's 1642 army may serve as an example. There were four 'Officers General of the Field' – the Captain-General himself; Sergeant-Major-General Philip Skippon, who was President of the Council of War; the Provost Marshal General and the Carriage Master General. Then there were the 'Officers of the Lord General's Train', who were his personal staff. They included the Treasurer at Wars; the Muster-Master General; the Advocate, the Secretary and the Auditor of the Army.

The cavalry had their own staff including the Lord General, the Earl of Bedford; the Lt-General, Sir William Balfour; the Quarter-Master-General, John Dalbier; the Commissaries for the Horse and for Provisions and a Provost Marshal General.

The Train of Artillery included gunners, engineers and pioneers as well as the pontoon-train. It also had a separate staff headed by the General of the Ordnance, the Earl of Peterborough, and the Lt.-General, Philibert Emanuel de Boyes, a foreign expert who failed to give satisfaction and was replaced after Edgehill.

The Scoutmaster-General does not appear in the earliest list of Essex's army, but Sir Samuel Luke was commissioned as such on 14 January, 1643, and was responsible for intelligence.

Essex had previous military experience as had Balfour and Skippon, but Bedford and Peterborough and many of the regimental commanders had never seen a shot fired.

There was no standing army at this period, except in Ireland, but armies had been raised to fight the Scots in 1639 and 1640, and although there had been little action, those who had taken part must have learned something of drill, discipline and camp life. On the continent there were four English regiments of foot in the Dutch service, three in the French and one in the Spanish. Many officers had fought in the Thirty Years War, and numbers of these now came home, though the great majority fought for the King. The professional talent available, even on the Royalist side, was not nearly sufficient to go round. The campaign of 1642 was indeed fought by armies of amateurs.

HORSE

Cavalry was the most important arm at this period. The men were for the most part armed with a sword and a pair of pistols. Ordinarily their defensive armour consisted of back and breast plates, pot helmet and a buff coat. Cuirassiers, or 'Lobsters', in three-quarter armour were not unknown.

Regiments usually consisted of six or more troops and numbered about 300 to 500 men. Pairs of troops often formed 'divisions' or squadrons. The men were generally drawn up for battle in three ranks, but one finds several instances of the Parliamentarians fighting six deep.

In 1642 a troop consisted of a captain, a lieutenant, a cornet, a quarter-master,[1] three corporals, two trumpeters, a sadler, a farrier, and 60 horse. The cornet carried the standard of the troop.

Cavalry is an arm designed for shock action. The great cavalry commanders of history have taught their men to charge home at the gallop, sword in hand, without using their firearms – at least until the enemy was broken. When the Civil Wars began cavalry tactics varied according to the ideas of the commanders. Prince Rupert quickly taught his regiments the true method; others contented themselves with trotting about blazing away with their firearms, or, even worse, sat still and received their enemy with carbine and pistol, thus throwing away the advantage given by the impetus of their chargers. Basically the cavalry of the Civil Wars were equipped much like the cuirassiers of Napoleon's time or the Lifeguards of today.

One last point must be remembered about cavalry. It takes a long time to train them. Not every trooper who enlists is a born horseman, nor will he necessarily know how to care for his mount. It is not easy to teach the horses to stand straight in the ranks. An unruly horse may run away with his rider, however much that warrior may wish to rejoin his troop at the end of a mêlée. It takes time to teach men to ride in a troop, keeping their dressing by the cornet in the centre of the front rank, and keeping a horse's length between each rank. Outpost duty has to be learned, the men have to be taught to rally after a charge. Let us not be surprised if we discover strange things happening on the battlefields of the Civil Wars.

DRAGOONS

Dragoons were still mounted infantry, their sub-unit being usually called a company, not a troop. They rode nags which were too light or otherwise unsuitable for cavalry work, and almost always dismounted to fight.

They were armed with sword and carbine, or sometimes fowling–pieces, which, being better made, were more accurate.

At Naseby Colonel John Okey's regiment mounted at the end of the battle and charged into the Royalist foot, but this was quite exceptional.

FOOT

Infantry regiments were in theory 1,200 strong, and in theory had ten companies. Each company had a captain, a lieutenant and an ensign[2], two sergeants, three corporals, two drummers and, sometimes, a 'Gentleman of the arms'. One third of the common soldiers were pikemen and the rest were musketeers.

The pikemen carried a pike 16 or 18 feet in length and a sword. They wore helmets, breast and back plates and tassets to guard the thighs, and were, therefore, far from mobile. They marched at only about 60 paces to the minute.

The musketeers were mostly armed with matchlocks, though a few already had firelocks or snaphances – early flintlocks.[3] A musket bullet would travel 400 yards, but even in Napoleon's day few musketeers could hit a man-sized target at more than 100 yards. The rate of fire was very slow, perhaps no more than one round every two minutes as the weapon took a long time to reload, and the wooden ramrod was liable to snap. In addition to this musketeers seem to have carried no more than 12 cartridges per man, and so although they had swords as well, and were more mobile than the pikemen, they were far less effective than, say, the infantry of Marlborough's time who had the ring bayonet. Even the plug bayonet was a thing of the future in Cromwell's day.

The characteristics of such infantry compelled them to draw up in a deep formation, usually six or eight or even ten ranks deep, with the stand of pikes in the centre. In this way the musketeers could keep up a rolling fire, and could take cover in the intervals of the pikemen if threatened by cavalry.

The infantry of the period are still represented by the Company of Pikemen of the Honourable Artillery Company.

ARTILLERY

Artillery was invaluable for sieges, but seldom played a decisive part in the battles of the period. There were various reasons for this. One was the slow rate of fire of mid-seventeenth-century guns. At the siege of Pontefract we find Parliamentarian guns bombarding for an hour and a half at a rate of about one round every seven minutes. Even if field guns could manage, say, one round in five minutes it is obvious that one would need very many to do decisive damage. And numbers of guns were not available. Both at Edgehill and at First Newbury the main Royalist army had 20 guns, at Naseby 12. The train of artillery was expensive – 'a sponge that can never be filled or satisfied',[4] and the equipment was heavy, requiring many horses or oxen. Guns were drawn by horses harnessed tandem, the more economical modern system of traction by six or eight horse teams harnessed in pairs had not yet been thought out.

Range was no great problem since armies drew up near each other in those days. In practice even heavy guns would seldom fire at over 1,000 yards. For siege work the gunners liked to be close to the target to get the maximum effect.

Mortars firing a primitive shell already existed and were very useful in a siege. The ordinary cannon fired caseshot or roundshot.

The Royalists had what they called galloping guns, small brass pieces mounted on a carriage, whose gunners rode on horseback. This was the germ of horse artillery.

William Eldred in *The Gunners' Glasse*, 1646,[5] gives details of artillery used in the Civil Wars.

	Calibre in inches	Weight of piece in lbs.	Length of piece in feet	Weight of shot in lbs.
Cannon Royal	8	8,000	8	63
Cannon	7	7,000	10	47
Demi-cannon	6	6,000	12	27
Culverin	5	4,000	11	15
Demi-culverin	$4\frac{1}{2}$	3,600	10	9
Saker	$3\frac{1}{2}$	2,500	$9\frac{1}{2}$	$5\frac{1}{4}$
Minion	3	1,500	8	4
Falcon	$2\frac{3}{4}$	700	6	$2\frac{1}{4}$
Falconet	2	210	4	$1\frac{1}{4}$
Robinet	$1\frac{1}{4}$	120	3	$\frac{3}{4}$

HEAVY ARTILLERY

It is doubtful whether the cannon royal or the cannon were ever used except for a siege. The King had two demi-culverins in his train at Edgehill, First Newbury and Naseby, and although these were used as siege guns on occasion, we may count the demi-cannons, culverins and demi-culverins as Heavy Field Artillery.

LIGHT ARTILLERY

The saker was a popular field gun. All the lesser types seem to have been classed as drakes. On contemporary battle plans, such as that of Naseby, one sees guns right up in the front line. These would be drakes and probably played much the same rôle as heavy machine guns in more modern times. Perhaps they should be classed as 'battalion guns'. Guns were seldom concentrated in battle, but generally seem to have been used in pairs.

At the beginning of the war, since the Parliament controlled the magazines of Hull and the Tower as well as most of the main ports, the Roundhead soldiers were much better armed than the Cavaliers, though not perhaps as well mounted.

[1] A commissioned officer.
[2] Who carried the colour.
[3] They were used to guard the Train of Artillery, being less prone to explode the powder barrels by accident.
[4] Clarendon.
[5] A. R. Hall. *Ballistics in the Seventeenth Century*, p. 168.

The Battle of Edgehill

THE CAMPAIGN

1642

22 August	*King Charles raises his Standard at Nottingham.*
9 September	*Essex leaves London to join his army at Northampton.*
13 September	*King Charles leaves Nottingham.*
20 September	*King Charles reaches Shrewsbury.*
23 September	*The action at Powick Bridge. Prince Rupert routs a force of Parliamentarian cavalry.*
24 September	*Essex enters Worcester.*
12 October	*King Charles advances from Shrewsbury.*
23 October	*The Battle of Edgehill.*
27 October	*The Royalists take Banbury.*
29 October	*King Charles enters Oxford.*
12 November	*The Royalists storm Brentford.*
13 November	*Turnham Green. The unfought battle.*
9 December	*The Royalists settle in their winter quarters.*

THE BATTLE

23 October, 1642

'But look, the morn in russet mantle clad,
Walks o'er the dew of yon high eastward hill.'

HAMLET, ACT I, SCENE I

PEER EASTWARDS FROM the battlements of Elsinore and you will see the waters of the Kattegat. Look eastward from Stratford on Avon and in the distance you will see Edge Hill. There, half way between Warwick and Banbury was fought the first great battle of a struggle as dramatic as any that inspired Shakespeare.

The strategy of the Edgehill campaign was straightforward. The Parliamentarians, with the resources of the City of London behind them, were able to raise an army and take the field before the King was ready. But their Captain-General, the Earl of Essex, was a lethargic person and contented himself with occupying Worcester, Hereford, Coventry and Banbury, while leaving the King to take the initiative. This Charles did when on 12 October he set out from Shrewsbury to advance on London, hoping to end the war at a blow.

Both armies were new to their work, and neither was capable of proper reconnaissance. Consequently they wandered slowly through the Midlands for more than a week with only the remotest idea of the whereabouts of their opponents. When eventually, on the evening of 22 October, the quartermasters of both armies clashed, the King at Edgecote was actually nearer London than Essex at Kineton.

The Royalists, who had intended to attack Banbury on the 23rd, took counsel during the night and resolved instead to march next day to the high ridge of Edge Hill and offer battle. By this time the various regiments had dispersed to their quarters in the neighbouring villages, and it would take some hours to concentrate them.

Essex's army was even more spread out than the King's. Two

regiments of foot had been left at Worcester, and others at Coventry and Hereford. Hampden's brigade and part of the train of artillery were a day's march to the rear, while a few of the troops of horse, including that of Captain Oliver Cromwell, arrived late presumably through bad staff work.

No sensible general likes to fight a pitched battle without first concentrating the largest possible army, but Essex no doubt was anxious for his garrison of Banbury, and on the morning of the 23rd he drew out his army and ranged it in battle array between Kineton and the 300-foot ridge upon which the Royalists were assembling.

Sir Richard Bulstrode, who was in the Prince of Wales' Regiment, tells us that they had orders to be upon their guard all night and to be at the rendezvous upon Warmington Hills by eight in the morning. When the King himself arrived soon afterwards he held a general Council of War to debate whether to continue to march on London or to fight the enemy, whom they could see embattling their army, 'in the bottom near Keinton'.[1] According to Sanderson the Parliamentarians were only a mile away. The Royalist Council of War decided to fight, and 'great preparations were made, and precautions taken for descending the hill, which was very steep and long, and had been impracticable if the enemy had drawn nearer to the bottom of it ; . . .'[2]

THE ROYALIST ARMY

King Charles commanded his army in person. The Earl of Lindsey was his Lieutenant-General, but according to Bulstrode the King asked him to permit Patrick Ruthven, Lord Forth, an old Scots officer, who had long served under Gustavus Adolphus, to draw up the army and to command it that day, 'being an old experienced general ; to which the Earl of Lindsey (being wholly made of obedience) willingly complied'. In fact Lindsey's resignation does not appear to have been so graceful, and it is generally accepted that there was a quarrel as to how the infantry should be drawn up, Rupert and Ruthven advocating the formation known as the Swedish Brigade, which was rather too complicated for untrained troops.

Horse

The cavalry, as yet unbrigaded, were divided into two wings, the right under Prince Rupert and the left under Lord Wilmot. Counting the King's Lifeguard as a regiment, there were ten present. They varied considerably in strength, several being as yet incomplete. Rupert's wing was rather stronger than Wilmot's. Each unit was drawn up in three ranks. Except for the Gentlemen Pensioners, perhaps 100 strong, no cavalry were left in reserve, though each wing had a second line in support of the first. The cavalry totalled 2,500, thus there was only about one cavalryman to every four foot soldiers, a much lower proportion than in the later battles of the war.

Foot

The foot, drawn up in the centre, were commanded by their Sergeant-Major-General, Sir Jacob Astley, a silver-haired veteran of the Dutch service, who was a very competent officer. All the five brigade (tertia) commanders had seen some previous service. Charles Gerard, for example, had been a captain in the Dutch Army. Some of the regimental commanders were wealthy magnates like Sir William Pennyman, the M.P. for Richmond, Yorkshire, who had voted against the attainder of Strafford; Sir Edward Fitton and Lord Molyneux. Others were professional soldiers : Sir Thomas Lunsford had been in the French service and Lord Willoughby d'Eresby had been a captain in the Dutch army. Most of the regiments had a sprinkling of experienced officers, though the majority of company commanders were drawn from the country gentry.

The infantry units fell in six deep. Like the horse the brigades were originally drawn up in two lines, but when the advance began those in rear came up into the intervals of the first line, and the whole advanced together. There were no infantry in reserve, though there was a company[3] of firelocks to guard the train of artillery. A number of the foot were as yet ill-armed, having nothing but scythe blades mounted on poles, pitchforks or even cudgels.

Dragoons

The dragoons under Sir Arthur Aston, an officer who had fought as far afield as Russia, were employed in skirmishing on the outer wings of the cavalry, one regiment on the right and two on the left.

Artillery

Sir John Heydon, the Lieutenant-General of the Ordnance and a noted mathematician, commanded the artillery. There were six heavy guns planted as one battery, perhaps as far back as Bullet Hill, and fourteen smaller pieces, which would be distributed in twos and threes with the brigades of foot.[4]

THE PARLIAMENTARIAN ARMY

When he reached Northampton on 10 September the Earl of Essex had 20,000 men at his command. He failed to concentrate more than about 14,500 of them at Edgehill.

Though no strategist Essex showed both at Edgehill and First Newbury that he was a sound tactician. Bulstrode gives the best description of the manner in which the Earl drew up his host. '... putting several bodies of foot with retrenchments and cannon before them, and all their foot were lined with horse behind them, with intervals betwixt each body, for their horse to enter if need required ; and upon their right wing were some briars covered with dragoons, and a little behind, on their left wing, was the town of Keinton, which supplied them with provisions and where their baggage and carriages were.'[5]

Horse

The regimentation of the Parliamentarian cavalry was, it seems, as yet incomplete. There were 24 troops on the left wing under Sir James Ramsey, and three regiments on the right. One of these, that of Lord Feilding, was on the right flank of the foot.

The other two, Stapleton's and Balfour's, seem to have been drawn up in support of the right hand brigade of foot.

Ten troops, most of which seem to have been in Ramsey's command, had been routed by Rupert at Powick Bridge (23 September) and their morale had suffered accordingly.

The General of the Horse, the Earl of Bedford, owed his appointment to his social rank. The Lt.-General was an excellent officer, Sir William Balfour, a Scot.

Foot

Three brigades of foot were present. Their commanders Sir John Meldrum, Charles Essex and Thomas Ballard, were all experienced officers, while old Sir William Constable had served under the first Earl of Essex in Ireland, but the regimental officers were for the most part seeing action for the first time.

Essex had prudently commanded that his infantry should be drawn up in plainer order than the Royalists, and they fell in eight deep in the simple linear formation that the Earl had learned in the Dutch army. When they were at Worcester he had told his officers to be careful in training their men, and to 'bring them to use their arms readily and expertly, and not to busy them in practising the ceremonious forms of military discipline'. They were to instruct them well 'in the necessary rudiments of war', so that they would 'know to fall on with discretion, and retreat with care'.

Meldrum's brigade was on the right of the foot – probably supported by Balfour and Stapleton with their horse – while Charles Essex was on the left supported by Ballard.

Dragoons

Essex appears to have had two regiments of dragoons, each of at least six companies. Doubtless they set to partners with the Royalist dragoons on the right wing, a role which seems to have been played by musketeers from the foot regiments on the left wing.

With the resources of the Tower at his disposal there can be no doubt that Essex had a good train of artillery, but thanks to the inefficiency of the Lt.-General of the Ordnance, a foreigner named Philibert Emanuel de Boyes, a large number of guns had fallen behind the army. How many were actually present cannot be said. Ludlow says the best field-pieces were planted on the right wing.

The General of the Ordnance was the Earl of Peterborough, a person of no military experience.

The two armies were fairly equal in strength.

| | Royalists | | Parliamentarians | |
	Regiments	*Strength*	*Regts/Troops*	*Strength*
Horse	10	2,800	42	2,150
Foot	17	10,500	12	12,000
Dragoons	3	1,000	2	720
Guns	—	20	—	30-37
		14,300		14,870[6]

Essex had made no move – and with good reason. Hampden had not yet come up, and the idea of storming Edgehill was unattractive.

The Royalists may have begun to descend the hill as early as 10 o'clock. First went Lt.-Colonel Henry Washington with Usher's regiment of dragoons, who occupied some enclosures and briars on the right of the army. Next followed a forlorn hope of 600 horse. The foot were ordered to descend as well as they could, straight down the hillside, a movement which must have caused considerable disorder. Rupert and Wilmot probably descended the hill by the two roads that run from Edge Hill to Kineton. As for the artillery 'the carriage horses of the cannon were put behind the carriages, excepting a horse or two before. . . .'[7]

One cannot tell precisely where the Royalist army drew up, but de Gomme's plan seems to indicate that it was about eight hundred yards from Edgehill and just clear of Radway. At this stage the two armies may have been about half a mile apart.

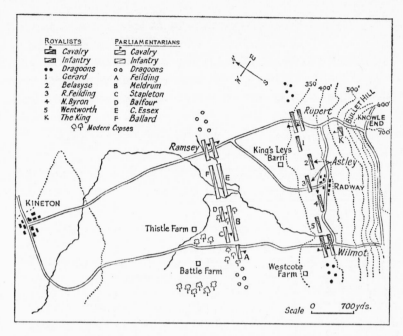

THE BATTLE OF EDGEHILL, 1642

De Gomme's plan is disappointing in that it fails to show the Royalist dragoons, their artillery or the village of Radway. Nevertheless, assuming that the Royalist horse and foot drew up on a front of rather more than 2,000 yards, de Gomme does seem to indicate that the Royalist line was a good deal nearer the hill than most modern historians have shown it.

If both sides seem to have been reluctant to begin the battle, the simple explanation is that they were both waiting for their rearmost units to come up – some of the King's foot had seven or eight miles to march from their quarters to the rendezvous. The battle began with a cannonade which lasted for about an hour, but did little damage. While this was going on the King, dressed in a black velvet coat lined with ermine, and a steel cap covered with velvet, rode to each brigade in turn, exhorting the men to do their duty, and being received with loud cheers. This done his generals urged him to withdraw 'to a rising ground, some distance from thence, on the right (Bullet Hill?) . . . from whence he might see the issue of the battle, and be out of danger ; and that otherwise the army

137

would not advance towards the enemy'.[8] Charles reluctantly agreed and rode off accompanied only by the young Prince Charles, the Duke of York, and the band of Gentlemen Pensioners. His Lifeguard, stung by being dubbed 'The Troop of Show', had insisted on being allowed to station themselves on the right of the front line of horse.

Prince Rupert rode from wing to wing 'giving positive orders to the horse, to march as close as was possible, keeping their ranks with sword in hand, to receive the enemy's shot, without firing either carbine or pistol', until the enemy were broken, 'which order was punctually observed'.[8]

The battle began with the dragoons on the flanks disputing possession of the hedgerows. Washington on the right and Sir Arthur Aston on the left beat back the Parliamentarian dragoons and cleared the way for the Royalist horse. This done, the Cavaliers made a general advance. In the centre old Astley made his famous prayer : 'Oh, Lord! Thou knowest how busy I shall be this day. If I forget thee, do not thou forget me. March on, boys !' On the wings Rupert and Wilmot quickly drew away from the foot.

As Rupert advanced the Roundheads saluted him with three cannon from Ramsey's wing, but though the second shot killed a quartermaster in the rear of the Duke of York's troop, the rest flew harmlessly overhead.

Lord Bernard Stuart, who commanded the King's Lifeguard, describes how the enemy

'stood still all the while upon the hill expecting the charge so that we were fain to charge them uphill and leap over some 5 or 6 hedges and ditches. Upon our approach they gave fire with their pistols, but finding that did nothing dismay the King's horse and that they came more roundly to them with all their fire reserved, just when our men charged they all began to turn head and we followed in execution upon them for 4 miles together. . . . A great many of them saved their lives by getting our [field] word "For God and King Charles". Had our reserve of horse [Sir John Byron] not mistaken, but stood still in their place they were commanded, we had given them as absolute a defeat both of horse and foot as ever was given.'[9]

To make matters worse for Ramsey, just at the moment when Rupert's horse was approaching, Sir Faithfull Fortescue and his troop deserted, firing their pistols into the ground and tearing off their orange tawny scarves.

Rupert succeeded in stopping three troops on his wing,[10] but the rest carried away with the excitement of the chase, thundered off in the direction of Kineton. The broken enemy were a tempting prey, and included besides Ramsey's troopers, the whole of Charles Essex's brigade of foot, except for a few officers. Holles' Londoners (Ballard's brigade) were actually broken by their own horse, but bravely rallied about their Colonel.

Bulstrode, pursuing the chase as eagerly as any, tells us that he was wounded in the head by a Roundhead who turned and struck him with his pole-axe, and was 'seconding his blow', when Sir Thomas Byron shot him dead with his pistol.

Through Kineton and beyond the Cavaliers pursued, many stopping only to plunder the baggage waggons – though according to the Parliamentarian Captain Kightley the worse pillagers were the foot and dragoons of Essex's own army.[11] Some of the Royalist horses did not draw rein until they found themselves confronted by Hampden's brigade coming from Warwick.

On the left wing things followed the same pattern, but Wilmot's charge only disposed of one Roundhead cavalry regiment, that of Lord Feilding, and one regiment of foot, Sir William Fairfax's, which fled without a blow. Nobody has ever explained precisely how he came to miss the cavalry of Balfour and Stapleton, but the explanation must surely be that they were drawn up *behind* Meldrum's brigade.

Most of Wilmot's men galloped off in the direction of Kineton, but Lt.-Colonel Sir Charles Lucas,[12] with great presence of mind, rallied 300 horse and fell upon the rear of the Parliamentarians.

Lord Bernard Stuart says that Lucas cut off four infantry regiments and took 'a whole bag full of their foot colours', so presumably he met Charles Essex's already broken brigade quitting the field. It was fortunate for the Parliamentarians that Lucas' attack did not fall on Meldrum or Ballard, who by this time were at push of pike with Astley's foot. Things looked black for Essex. In little more than a quarter of an hour he had seen his army reduced to a force of two cavalry and seven foot regiments. Ballard's brigade had come up on Meldrum's left, and seizing a pike the Earl led his own regiment into action, resolved to take no quarter. Colonel Charles Essex, abandoned by his men, was one of the first to fall, hit by a musket ball.

At this crisis Sir William Balfour turned the fortunes of the day. Leading his regiment out through the intervals between the Roundhead foot regiments he launched them in a desperate charge against Richard Feilding's brigade. How much resistance he encountered cannot be told, but certainly disaster overtook the Royalists. Richard Feilding[13] and two of his colonels, Lunsford and Stradling, were taken. Stradling's lieutenant-colonel, William Herbert, M.P. for Swansea, was killed, and Captain Howell Gwynn was wounded.[14] Among the few colours captured by Essex's army was one bearing the cinquefoil of Stradling, and clearly belonging to his fourth captain.[15]

Pushing on, Balfour reached the main Royalist battery. At one moment it looked as if his men would carry off the young Prince Charles, who, quite unmoved, was seen winding up his wheel-lock pistol, but, by the merest chance, the Roundheads ignored the Gentlemen Pensioners. Having failed, for lack of nails, to spike the Royalist guns, Balfour's men rode back towards their own lines.

Meanwhile Sir Nicholas Byron's brigade on Richard Feilding's left, carrying the Banner Royal in its ranks, had borne down on the part of the line where Stapleton's regiment was posted. The redcoats of the King's Lifeguard were within musket shot, when Sir Philip, seeing none of the King's horse to encounter, charged them. He was less successful than Balfour, for though he suffered little loss from their musketry, he had some from the hedgehog of their pikes, and being unable to break them fell back to his former station. Arrived there he found that the escort of the artillery 'were marched off'[16] (in other words had taken to their heels). Stapleton's troopers promised to stand by him in defence of the guns, and ordered a servant to load one of them. He had scarcely levelled it, when a body of horse appeared advancing from the direction of the Royalists.

'We fired at them with caseshot, but did no other mischief save only wounding one man through the hand, our gun being over loaded, and planted on high ground.'[17] The target turned out to be Balfour's men, and the wounded man had been signalling to them not to fire!

Essex now came on the scene and ordered two regiments of foot to attack Byron's brigade : still Sir Nicholas stood his ground. But a third attack in which Balfour attacked the rear of the Royalist brigade, Stapleton the flank, and the infantry the front, was successful : Byron's men broke and ran away towards the hill. They had suffered heavily. Byron himself was wounded ; the Earl of Lindsey fighting at the head of his regiment had his thigh broken by a musket ball and was captured. Lord Willoughby d'Eresby, after slaying two Roundheads with his half-pike 'piously endeavouring the rescue of his father', Lindsey, was himself taken. Sir Edmund Verney, the Knight Marshal, was struck down, and the Royal Standard was carried away in triumph, an exploit which has been attributed to several different Parliamentarians.[18]

There was now a great gap in the Royalist line, and Essex made an attempt to exploit the success. It was not easy. Both his cavalry regiments had charged twice and their horses were pretty well blown. Only seven regiments of foot remained to him, while the Royalists still had at least nine. On the right the brigades of Charles Gerard and John Belasyse were engaged in a fire-fight, which had followed upon the first attack at push of pike. James II, an eyewitness, though a youthful one, wrote : 'Each, as if by mutual consent, retired some few paces and stuck down their colours, continuing to fire at one another even until night.' Wentworth's brigade on the left may have been similarly engaged.[19]

A Royalist account[19] describes this phase.

'The left side of our foot being put into disorder all the rest gave way, yet those of the right hand were never put into disorder, but, seeing some of the cannon in danger to be lost, advanced again and made the place good, the left hand of the rebel's foot coming on a pace to charge them: By this time the right wing of our Horse was returned ... and were in some confusion ... but seeing our foot and cannon in some danger to be lost ... ours made a stand and soon rallied together, having some dragooners with them, and so advancing made the dragooners give them a volley or two of shot, which made the rebels retire.'

The Royalists were able to bring their big guns into action, firing caseshot, and this too tended to discourage any further advance on the part of Essex's tired soldiers.

With their line restored, and their cavalry returned the fortunes of the battle had changed once more. Falkland even urged Wilmot to make a last charge against Balfour, whose men were now drawn up in the Roundhead centre, only to be told: 'My Lord, we have got the day, and let us live to enjoy the fruit thereof.'[20]

In the rear of Essex's army all was confusion. Captain Edward Kightley[21] describes how he brought his troop from its quarters five miles away, and met two other troops. Entering the field 200 horse

> 'came by me with all the speed they could ... saying that the King had the victory, and that every man cried for God and King Charles. I entreated, prayed, and persuaded them to stay, and draw up in a body with our troops, for we saw them fighting and the field was not lost, but no persuasions would serve, and then I turning to our three troops, two of them were run away, and of my troop I had not six and thirty men left'.

When such chaos reigned it is hardly surprising that the Parliamentarians failed to retain their best trophy: the Banner Royal. Captain John Smith had taken part in Lucas's charge, and was making his way back to the Royalist position, when a boy told him that a party of Roundheads were carrying off the Standard. They were seven strong, six being mounted, but saying: 'They shall have me with it, if they carry it away,' Smith charged them with his rapier, killed one, wounded another, and routed the rest. The recapture of the Banner Royal won him a knighthood.

The battle was not a long one. Perhaps not more than two hours elapsed between the time when the armies engaged, and the time when 'night (the common friend to wearied and dismayed armies), parted them'.[22] By that time perhaps 5,000 of the 28,000 combatants had fallen, that at least is the figure Clarendon gives. It is a high one, probably too high. Yet Bernard Stuart estimated the King's losses in 'killed and run away' at about 2,500, and it is likely that Essex lost at least as many men as Charles.

On the Royalist side very few of the cavalry were hurt, Lord d'Aubigny being the only officer of note.[23] The total seems to have been about 40.

The infantry suffered much more severely. Astley was

wounded, and two brigadiers, Byron and Charles Gerard, the latter very severely. The captive Earl of Lindsey died of his wounds. Ludlow saw 'three-score lie within the compass of threescore yards upon the ground whereon that brigade fought in which the King's standard was'.

On the Parliament side the most notable men slain were Lord St. John and Colonel Charles Essex. But the rank and file were hard hit. Ballard, whose regiment numbered 776 men on 17 October, could only muster 439 three weeks later. Cholmley had 1,200 men on 1 October and only 552 on 23 November.[24] Ballard's regiment had been in the thick of it at Edgehill, while Cholmley's had fled among the first. It must be assumed that desertion accounts for many of the men missing, but it looks as if the regiments that ran got cut up just as badly as those that stood their ground. Not all Rupert's troopers were bent on plunder, some had grimmer work in mind. It is very difficult to estimate Essex's losses, but judging by the casualties in these two regiments and assuming that only half of them were battle casualties, it seems likely that Essex lost about 25 per cent of his infantry, or 2,750 men at Edgehill. Presumably the cavalry, departing 'loose rein and bloody spur' got off more lightly.

The day had been a fine, cloudless one and the night that followed was cold and frosty. Ludlow, who had come off his horse in a charge at the end of the day, spent the night stamping up and down in his 'Lobster's' armour trying to keep warm. Sir Gervase Scrope,[25] lying amidst the wreckage of Byron's brigade with sixteen wounds, owed his life to the frost which stopped the bleeding.

The King spent the night in the field, and found in the morning that the Earl, reinforced by Hampden's brigade 2,000 strong, had done likewise. The two armies spent the 24th looking at each other, and then Essex fell back to Warwick, while the King sent his regiments into their old quarters in the neighbourhood of Edgecote, where they found many of their missing men had arrived before them in search of food and warmth.

The wounded Bulstrode thought the Royalists had 'no great

reason to brag of a victory', but in fact the King had rather better of his first battle. He was now much nearer London than Essex. He was able without opposition to occupy Oxford, a city which made a convenient capital and fortress for the rest of the war. He now had a real opportunity to reach London before Essex could return to its defence. If the speed and resolution needed for such an operation were lacking, this was not because he had been defeated at Edgehill. Indeed he had some reason to be satisfied with his army.

Rupert's horse had increased their moral superiority ; if some of the Royalist foot had been routed, at least it was not without a fight ; those who were only armed with cudgels had been seen to snatch up the arms of their slaughtered comrades. The artillery train had been increased by seven captured cannon.

Essex on the other hand can scarcely have been reassured by the conduct of his ill-disciplined levies. The regiments of Mandeville, St. John and Wharton indeed had done so badly that they appear to have been disbanded. As to the cavalry he would probably have agreed with Captain Oliver Cromwell when he told his cousin, Hampden 'Your troopers, are most of them old decayed servingmen and tapsters. . . .'

But if, strategically speaking, King Charles had the better of Edgehill fight, the tactical honours lay with Sir William Balfour, who at the crisis of the battle had shown his less experienced comrades how to combine horse and foot in one effective onslaught.

[1] Bulstrode.
[2] Bulstrode.
[3] 'Colonel Leg's firelox'. Will. Legge did not in fact become a Colonel until 1645.
[4] Two demi-cannon; two culverins; two demi-culverins; six fawcons; six faw-conetts; two rabonetts. (Burne & Young. *The Great Civil War*, p. 107).
[5] Bulstrode.
[6] Godfrey Davies calculates: Horse, 2,000; Foot, 11,000; Dragoons, 700-1,000 E.H.R. 1934). It seems unlikely, however, that the horse averaged less than 60 per troop.
[7] Bulstrode.
[8] Bulstrode.
[9] BM. Harleian MS. 3783. f. 60.
[10] Prince Rupert's Diary.
[11] BM. E. 126/13.

[12] Caernarvon's regiment.

[13] He was rescued later by Captain John Smith.

[14] He came from Llanbrayn, Carmarthen, so it may be assumed that he served in Stradling's regiment, the only one from South Wales.

[15] MS. in Dr. William's Library. BM. Harleian MS. 986.

[16] Ludlow.

[17] Ludlow.

[18] Ludlow saw Lt.-Colonel Middleton displaying the Banner, while Mr Lionel Copley is said to have killed Sir Edmund Verney. (E. 126/1. Special Passages.)

[19] E. 126/24. *A Relation of the Battaile*. Printed at Oxford by Leonard Lichfield.

[20] Clarendon.

[21] E. 126/13.

[22] Clarendon.

[23] Duke of York's troop. Prince of Wales' Regiment.

[24] Excluding officers in each case.

[25] Captain in the Lord General's Regiment of foot.

The First Battle of Newbury

THE CAMPAIGN

1643

26 *July*	*Prince Rupert storms Bristol.*
10 *August*	*King Charles lays siege to Gloucester.*
26 *August*	*Essex marches from Colnbrook.*
30 *August*	*The London trained bands join Essex at Aylesbury.*
4 *September*	*Action at Stow-on-the-Wold.*
5 *September*	*King Charles raises his siege of Gloucester.*
8 *September*	*Essex enters Gloucester.*
15 *September*	*Essex surprises Cirencester.*
18 *September*	*Rupert attacks Essex at Aldbourne Chase.*
20 *September*	*First Battle of Newbury.*
21 *September*	*Action near Aldermaston.*
22 *September*	*Essex reaches Reading.*
28 *September*	*The trained bands reach London.*

THE BATTLE

20 September, 1643

THE EVE OF the first Battle of Newbury found the Earl of Essex in his usual strategical situation : cut off from his base. At Edgehill this had not proved disastrous, but at Newbury the strategical situation was infinitely worse : the Parliamentarians, tired and hungry after long marches, their cavalry outnumbered, were in real danger of annihilation.

King Charles was at the head of as fine an army as he ever commanded during the whole war. If he could now destroy Essex's army the way to London would lie open, and if he could regain his capital the war would be as good as won. Thus far the Cavaliers had had much the better of the fighting, but their financial resources were strained ; a long war was bound to go against them. It behoved them to take advantage of an opportunity that might never recur.

The siege of Gloucester had lured Essex far from his base. It may be that the Royalists with their superior cavalry would have done well to meet the Parliamentarians in a pitched battle in the Cotswolds. This they had failed to do, and on 5 September, when the garrison had only three barrels of powder left, they had raised the siege. Three days later the Earl entered the city. His problem now was to get home again. He chose to do so by marching round the south of the circle of Royalist fortresses that defended Oxford. His goal was Reading, which he had captured in the previous April. It was a long hard march, but on 15 September Essex caught 200 Cavaliers 'napping in their beds'[1] at Cirencester and seized 30 or 40 carts of bread and cheese ; provisions which enabled his men to keep going for the next few days.

On the 18th Prince Rupert and 3,000 horse fell on the Parliamentarians at Aldbourne Chase, handling them so roughly that they crossed the Kennet at Hungerford. They hoped that with the river between them and their pursuers their march would be undisturbed, and naturally the Earl did not want to fight a pitched battle with the Kennet at his back. The delay caused by his detour gave King Charles and his main body just sufficient time to reach Newbury ahead of Essex. But it was a near run thing, so near in fact that the battlefield was insufficiently reconnoitred, though according to Sir John Byron there was still light enough to have done so. The account, attributed to Digby, states specifically that they failed to observe . . . 'a round hill . . . from whence a battery would command all the plain before Newbury, where the King's Army stood'.

The King and his generals were well pleased at having caught up the enemy. 'The Rebels thus happily overtaken in their flight, consultation was held of the way to prevent their further evading us. . . .' They resolved to bivouac in a large field on the south side of Newbury, though they spent the night in some uncertainty, fearing that the Roundheads had marched away. Had they occupied the high ground that evening they need have suffered no such doubts. Rupert sent a body of cavalry on to the plateau, whose commander[2] sent out patrols all night, but that was all.

Essex's army spent the night at Hamsted Park and Enborne.[3] Local tradition has it that the Earl himself spent the night at Bigg's Cottage.

THE ROYALIST ARMY

The King's army was not less than 14,000 strong, 6,000 horse and 8,000 foot. It may have been considerably stronger. Clarendon puts the horse as low as 4,000, but in view of the number of regiments present the higher figure is the more probable.

The exact number of brigades present is uncertain. There were at least four of each arm, and possibly five.[4] The train of artillery included 20 pieces of ordnance, 16 of brass and four of iron.[5] Of these the smaller pieces were probably employed in close support of the infantry brigades; eight guns were used as one battery in the Royalist centre.

King Charles commanded his army in person, having the professional assistance of Patrick Ruthven, Lord Forth, who, as Lord General, acted more or less as Chief of Staff. This veteran had seen many years of service in the Swedish army, then the best in

Europe. He had been known to his comrades there as Pater Rotwein – and not entirely because they could not pronounce his name.

Prince Rupert commanded the cavalry, which was now far stronger than it had been at Edgehill, and far more experienced and considerably stronger than Essex's horse.

Sir Jacob Astley was present once more to take overall command of the foot. These may have been about 2,000 fewer than at Edgehill, which was a serious disadvantage in enclosed country.

The guns, generally speaking, were heavier metal than at Edgehill. The General of the Ordnance was Lord Percy, an inefficient amateur.

THE PARLIAMENTARIAN ARMY

Essex had some 15,000 men when he set out to relieve Gloucester,[6] but by 20 September casualties, sickness, hunger and desertion had probably reduced his numbers to nearer 14,000.

On 31 July the Earl had reported that he had only 2,500 horse. Since then he had been joined by Harvey's London regiment and Norton's from Hampshire, besides being assisted to some extent by the recruiting drive made by Parliament when Gloucester was besieged. Altogether the Earl had 12 or 13 regiments of horse (though the number of troops in each varied), besides his troop of Lifeguards and several companies of dragoons. They were divided into two wings, commanded by Sir Philip Stapleton and Colonel John Middleton. The cavalry probably mustered at least 4,000 men.

The Earl had 18 regiments of foot, 13 of his own and five from London. His own infantry were divided into four brigades each of three regiments, his own regiment remaining unbrigaded. The London trained bands did not fight as a brigade. On 31 July the Earl had reported that he had 3,000 foot able to march and 3,000 sick. His army had been recruited by impressment, but it is difficult to say how effective this had been. The London trained bands were about 5,000 strong when they joined him. Allowing for wastage 10,000 would be a moderate computation of the strength of his foot at Newbury.

Essex had at least four great guns, besides demi-culverins, small field guns and drakes of which about 15 figure in various accounts of the fight. The precise composition of his train has not come to light, but he probably had at least as many guns as the King. Sir John Merrick commanded the Parliamentarian artillery, and his 'skill and care' were particularly commended. A number of the guns belonged to the infantry regiments.

There was a shortage of experienced senior officers in the Parliamentarian army, and the burden of command fell upon Essex and the Sergeant-Major-General of the foot, Philip Skippon. The latter was an able and gallant veteran, who had risen from the ranks in the Dutch service. During the battle Essex, besides exercising overall command, commanded the right – an untidy arrangement. Skippon commanded the left and the reserves.

The armies seem to have been fairly equal in numbers, but the King certainly had more cavalry than Essex.

	Royalists		Parliamentarians	
	Regiments	Numbers	Regiments	Numbers
Horse[7]	23+	6,000	13?	4,000
Foot	24-26	8,000	18	10,000
Guns	—	20	—	20+?
		14,000 +		14,000

The battlefield lies to the south-west of the town and, though more built-up, is now less enclosed than it was in 1643. The heaviest fighting took place on the plateau which forms the southern half of the field.

Both armies were afoot betimes on the 20th, but the Parliamentarians were evidently on the move first: 'by break of day[8] order was given for our march to an hill called Big's-hill, near to Newbury, and the only convenient place for us to gain, that we might with better security force our passage'.[9] Essex had 'perceived' that the Royalists had possessed themselves of the hill, and led a column of infantry up the Bigg's Hill lane to dislodge them. In fact the enemy he could see was no more than the cavalry patrols Rupert had sent out the previous evening and Essex's column reached its objective without difficulty. Gaining the top

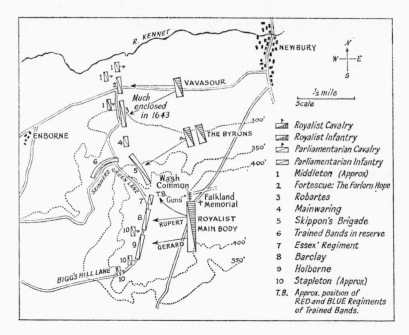

Royalist Cavalry
Royalist Infantry
Parliamentarian Cavalry
Parliamentarian Infantry
1 Middleton (Approx)
2 Fortescue: The Forlorn Hope
3 Robartes
4 Mainwaring
5 Skippon's Brigade
6 Trained Bands in reserve
7 Essex' Regiment
8 Barclay
9 Holborne
10 Stapleton (Approx)
T.B. Approx. position of
RED and BLUE Regiments
of Trained Bands.

THE FIRST BATTLE OF NEWBURY, 1643

of the hill he marched his men down the lane to his left almost as far as Skinner's Green Lane, and then deployed them in the hedges ready to withstand the expected counter-attack. Essex's Lifeguard and the regiments of Stapleton and Dalbier followed and, emerging from the lane, arrayed themselves partly between the bodies of foot and partly on their right.

Simultaneously Skippon's brigade, commanded presumably by the senior colonel present, marching up Skinner's Green Lane, had occupied Round Hill.

Skippon meanwhile had been ordering the march of the train of artillery and the rest of the foot regiments. This done he had hastened to join Essex. Looking from the top of the hill towards Newbury he saw 'a great strength of the enemy both horse and foot in divers great bodies advancing directly towards the way which all our train was of necessity to march'. These Royalists doubtless belonged to the foot brigades of Sir William Vavasour and Sir Nicholas Byron, and the cavalry brigade of Sir John Byron.

Skippon lost no time in deploying more infantry to cover the valley between Round Hill and the Kennet. On his right, on the

151

slopes of the hill, he placed the Red Auxiliary Regiment, next Lord Robartes' brigade and four or five small guns 'just where the enemy advanced', and on his left four drakes and a strong body of foot, called the forlorn hope, under Major Fortescue, 'upon the high way that came from Newbury just upon us'.[10] Skippon still had four of the London regiments in reserve.

Most of Middleton's cavalry must have been on Fortescue's left, though some may have been placed to support him and Lord Robartes. Owing to the number of hedges Middleton's men and the right wing of the Royalist horse were only able to engage in small parties.[11]

The battle began at about 7 o'clock, and it is clear from Digby's account that Essex was already in position before the Cavaliers advanced, even though they may have hoped to gain possession of the hill before Essex. Digby describes the Parliamentarian position. They had

> 'lodged their baggage and principal reserves, both of horse and foot, upon a hillside under a wood near Hampsted, fenced by hedges and ditches inaccessible, but by such and such passes, and having disposed, another principal part of their strength betwixt that and a place called Enborne, in strong hedges and houses, with apt batteries on both sides, for bravadoes' sake, or to invite us, they had drawn out into battalia into a little heath on the south side of Enborne three[12] bodies of foot, both lined and flanked with strong bodies of horse,[13] and under favour of cannon.'

He goes on to mention that Round Hill was 'within the enemy's dominion'.

In a sense the first round had gone to the Parliamentarians, without a shot being fired. They had established themselves in a strong defensive position, eminently suitable to an army whose strength was its infantry. Even so the King was still between them and London and there was nothing to prevent him drawing up his men to the east of the Earl's position, and adopting a defensive posture: nothing except the nature of his army. As Clarendon tells us the King had 'some young officers, who had good commands, and who unhappily always undervalued the courage of the enemy', while his horse had 'a kind of contempt' for their foes. These gallants were in no mood for passive defence.

The Royalist onslaught, generally speaking, consisted of two main thrusts, and two minor ones. On their left, where the ground was more suitable for cavalry, a strong body of Royalist horse attacked Stapleton and Essex. In the centre the Byrons attacked Round Hill and on the right there were attacks on Robartes and Fortescue. These were probably made by Vavasour's Welshmen. They do not seem to have been very fierce, and may perhaps be described as holding attacks.

On Essex's front the Cavalier advance was led by 1,000 musketeers under Lt.-Colonel George Lisle. The Parliamentarians were hotly charged by both horse and foot and much prowess was shown on both sides.[14] But before Lisle's foot could be supported they retreated, and the cavalry officer who commanded Rupert's outposts the previous night gives a picture of the confused fighting that followed, how he drew his horse into the next 'close' though not before they had suffered casualties from artillery and musketry, how his horse was shot in the near shoulder.

> 'But the foot crying out for ye horse, I returned into ye first mentioned close and was very slowly followed by reason of the straitness of the passage, but when I thought I had men enough to do ye service, I went to ye furthest part of ye said close where were near about 1,000 of ye enemy's foot drawn up in order and one piece of artillery, and as I was charging my horse was shot again into ye breast and faltered with me, so that, I being out of hopes to do other service than to lose myself, I gave orders to ye party in these very words in Major Smith's[15] hearing – "Fall on, my Masters! for I must go change my horse!" '

One cannot be certain, but it seems likely that this was an attack on Barclay's brigade.

On the Royalist left Wash Common was good cavalry country. Here Rupert deployed most of his horse, and determined to clear Stapleton from the heath. It took him three charges to do so, but in the end the Cavaliers prevailed.

In the first charge Stapleton's men held their fire until the Royalists were at close quarters, routed them and pursued them with much execution, almost up to their main body of horse, but Colonel Dalbier and Commissary Copley[16] were wounded and the latter lost his standard. Meanwhile the rest of the Roundhead right wing were able to come up the lane and deploy, and Stapleton rallied on them.

Fresh regiments of Cavaliers now galloped down on Sir Philip only to be repulsed, but while Stapleton was endeavouring to get his men into some order again, the whole body of Royalist horse thundered down on them. Once more a brave charge was bravely received. Stapleton found himself attacked both in front and flank ; his men had not had time to reload their pistols, and a terrible hack and thrust mêlée followed, both sides mingling in great confusion, and the Cavaliers gradually forcing the Roundheads back into the lane's end. Here the Cavaliers endeavoured to disengage for the Roundhead foot were close by. 'Those that entered the lane, with ours,' writes the Parliamentarian chronicler, 'were most of them slain.'

In the third charge Captain Robert Hamond and Cornet Charles Doyley of Essex's Lifeguard, and Captains Charles Fleetwood and Charles Pym (Dalbier's regiment) were wounded. Captain Draper, who led a forlorn hope of Stapleton's men, and the dragoon captains, Abercromy and Shibborne, are mentioned for their gallantry. Three Royalist standards[17] fell into the hands of the Roundheads, but Charles Gerard, whose brigade had finally driven Stapleton off the heath, had taken two Parliamentarian cornets.[18] Sir Philip's men had fought stoutly, but Essex's foot were now left to their own devices.

It was in one of these charges that the Earl of Caernarvon who had routed a body of horse, 'coming carelessly back by some of the scattered troopers, was by one of them, who knew him, run through the body with a sword, of which he died within an hour'.[19] Stapleton's wing played no further part in the fight that day.

The attack on Round Hill, which began about the same time as the attacks on Essex and Stapleton, is well described by Sir John Byron, who tells us that he got his orders to move about 5 o'clock in the morning and 'to march towards a little hill full of enclosures, which the enemy (through the negligence before mentioned) had possessed himself of'. The Parliamentarians had brought up two small field pieces and were bringing more, and the hill being 'extreme unfit for horse service', Byron's orders were to support Lisle's commanded foot, with his own regiment and Sir Thomas Aston's. Lisle's musketeers were, of course, heavily outnumbered by the regiments Essex and Skippon had brought into line, and were unable to hold their ground. Sir Nicholas Byron, Sir John's uncle, therefore, brought up part of the Lifeguard, Prince Charles' regiment and Charles Gerard's. The fight grew hot. Soon eleven of the twelve ensigns of Gerard's regiment were down and his lieutenant-colonel[20] had been shot through the shoulder. Again the cry of 'Horse! Horse!' went up, and Sir John Byron brought his two regiments to the front, halted them, and went to reconnoitre. He found the Roundhead foot 'enclosed with a high quick hedge and no passage into it, but by a narrow gap through which but one horse at a time could go and that not without difficulty'. He was giving orders for widening the gap when his horse was shot in the throat and its bit broken. While he was getting another horse 'Lord Falkland (more gallantly than advisedly) spurred his horse through the gap, where both he and his horse were immediately killed.' When the passage had been widened, Byron led his own troop through first, ordering the rest to follow, and charged the enemy, 'who entertained us with a great salvo of musket shot, and discharged their two drakes upon us laden with case shot, which killed some and hurt many of my men, so that we were forced to wheel off and could not meet them at that charge'. Undismayed by this rough reception the dogged Byron rallied his men, but before he could charge again, the Roundheads had got their guns away 'for fear of the worst, seeing us resolved not to give over. . .' Sir Thomas Aston's regiment came up, and Sir John charged a second time, beating the Parliamentarians to the end of the close, where with a hedge at their backs they faced about again, pouring in another volley of shot. Aston's horse was killed under him, and the Roundheads kept off the Cavaliers with their pikes, forcing them to wheel off once more, and won themselves sufficient breathing space to retreat into another little close and then hasten back into Skinner's Green Lane.

Once more Byron rallied his horse, and made his third charge, this time utterly routing his opponents, 'and had not left a man of them unkilled, but that the hedges were so high the horse could not pursue them, and besides, a great body of their own foot advanced towards the lane to relieve them'. Skippon had thrown in the London trained bands.

Sir John now drew his horse back 'to their former station', while his uncle's men held the ground gained. The three charges had cost Byron 100 men from his own regiment, and 26 from his own troop. Still it was a remarkable achievement to have driven an infantry brigade[21] from so strong a position.

Down in the valley Lord Robartes had been attacked but the Cavaliers met with 'so warm an entertainment that they ran shamefully', though not before they had shot Robartes' lieutenant-colonel.[22]

Another body of Royalists attacked Fortescue and got up so close that they captured the limber of one of his drakes, though the exploit cost them a number of lives. This attack was sufficiently severe to make Skippon spend more of his reserve. He sent the Blue Auxiliary Regiment to relieve Fortescue.

Essex too was hard-pressed and to relieve his brigades which had now been in 'very hot service' for about four hours he sent for the Red Auxiliaries, which had not been attacked. The time must have been about 11 o'clock.

Thus far things had gone well enough for the Royalists. Stapleton had been disposed of, Essex had his hands full; and part at least of Round Hill had been overrun. Only in the valley was the situation a comfortable stalemate. The crisis of the battle was at hand. If the Cavaliers could follow up their advantages Essex's whole army might be routed, but except for Sir Nicholas Byron's brigade the Royalist infantry did little to distinguish themselves that day. According to Digby 'our foot having found a hillock in the heath that sheltered them from the enemy's cannon, would not be drawn a foot from thence'. This is no doubt a generalisation which only applied to Belasyse's[23] brigade, but even so it accounts for much that follows.

On Essex's right wing the battle became a struggle of horse against foot. Time after time Rupert's cavalry, inspired by his example, charged the unbroken foot suffering heavy losses, particularly in officers, and inadequately supported by their foot.

But it was in the centre, at Round Hill, that the vital ground lay, and here it was that Skippon changed the fortunes of the day. When he had put the left wing in order the veteran had ridden back once more to the top of the hill. Over to his right some Cavaliers had got into a house and were pelting Barclay's and Holbourne's brigades at close range. There were two demi-culverins in position at the top of Skinner's Green Lane, probably engaging the Royalist's eight gun battery near the tumuli. Skippon ordered the gunners to open fire on the house, and they fired eight or ten rounds at it. But this was no more than an interlude. His real problem was the use of the remaining reserves.

His first move was to put the Red and Blue Regiments of the London trained bands into one body and post them to cover the mouth of the lane, the place where the train of artillery was to come to the top of the hill.

Next he asked Major John Boteler to place the musketeers of Essex's regiment on the right flank of the demi-culverins and somewhat to their front. The Red Auxiliaries, summoned to his aid by Essex, came up and Skippon placed them on the left of the two guns, which up to this time had been slenderly guarded. These movements must have been those noted by Sir John Byron at the end of his charge. Skippon now had only one regiment left in reserve, the Orange Auxiliaries, but he had stabilised the Parliamentarian centre. It was now possible to bring up the big guns. Things indeed had improved so much that Major Boteler led Essex's regiment in a local counter-attack against Sir Nicholas Byron, which recovered two pieces belonging to Skippon's regiment and a drake of Sir William Brook's.[24] These guns no doubt had been lost in Byron's onslaught. Boteler's counter-attack did not get far : in the words of Sir John Byron 'The enemy drew up fresh supplies to regain the ground again', but thanks to Sir Nicholas '(who that day did extraordinary service) was entirely beaten off.'

The brunt of the fighting now began to fall on the London trained bands. Sergeant Henry Foster (Red Regiment) has left a spirited account of their adventures. Morale was high when they marched off that morning, and the news that on the left Robartes was already engaged put them into 'a running march till we sweat again, hastening to their relief and succour'. But in fact it was not to support Robartes that Skippon eventually launched them, but in a much hotter part of the field. They found themselves opposite the main Royalist battery (eight guns), 'far less than twice musket distance away'. He tells us that it was more than half an hour before any of their own guns could get up to them and complains that 'our gunner dealt very ill with us, delaying to come up to us'. He may only be referring to the regimental artillery, but clearly Skippon could not bring the train up Skinner's Green Lane until its mouth was secured, and drawing seventeenth-century guns up a narrow lane, the horses dragging them tandem, was no easy matter. When the guns did arrive 'our noble Colonel Tucker fired one piece of ordnance . . . and aiming to give fire the second time, was shot in the head with a cannon bullet. . . .'[25]

The Royalist cannon were concentrating on the Red Regiment and 'did some execution . . . at the first, and were somewhat dreadful when men's bowels and brains flew in our faces : but blessed be God that gave us courage, so that we kept our ground, and after a while feared them not ; our ordnance did very good execution upon them : for we stood at so near a distance upon a plain field, that we could not lightly miss one another : . . . .' Next day, near the field where Lloyd's regiment had been, Ensign Gwyn saw 'upon the heath . . . a whole file of men, six deep, with their heads struck off with one cannon shot of ours'.

Rupert was not the man to let the battle deteriorate into a mere cannonade. Two regiments of horse charged the Blue Regiment, but were beaten off several times. Once they came up wearing green boughs in their hats, the Roundheads' field sign, and shouting 'Friends ! Friends !', but the Cockneys were not so easily taken in and let fly, bringing many down and making the rest fly off with a vengeance. But the trained bands were too exposed and eventually out-flanked by horse and foot they were driven off the little hill they were on, and fell back to the main position. The Red Regiment alone lost 60 or 70 killed, though not all on the hill for 60 files of musketeers (360 men) were with Fortescue.

Digby records that the Parliamentarians made a thrust at 'a pass on our right hand near the river,'[26] but this was repulsed. The hottest fighting was certainly in the area of Round Hill and Wash Common, and even here it died down about 7 o'clock. As night drew on the Roundheads could still see their enemies, horse and foot, standing in good order on the further side of the green, and there they expected to see them when the next dawn came. About 10 o'clock at night the Cavaliers let fly a good round salvo against the Roundhead right – Barclay and Holborne – and thereafter all fell silent.

That night the King held a Council of War. Losses had been heavy, particularly among the horse, even so Rupert was for holding the ground they were on, and Sir John Byron, for one, was of his mind. They were overruled. Percy, who as General of the Artillery was responsible for the provision of ammunition, declared that 80 barrels of powder had been spent and that only 10 remained, and it seems that this argument clinched the matter. The King gave orders for a withdrawal towards Oxford. It was a fatal decision for which the blame must lie with Charles himself and his Lord General, Forth. No doubt they were supported by Wilmot, Digby and others who, more cautious than Rupert, were yet bold enough to cross him. But the ultimate responsibility lay with the King and his chief professional adviser. It may be that a bold front would not have been enough. Essex and his officers were encouraging their soldiers by God's help to force their way through or die next day. But they were glad enough when it pleased God, as they put it, to make their passage without blows.

As Essex's soldiers, weary and famished, trudged towards Reading, the tireless Rupert fell on their rearguard routing the horse, who, according to one disgusted Roundhead infantryman, behaved basely and 'rode quite through our foot in a narrow lane, pressed many of them down under their horses' feet, and for the present utterly routed us. . . .'[27]

As trophies the Prince carried off five orange colours, but this blow at parting could not conceal the fact that in his second great battle with his King, the Earl of Essex had achieved his purpose. He entered Reading on the 22nd.

Essex and his officers had played their parts worthily. The Parliament Scout tells us that the Lord General took 'unexpressable pains' and that his horse fell under him 'being tired with continual motion'. *Mercurius Civicus* records his surviving a near miss from a Royalist 24-pounder. Skippon 'rid down three horses

159

that day'. Lord Robartes 'never budged from his Regiment' doing his duty as bravely as any, while Colonel Barclay 'stood bravely to the business and gave full testimony of his valour'.

The Royalist tactics had left something to be desired. Had they seized Bigg's Hill on the 19th and lined the hedges, adopting a defensive posture on the 20th, it is difficult to see how they could have lost the battle.

We have no casualty returns for Essex's army, though White-lock puts his killed as low as 500. According to a *Relation*[28] printed on 26 September, 1643, 'The most we lost were out of the Blew and Red Trained-Bands, who neverthelesse have gained them-selves eternall honour.' It may be that the Red regiment of the trained bands with 60 or 70 killed, lost more heavily than the rest of Essex's infantry, but it would not be surprising if the ten regi-ments that were all day on Bigg's Hill or Round Hill lost as heavily. Robartes and the others who were in the valley had less of an ordeal, but even there the fighting was fierce for a time. Stapleton's wing of cavalry must have suffered fairly severely in its three charges, otherwise one would expect it to have rallied and attempted to come up the lane again. Middleton on the other wing probably lost but few men. Perhaps 2,000 is a reasonable estimate of Essex's losses, but it is a leap in the dark.

Judging by the number of officers hit the Royalist cavalry suffered severely. Rupert lost 30 of his troop, which was probably about 100 strong, and 300 of his regiment. It is true that his regi-ment had ten troops and was a very strong one, but even so these were grievous losses. Byron lost 100 from his regiment, probably about 25 per cent.

It is certain that the Royalist foot had 59 officers and 584 other ranks wounded,[29] and with killed their casualties must have been about 1,000. The losses fell very unevenly on the brigades. Sir Nicholas Byron's had more than 200, perhaps over 300, wounded; Sir Gilbert Gerard's 247 casualties, of whom 138 were hurt; Belasyse's apparently 123 wounded, and Vavasour, on the right where the fighting was not so heavy, only 48 wounded.

Charles Gerard's regiments had the heaviest casualties, 16 officers and 85 men wounded. The Prince of Wales and the Lord General had 75 and 74 wounded respectively. Other regiments,

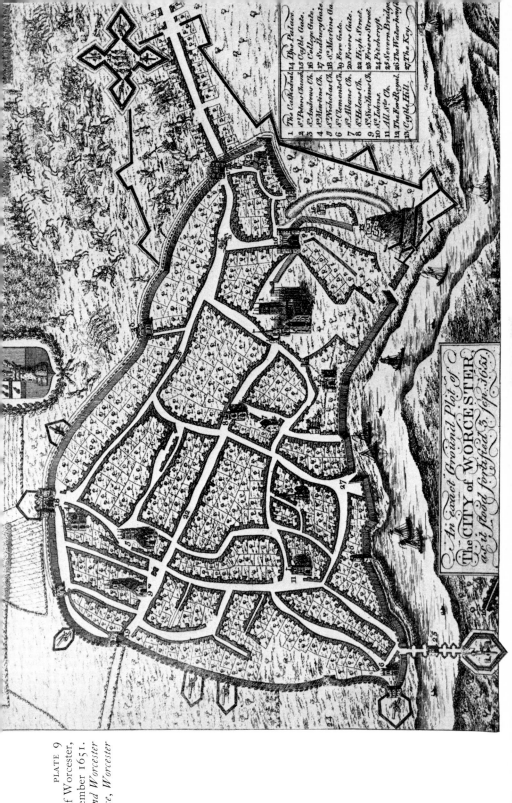

PLATE 10
Royalist Colours, Guidons and Standards   *W. Y. Carman*
Infantry Lt. Colonel   First Captain Lamplugh's Regiment
Lt. Colonel of Dragoons   Major of Dragoons
Horse   Horse

PLATE 11

Harquebus armour from the Littlecote House collection, now in H.M. Tower of London.

This is how one imagines a Cromwellian cavalry soldier might have looked, but it was the ideal of both sides in the Civil War. The basis is the buffcoat, which would keep out most sword cuts, and the lobster tail helmet, single or three bar, which was preferred to the Cavalier feather or beaver hat. The left arm guard is rather rare (although see plate 7) but very useful since the most vulnerable point of attack on a cavalryman is his bridle arm. It is questionable whether the protection afforded by the back and breastplates is worth the extra weight to be carried on a horse.

Littlecote House and the Armouries, H.M. Tower of London

The D. of Monm. landed at Lime in Dorset with 82 men Thursday Jun. 10. 1685, & he
He ordered his affaires so in those parts, as y he was able to enter in a Triumphant ma
er into Taunton, June 18, being y Thursday following w an army of about 3000 men.
At Taunton, Saturday Jun. 20, He was proclaimed King. And y next day, Sunday Jun. 21
marched into Bridgwater, with about 5000 men, armed about 4000, vnarmed 1000.
incamped on y North side in Castle-field. Munday June 22. He marched by Weston &
er the Moor to Glastonbury. His souldiers boasting that by Saturday night next the
would be in London, & place their King upon his throne. But the difficultyes w he m
in his motion Eastward; and y hopes he had of great additions from y Clubmen in Somerset
in the Marsh Country, gave the occasion of his return to Glaston; & thence by Weston
back to Bridgw: into w Town he came Thursday July 2. He was about to for
ty that place; & to that purpose summoned in Pioneers. But the Townsmen disapprovi
it, He desisted, & dismissed the Country men.
On Sunday July 5. The Kings Army consisting of about 4000 in all, marched from
Som̃ton. About noon they incamped in Zog; in y parish of Chedsey, vnder Weston.
2000 lodge in y Camp. 500 Horse quarter in y Town. 1500 Militia men quarter
Midlesy & Okersey. Benjamin Newton of Bridgw: parish being in y Moor to look
after Cattle, sees y manner of their incamping, goes into y town to the D. of Mon
tells him all; gives account of the way through North-moor, & had a Guinea for his pai
The D. forthwith goes up to y Church tower. There spends a considerable time in
viewing all with a Prospective glass. He calls a Councill of war; & with consent
in y Evening He marches forth; The townsmen being unwilling he should stay
there; as fearing that the Kings army would fire down the Town. He did not
take y nearest way to Weston, by w he went June 22 & returned July 2 bu
he took to y Long Cawsey. in w way some being in y trees & hedges by, heard
him animating his men with great zeale. He left y way through Chedsey by
the short Cawsey, though that was y nearer and more convenient, probably the
way to avoid the danger of being discovered. But He went by Bradney lane
which lane he also soon left to avoid being too near, to a loyall mans house as
likely; So by Marsh-lane, w is y farther about and lesser commodious He led y
Army into North-Moor.
About Sun-set A party of the Kings Horse came to Langmoor stone from y camp
& taking w them y Guard there; (about 12 or 16 Horse), went by North moor
into Bawdrip, & afterward up y Hill to Bristoll road. They passe by Long
Cawsey to Bridgwater townes end. And so round y next way to Weston. Whilst
they were about Bawdrip, The Dukes Army marched into North moor, with great
silence standing still, till this party of Horse was gone; for they were w in view
of them. this party is supposed to be Col. Oglethorps.
About Midnight (probably while y D. of Mon. was in North moor) Another
party of y Kings Horse came from Zog, by Langmoor stone, & step stones,
to Parchey Gate. So they Marched quite through Chedsey; & round as y suppo
osed to y Camp again. yet though they were so near to y Enemy marching
toward y Kings Army this Horse made no discovery of them. Guards and Centi
nels were placed in all the Avenues in y about y nearer way from Weston to Bridgwater,
& in y other & farther way about by w the Enemy designed to come, But all were gone
(particularly that most necessary Guard at Lang-moor stone, & y Centinels y stood near it,
before bed-time) A Watch of 8 Chedsey men was set at Chedsey Crosse. Two persons frie
to y D. Cause) who had seen his Army march as far as Bradney, came & told y that y
Army was marching, & that there would be a fight, & so they were going in hast that
y nearest way to the Mill to see it. But these men in y watch, whether thinking it might h
we

which seem to have belonged to Belasyse's brigade, suffered but lightly, Thomas Blagge's regiment had only 6 wounded.

The loss of Lord Falkland, though he fought only as a volunteer in Sir John Byron's troop, was a particularly heavy one, quite apart from his own nobility of character, for on his death King Charles appointed Lord Digby, an unscrupulous intriguer, to be Secretary of State in his place.

But a mere computation of the casualties can be misleading. It is quite likely that Essex lost as many men or even more than the King; but while the Earl achieved his aim of reaching Reading with his army more or less intact, Charles had failed to bring about the destruction of the main Parliamentarian army.

For the Royalists a quick and decisive victory was absolutely necessary. Their aim at First Newbury should have been simple enough. But in war even the simple is very difficult.

Within the week it was reported[30] in London that King Charles had described Newbury as 'a worse bout than Edgehill'. The long looked for crisis of a battle had passed, and with it his best chance of regaining his Kingdom.[31]

[1] E. 69.

[2] His report, unfortunately anonymous, is in the British Museum. Add. 18980-2.

[3] E. 69/10.

[4] *Brigade commanders.*

Horse	Foot
Prince Rupert	Sir William Vavasour
Lord Wilmot	Sir Nicholas Byron
Earl of Caernarvon	Colonel John Belasyse
Sir John Byron	Sir Gilbert Gerard
Colonel Charles Gerard	

[5] Demi-cannon, 2; Culverins, 2; 12-pounders, 2; 6-pounders, 5; Sakers, 1; Mynions (Iron), 2; 3-pounders, 4; Bases, 2. One of these pieces was a 24-pounder. (*The Great Civil War*, p. 107.)

[6] S. R. Gardiner.

[7] As a rule a troop of horse in Essex's army numbered at least 60. In the Royalist army a troop seldom seems to have exceeded 50, the average being rather lower.

[8] Sunrise: 5.56. Sunset: 5.45.

[9] Official Account.

[10] Official Account.

[11] Official Account.

[12] Essex's regiment; Barclay's and Holborne's brigades.

13 Stapleton.
14 Official Account.
15 Paul Smith. Wilmot's regiment.
16 Stapleton's regiment.
17 The devices on these cornets were:
    1. The harp with the crown royal; the motto LYRICA MONARCHICA.
    2. An angel with a flaming sword treading on a dragon with the motto QUIS UT
       DEUS.
    3. A standard with the motto COURAGE POUR LA CAUSE.
18   1. A red standard with the motto VINCERE SPERO. This belonged to Captain
       Sandys of Kent.
    2. A standard bearing the motto ONLY IN HEAVEN and a gold anchor. This was
       Captain Robert Mainwaring's cornet. He was a Londoner and belonged to
       Harvey's regiment.
    National Army Museum. MS. book of Parliamentarian Standards. f76 and 81.
19 Clarendon.
20 Ned Villiers.
21 His opponents must have belonged to Skippon's brigade.
22 William Hunter?
23 Prince Rupert's Diary mentions this incident.
24 Skippon's brigade.
25 A cannon bullet means a piece of grapeshot not a cannon ball, or roundshot. The
   range cannot have been more than 350 yards.
26 Apparently Guyer's Lane (Money).
27 E. 69/2.
28 E. 69/2.
29 *Hurt Souldiers of Newbery.*
30 E. 69/2.
31 For a detailed study of the composition of the rival armies at the First Battle of
   Newbury, see the article by Brig. P. Young in *The Army Historical Research
   Journal*, 1964.

The Battle of Marston Moor

THE CAMPAIGN

1644

19 *January*	*The Scots cross the Tweed.*
25 *January*	*Sir Thomas Fairfax defeats Byron at Nantwich.*
19 *February*	*Prince Rupert sets up his Headquarters at Shrewsbury.*
21 *March*	*Rupert's victory at Newark.*
11 *April*	*The Fairfaxes storm Selby.*
22 *April*	*Newcastle besieged in York by Lord Fairfax and the Earl of Leven.*
6 *May*	*Manchester reinforces the Allies before York.*
16 *May*	*Rupert leaves Shrewsbury.*
25 *May*	*Rupert takes Stockport.*
28 *May*	*Rupert storms Bolton.*
30 *May*	*Goring joins Rupert.*
7-11 *June*	*Siege and capture of Liverpool by the Royalists.*
23 *June*	*Rupert begins to cross the Pennines.*
26 *June*	*Rupert at Skipton.*
1 *July*	*Rupert relieves York.*
2 *July*	*The Battle of Marston Moor.*
16 *July*	*The surrender of York.*

THE BATTLE

2 July, 1644

IF YORK BE lost I shall esteem my crown little less. . . . But if York be relieved, and you beat the rebels' army of both Kingdoms, which are before it ; then (but otherwise not)[1] I may possibly make a shift (upon the defensive) to spin out time until you come to assist me. Wherefore I command and conjure you by the duty and affection which I know you bear me, that all new enterprises laid aside, you immediately march, according to your first intention, with all your force to the relief of York.' Thus wrote King Charles to his nephew, Rupert, on 14 June, 1644. When Lord Culpeper saw the copy of the letter he told his master : 'before God you are undone, for upon this peremptory order he will fight, whatever comes on 't'.

Rupert had left Shrewsbury on 'The Yorke March'[2] on 16 May, nearly a month before this curious operation order was penned. At this time he had no more than 2,000 horse and 6,000 foot, a force with which he could not hope to make head against the three Allied armies before York, whose strength seems to have been about 27,000. In order to fight the Allies with some prospect of success it was absolutely necessary to increase his army.

Rupert first marched into Lancashire, a county which had provided the 'Oxford Army' with two regiments of foot[3] in 1642, and in 1643 had raised many men for the Queen's Regiment of Horse and her Lifeguard of foot. In the absence of so many loyal soldiers the Roundheads had overrun the whole county, save only Lathom House which was bravely defended by the Countess of Derby. Rupert felt that if he could reconquer Lancashire recruits would flock to his standard, and when Stockport, Bolton and Liverpool fell in quick succession, he was proved correct. A further addition of strength came when Goring with Newcastle's cavalry, some 5,000 strong, arrived on 30 May. Early in June a contingent of about 500 Royalists from Derbyshire joined the Prince.[4] On the other hand a garrison had to be found for Liverpool so it was probably with no more than 13,000 men that the Prince set out from Preston on 23 June to cross the Pennines. The odds were still too long, but if he could join hands with Newcastle's garrison in York Rupert would be at the head of the biggest Royalist army yet assembled, for Newcastle's garrison in York was not less than 5,000 strong. And so Rupert set out on his attempt to break through the three beleaguering armies, double his own strength though they were.

It may be that the Prince's chief asset was the fact that he was opposed by a triumvirate. The Scots general was Alexander Leslie, Earl of Leven, a 55 year old veteran who had been made a field-marshal by Gustavus Adolphus. His cavalry was commanded by his son, Major-General David Leslie, who had also fought in the Swedish army, and his infantry were under Lt.-General William Baillie. The second triumvir was Lord Fairfax, a man of 60, whose most notable contribution to the Parliamentarian party was to have produced a fire-eating son in Sir Thomas, the mainspring of the Roundhead cause in Yorkshire. The third triumvir was that 'sweet, meek man,' the Earl of Manchester, an uninspired general if ever there was one. His horse were commanded by Lt.-General Oliver Cromwell and his foot by a fiery and outspoken young professional soldier, Major-General Lawrence Crawford. At the top level the Allied army was commanded by officers of very ordinary ability. All the thrust was at the next level down.

Rupert, advancing along the modern A59 by Clitheroe and Gisburn, reached Skipton, 43 miles from York, on 26 June. Here he spent three days putting his army in order, ensuring that his men were as well armed as possible, and that their muskets were properly 'fixed'. Messengers were sent into York.

On 28 June the triumvirate heard of Rupert's approach. They were reluctant to break up their siege, which had already cost them many lives and much labour, at a time when the garrison was hard-pressed. Yet they were doubtful whether they had enough men both to face Rupert and to continue the leaguer. They thought that the Prince had been reinforced by Colonel Sir Robert Clavering and a contingent from the northern counties. Their own reinforcements under Sir John Meldrum and the Earl of Denbigh had not yet arrived from Cheshire. Although they seem to have overestimated Rupert's strength their decision to break up the siege was probably sound. Had they left, say, 8,000 or 9,000 men to

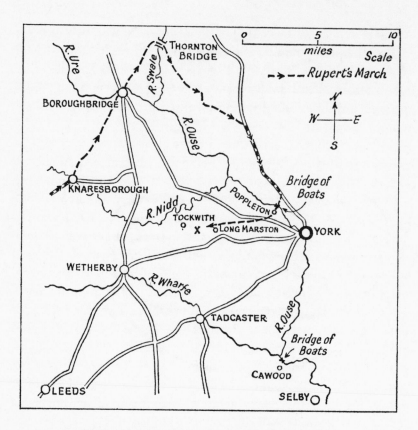

THE CAMPAIGN OF MARSTON MOOR

blockade York, and offered battle to the Prince with the remaining 18,000 or 19,000 they might well have suffered a crushing defeat. They were obeying one of the so-called Principles of War, Concentration of Force, by opposing the relieving army with every man at their disposal. They hoped by placing their 27,000 men between York and Skipton to prevent the Prince's 13,000 joining hands with Newcastle's 5,000. Such straight-forward strategy might have served against a lesser commander, but in Prince Rupert they were opposed to a master of mobility. In the days when an army looked upon 8 miles as a fair day's march the Prince could get 20 out of his; pikemen, train of artillery, sumpter horses and all.

On 29 June the Cavaliers resumed their advance, reaching Knaresborough, only 18 miles from York, on the 30th. It was on that night that the Allied generals finally decided to raise their siege. Next day (1 July) they drew up their great host on Marston Moor, which lies 6 miles due west of York on the Knaresborough road. As they expected Rupert's advanced guard was soon in sight, armour twinkling in the summer sun, but as hour after hour slipped by the serried ranks, keyed up for battle, waited in vain for the Prince's main body to appear.

Rupert had been early afoot, and after spending the night in Galtres Forest, had marched hard for Boroughbridge, 7 miles north-east of Knaresborough, where he crossed the Ure. Then pushing on he crossed the Swale at Thornton Bridge, and swept down on York along the north bank of the Ouse. Late in the day he surprised a regiment of Roundhead dragoons, guarding a bridge of boats at Poppleton, 3 miles north-west of York. Meanwhile the Allies, amused by no more than a cavalry screen, had spent a frustrating day on Marston Moor. Rupert's army had covered rather more than 20 miles and had completely outmanoeuvred them. York was relieved. The Prince now had something like 18,000 men at his disposal, excluding the three regiments of foot required as a minimum garrison for York.[5]

The Allied commanders were dumbfounded by this thunderbolt of war. That night they determined to march south-west towards Cawood and Tadcaster. This was sound enough. Meldrum could join them unmolested. By cutting off supplies from the East and West Ridings they would compel the Prince to fight.

But, unfortunately for his uncle's cause, the Prince was anything but reluctant to fight, even against odds of three to two. And even without his uncle's 'peremptory order' in his pocket one may be permitted to suspect that this ardent young general would have hazarded all on a pitched battle. The polished Newcastle had assured him in a letter of congratulation that he was 'made of nothing but thankfulness and obedience to Your Highness's commands'. Rupert, who was no courtier, accepted this assurance literally, and proceeded to give orders for battle on the morrow. Newcastle, and his 'Chief of Staff', James King, Lord Eythin, were horrified. Very sensibly, they wanted to await Clavering's arrival before fighting. No doubt, too, they felt that their men deserved some rest : after the strain of the siege such a reaction was only to be expected. Rupert, whose tireless frame could endure any amount of work, was far from appreciating such arguments. No doubt the Royalist generals conferred, and maybe quarrelled far into the night, but the Prince held the trump card: the King's letter. He would have been wise to spend a few days revictualling York, and putting his army in order – as he had done at Skipton Castle. However, he had his way and next day the Cavaliers trooped out on to Marston Moor, but not in the perfect order their commander desired. Many of Newcastle's foot surged into the enemy's abandoned lines in search of loot. Others celebrated their relief in drunken revelling. The afternoon was far spent before his famous Whitecoats reached the field.

The van of the Allied armies was nearly at Tadcaster before news reached their commanders that the Royalists were offering battle. With their great superiority in numbers they had no reason to reject the challenge. Countermarching they deployed for the second time on Marston Moor, but this time facing not west but north.

THE ROYALIST ARMY

Prince Rupert's Order of Battle has been preserved.[6] As was the practice of the time, especially when the battlefield was relatively free of obstacles, the army was drawn up with horse on the wings and foot in the centre. In addition there was cavalry in reserve behind the centre.

Lord Byron commanded the right; Lord Goring the left, and Rupert himself the reserve. The infantry were presumably commanded by their two Sergeant-Major-Generals, Henry Tillier of Rupert's army and Sir Francis Mackworth of Newcastle's. Newcastle and King seem to have been with the reserve, acting rather as critics than commanders.

The Right Wing consisted of 2,600 horse and 500 musketeers. Byron commanded the front line (1,100 horse and 500 musketeers). The second line consisted of Lord Molyneux's brigade and Prince Rupert's regiment, a total of about 1,300 horse. Covering Byron's right, and half way between the two lines was Colonel Samuel Tuke with 200 horse.[7]

The musketeers were drawn up in bodies of about 50 in support of the eleven squadrons of horse in the front line. Presumably they were intended to disorder the enemy by firing volleys into them as they advanced. Rupert and Maurice appear to have been the only commanders to have employed this tactical device during our Civil Wars. One suspects that they had learned it on the continent, and it would be interesting to know who was its originator, perhaps Gustavus Adolphus.

The centre consisted of about 10,000 foot and Sir William Blakeston's brigade of horse (800?) and, presumably, the 16 guns. The front was covered by musketeers lining a ditch, but the rest of the foot were divided into twenty-two more or less equal bodies of which fifteen belonged to Rupert's army and the remaining seven to Newcastle's. These last, because they arrived late, were placed in second and third line.

Well to the front, perhaps 300 yards, were posted three 'divisions' (750 strong?),[8] the 'forlorn hope'. There may have been a gap in the ditch at this point. The plan may have been to support the musketeers in the ditch, but it seems much more likely that they were to fire into the opposing cavalry as they approached Byron, and indeed they were drawn up ahead of his left hand regiment, Marcus Trevor's.

The front line proper consisted of eight divisions of Rupert's army, the second of seven covering the intervals in the first; the right hand three being Newcastle's men. The next line was Blakeston's horse. Behind him and to the right were four divisions of Whitecoats.

The Left Wing consisted of 2,100 horse and 500 musketeers. The front line was 1,100 horse and 500 musketeers, under Goring and Lucas, the second line was Sir Richard Dacre's brigade (800), while Colonel Francis Carnaby (200) covered Lucas' left, in the way Tuke did Byron's right.

As a reserve Rupert had about 650 horse, including Sir William Widdrington's small brigade (400) and his own Lifeguard.

Except that one would like to have seen a larger reserve of horse, the Prince's dispositions appear reasonable enough.

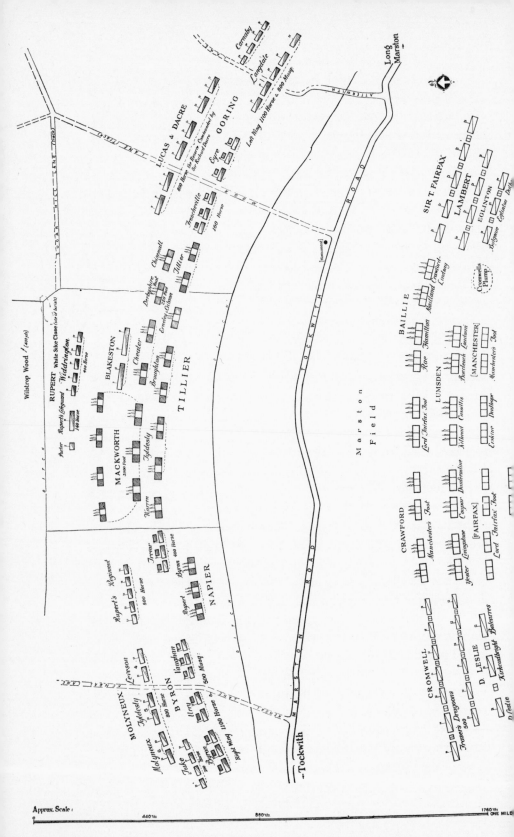

THE BATTLE OF MARSTON MOOR, 1644

Lumsdon's plan survives to show us the dispositions of the three Allied armies. Except that they had no reserve, the Allies 'set to partners' with the Royalists in the conventional style. Sir Thomas Fairfax commanded the right wing of horse and Oliver Cromwell the left. The Scottish horse, being less formidable one supposes than, say, the Ironsides, were divided and placed in rear of Fairfax and Cromwell.

	Royalists	*Allies*
Horse	6,500	7,000?
Foot	11,000	20,000?
Guns	16	25
	17,500	27,000

The Duke of Wellington once said that one might as well attempt to write the history of a ball as a battle. Accurate description defies even the most level-headed observer. Marston Moor began in a thunderstorm and ended by the light of a harvest moon. The decisive blows were struck by swift-moving bodies of cavalry, who, in the nature of things, hardly stood still for more than a few minutes at a time. No wonder if the details are more than ordinarily obscure. Yet the main lines are clear enough.

The day was spent in marshalling the five armies. Rupert showed Lord Eythin a plan – de Gomme's is no doubt the fair copy – to be told rudely, 'By God, sir, it is very fine on paper, but there is no such thing in the field.' Coming from the Chief of Staff of a contingent that had arrived late and with many of its men half drunk this speech was hardly calculated to please the Prince. However, he seems to have controlled his temper, and even to have offered to alter his dispositions – only to be told that it was now too late. Eythin, a Scots mercenary from the Swedish service, had been in command at Vlotho[9] in 1638, when Rupert as a young colonel had fallen into the hands of the Imperialists. On that occasion it was said that, fearing the worst, Eythin had sent away his own baggage before the battle began. He had certainly failed to support Rupert, blaming the latter for his 'forwardness'. Although he had recently been in correspondence with Leven, a former comrade in arms, it is his competence rather than his loyalty that is in doubt. He was an uninspired, methodical, professional soldier, who, after two years under Newcastle, a grandee, who left all the details to him, resented serving a talented young general who meant to be obeyed.

As the day wore on it gradually became increasingly clear to the Allied commanders that the Royalists did not mean to attack that day. It may be supposed that they conferred, probably on the hill, now crowned by the trees known as Cromwell's Plump. Rupert had been first in the field and had chosen his ground, a slightly concave front of nearly 2 miles with its left flank just north of Long Marston and its right stretching almost to Tockwith. Behind the Royalists lay the open moor, in those days unenclosed. The Allies were drawn up not on moorland, but in fields of rye.

By about 4 p.m. both armies were fully deployed, but still there was no move. The Allied commanders, relieved that Rupert had not seized the initiative before their rearmost units could come up from Tadcaster, now began to think of attacking themselves. The hours crept slowly by and then about 7 p.m. they saw the smoke of fires beginning to rise from the Royalist lines as they cooked their evening meals. Through their perspective glasses they could make out cavalrymen dismounting. Now was the time. A cannon was fired as the signal for the advance. Almost immediately the darkening skies opened as peals of thunder heralded the battle. The Ironsides began to move down the gentle slope towards Byron's line.

Across the moor Rupert, having told Newcastle 'We will charge them tomorrow morning,' was sitting on the ground eating his supper; the stately Marquis, comfortably installed in his coach, was smoking his pipe. The cannon that signalled the Allied charge, served also as a summons to the Cavaliers. Everywhere officers hastened to dress the ranks, troopers hastily remounted. But the initial surprise sufficed to carry the Allies across the ditch, though it proved a serious obstacle on their right.

Sir Thomas Fairfax with the right wing of horse tells us that his men were put into great disorder 'by reason of the whins (gorse) and ditches which we were to pass over before we could get to the

Enemy . . . .' Nevertheless he drew up a body of 400 horse, but because Goring's men 'were lined with Musketeers, which did us much hurt with their shot, I was necessitated to charge them. We were a long time engaged one with another; but at last we routed that part of their wing. We charged and pursued them a good way towards York'. Sir Thomas himself, alone, returned immediately to bring up the rest of his men, but only to find that the Cavaliers opposite them 'perceiving the disorder they were in, had charged and routed them. . . . So that the good success we had at first was eclipsed much by this bad conclusion'. In this first charge his brother, Charles, 'being deserted of his men', was sore wounded, and of his officers hardly one escaped unscathed. Colonel John Lambert, who should have seconded Fairfax, could not get to him, but 'charged in another place'. His Major, another Fairfax, received at least thirty wounds, of which he died.

We have no account of this fight from any Royalist source, but it is evident that Goring's men were everywhere successful and swept not only the horse from the field, but much of the foot as well. Lucas, once the opposing cavalry were routed, repeated his Edgehill manoeuvre on a bigger scale by leading his brigade against the enemy foot, who by this time were doubtless at push of pike with Tillier's command. Lord Fairfax himself, who was with his infantry, fled to his house at Cawood – and went to bed! Confusion spread down the Allied line and 'amazed with panicke feares' many, both English and Scots, quit the field. Only the stubborn resistance of two Scottish regiments, the Earl of Lindsay's and Lord Maitland's, checked the rout. Twice they repelled the Royalist horse, before Baillie and Major-General Lumsden brought regiments from the second line to their support. Lucas leading his men against a hedgehog of pikes was unhorsed and taken. The tide had turned.

On the other wing events took a very different course. Cromwell's horse, not less than 3,000 strong, rode down on Byron 'in the bravest order, and with the greatest resolution that ever was seen', according to Scoutmaster-General Watson. 'In a moment we were past the ditch into the Moor, upon equal grounds with the enemy, our men going in a running march.' Byron – wrongly as Rupert thought – advanced to meet the Ironsides. No doubt he preferred to get up speed before the impact, but in doing so he masked the fire of his own musketeers. In the short mêlée that followed most of Byron's command was routed, but not before a Royalist colonel, Marcus Trevor, had wounded Cromwell himself.[10] Nevertheless, the latter was able to rally his men ready for a second charge.

When the battle began Rupert was quickly in the saddle, and was not slow to see that it was on the right that his presence was needed. Putting himself at the head of his reserve he rode at once in that direction. Men of his own regiment – the left of Byron's second line – came galloping by. 'Swounds, do you run?' he shouted, 'follow me.' More frightened of the Prince than of any Roundhead, the dismayed Cavaliers turned and followed him, rallying on the 600 or so fresh men that he led.

Meanwhile Cromwell had gone off to Tockwith to have his wound dressed, leaving Lawrence Crawford temporarily in command of his Ironsides. In his absence his men 'had a hard pull of it, for they were charged by Rupert's bravest men both in front and flank. They stood at the sword's point a pretty while, hacking one another ; but at last (it so pleased God) he broke through them, scattering them before him like a little dust'.[11]

Other things being equal, the victor in any cavalry battle is the last man to have an effective reserve to put in. So it was now. It was David Leslie and some 800 Scots, who made up Cromwell's third line, that finally swung the battle against Rupert. Cut off from his Lifeguard the Prince was compelled to conceal himself in a beanfield.

It may have been about this time that Colonel Sir Philip Monckton, an officer of the Northern Horse, met Urry, and pointing to a large body of horse that had been rallied, urged him to counter-attack. 'Broken horse, won't fight,' was all the answer he got before Sir John (who had already changed sides once in the war and was to do so twice more) galloped from the field.

All was confusion. Sir Henry Slingsby, an eye-witness, describes the rout of the Royalist right. 'They fly along by Wilstrop woodside as fast and as thick as could be....'[12] Arthur Trevor arriving on the battlefield with a message for Rupert tells us 'in the fire, smoke and confusion ... I knew not for my soul whither to incline', and describes the runaways from both sides, 'so many, so breathless, so speechless, so full of fears. . . .' The cornet of a troop rode by with only four of his men left ; then 'a little foot officer without hat, band, sword or indeed anything but feet and so much tongue as would serve to enquire the way to the next garrison'. A band of Scots swept past with 'Wae's us, we are all undone !' – an opinion shared by their commander, Leven, who had also departed. Of the triumvirs only Manchester, it seems, remained. He apparently rallied 500 men and brought them back to the field. It rather looks as if he too, like his distinguished subordinate, had left the field for a time. But Cromwell could at least plead that his wound had put him *hors de combat*.

Cromwell's return to his command may have coincided, more or less, with the arrival of Sir Thomas Fairfax who having 'gotten in among the Enemy', had taken the field sign, a white handkerchief or a piece of paper, from his hat, and, passing for a Cavalier commander, had made his way to the Roundhead left. In battle early and accurate information is a pearl of great price. Sir Thomas Fairfax was ever a man of few words, but it needed few to show Cromwell that his next move must be to try conclusions with Goring. Marching round behind Wilstrop Wood his men fell on the rear of the surviving Royalist cavalry, who by this time were somewhat scattered. Some had pursued Fairfax's troopers from the field, others were plundering the baggage waggons, still more had followed Lucas against the Scots foot. And so, at the moment when victory seemed assured, Goring in his turn was routed.

Newcastle's Whitecoats were still to be reckoned with. With their right flank in the air they had fallen back gradually to White Sike Close, where, assailed on all sides by horse and foot, they fought it out to the bitter end, refusing quarter.

Next day Sir Charles Lucas was taken to view the dead and identify the senior officers. When he saw their numbers that stern officer, whom the Cavaliers in Colchester (1648) thought more terrible than the siege, could only weep and exclaim 'Alas for King Charles ! Unhappy King Charles.' It is said that the Royalist dead numbered 4,150, while 1,500 were taken.

It is doubtful whether as many as 10,000 of Rupert's army had escaped. Nevertheless the Prince had no thought of abandoning the struggle. But he could not bring Newcastle to attempt to rally his army. 'I will not endure the laughter of the court,' said the Marquis. He and Eythin took ship for Hamburg and played no further part in the war.

The Allies' losses were not nearly so severe as Rupert's. Perhaps 300 were killed, though many more were wounded, the losses falling heaviest on Sir Thomas Fairfax's wing. Their trophies, besides numerous colours, included all Rupert's artillery – and the corpse of his 'familiar', the dog Boye.

There is a Chinese proverb which says, 'It is easier to gain a victory than to secure its advantages.' Marston Moor should have been the decisive battle of the Civil War, but the Allies failed so dismally to follow up their success that the war dragged on for another two years. After the fall of York the three armies each set about a separate task instead of concentrating against the 'Oxford' Army, whose destruction was absolutely necessary if the Parliament was to win the war. The Fairfaxes contented themselves with the reduction of the surviving Royalist fortresses in Yorkshire. The Scots were soon distracted by Montrose's astonishing series of successes, and were compelled to send powerful forces home. Manchester's operations were the least useful of any. His heart was no longer in the war. 'If we beat the King ninety and nine times,' he said, 'yet he is King still, and so will his posterity be after him ; but if the King beats us then we shall be hanged.' During the next four months the only exploit of his army was the capture of Tickhill Castle (26 July) which was done against his will !

Yet Marston Moor was a turning point of the war. The loss of Newcastle's Army and the North was a crippling blow to the Royalists. The reputation of their best general, Rupert, was seriously lessened ; those of Sir Thomas Fairfax and of Cromwell were greatly enhanced. The Parliament was no longer compelled to rely upon lethargic grandees like Essex and Manchester. Cromwell's Ironsides had shown such an experienced observer as David Leslie that Europe had not their equal.

Had the Cavaliers won Marston Moor the King might have spent the winter of 1644, not in Oxford, but in London. Now with his numbers steadily diminishing and his financial difficulties ever increasing, Charles' prospects of final victory were poor indeed.

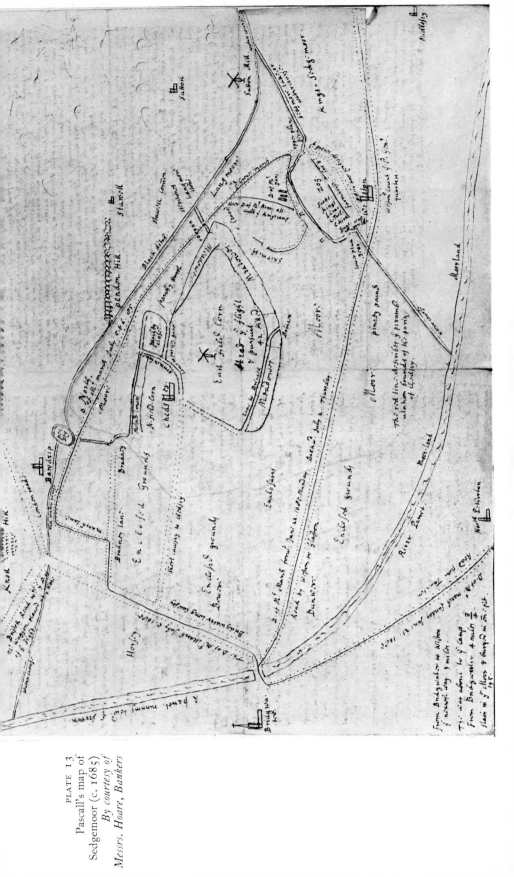

PLATE 13
Pascall's map of
Sedgemoor (c. 1685)
*By courtesy of
Messrs. Hoare, Bankers*

PLATE 14   The Battle of Culloden   *Thomas Sandby*

PLATE 15 'An Incident in the Rebellion of 1745' *David Morier* (1705–1770)
It is said that Morier used Scots captured at Culloden as models for the Highland soldiers in the picture.
Barrell's Regiment of the 4th Foot appear to be dressed for the parade ground, although they are unshaven.
Reproduced by gracious permission of Her Majesty Queen Elizabeth II

PLATE 16
Francis Hawley, 3rd Foot Guards. The earliest known portrait of a British Grenadier.
Note his bayonet, grenade and match.
Private Collection

1 Inserted by Lord Wilmot.
2 The Journal of Prince Rupert's Marches.
3 Those of Lord Molyneux and Sir Gilbert Gerard.
4 Calendar of State Papers, Domestic. 1 June, 1644.
5 The regiments of John Belasyse, Sir Thomas Glemham and Sir Henry Slingsby.
6 It was drawn by Bernard de Gomme, Prince Rupert's Walloon Engineer and Quartermaster-General, and is in the British Museum. 'Ordre of his Maj:tie Armée of iiooo foot, and 6500 horse, with 16 pieces of Ordinance as they where Drawne unto seuerall Bodyes, at the Battle of Marston More, the 2 July 1644. Command by his heighnesse Prince Rupert, against the schots and the parliaments Armée, In the Relieuing of the siedge of the Citty of Yorck.' De Gomme may not include officers in his totals.
7 The Duke of York's Regiment.
8 Rupert's Bluecoats and Byron's regiment.
9 Or Lemgo.
10 There are several explanations of how Cromwell came by his wound, but considering that Trevor's regiment was exactly opposite the part of the line where Cromwell, as lieutenant-general, would be posted, this seems the most likely.
11 Watson.
12 Sir Henry had local knowledge. He tells us that Cromwell 'came off the Cows-Warrant by Bilton-Breame to charge our horse . . .' at the beginning of the fight.

The Lostwithiel Campaign

THE CAMPAIGN

1644

26 *July*   *King Charles reaches Exeter.*

28 *July*   *Essex reaches Bodmin.*

7 *August*   *Essex, in Lostwithiel, called upon to surrender by the King.*

11 *August*   *Grenvile arrives at Bodmin.*

14 *August*   *Essex's relieving force under Middleton is defeated.*

21 *August*   *The battle of Beacon Hill.*

31 *August*   *Balfour escapes. The battle of Castle Dore.*

2 *September*   *Parliamentarians surrender.*

ON 7 JULY a Royalist Council of War at Evesham advised the King to move against Essex, who by this time was in Devon. The advice was welcome to Charles, who was anxious for the safety of the Queen ; a week later she left Falmouth for France, her voyage attended as usual by the salvoes of Parliamentary men-of-war.

After reinforcing Lyme Essex had occupied Weymouth and Melcombe Regis ; then, his army somewhat diminished by the garrisons left behind, he had pushed westwards. He reached Tavistock on 23 July while the King was still in Somerset. He wrote that day to the Committee of Both Kingdoms announcing his intention to adhere to a former resolution of relieving Plymouth, and expressing a hope that Waller would 'take care of the King's army'.

Sir Richard Grenvile now abandoned the siege of Plymouth, and assembling the small garrisons of Saltash, Mount Stamford and Plympton, marched north to guard the passage of the Tamar at Horsebridge.

On the very day (26 July) that the King reached Exeter Essex decided to invade Cornwall. He was encouraged in this course by Lord Robartes, who over-estimated his own influence in that county, and who pointed out that the King depended on the export of Cornish tin for the import of munitions.

Brushing Grenvile aside Essex reached Bodmin on 28 July. There on 2 August he heard that the King was hard on his tracks and had reached Launceston only 20 miles away. Thoroughly alarmed, he moved to Lostwithiel so as to keep open his communications with the sea, while a detachment was sent to hold the little port of Fowey. On 4 August Essex wrote to the Committee that three armies under the King, Maurice, and Hopton were approaching from the east, 'and the country rising unanimously against us, with the exception of a few gentlemen. We must expect another army from the west.' This was a reference to Grenvile's force, which on the previous day the King had ordered to advance to Tregony, 15 miles south-west of Lostwithiel, in order to check the Roundhead foraging parties. Already Essex's army was short of bread, and hoped for supplies from Plymouth. 'Then', says the Earl, 'we shall sell our lives at as dear a rate as may be, for I have never seen soldiers more willing to undertake anything nor to undergo wants with more patience.' The soldiers may have been resolute : their commander was badly rattled.

Essex still had an army of some 10,000 men, but the King now had not less than 16,000 horse and foot at his disposal. The Cornish peasantry, their traditional loyalty inspired by the presence of the monarch and by hatred of the 'foreigners', were wholeheartedly for the King. Provisions and intelligence, both denied to the Parliamentary army, were offered to the Cavaliers. No Roundhead straggler was safe.

On 7 August Charles called on Essex to surrender. The negotiations, a symptom of war-weariness, consumed several days, but to his credit the Earl resisted all appeals.

Though Essex was now in a difficult position, all was not well with the Cavaliers. Wilmot, the Lieut-General of the Horse, out of pride and vanity had been talking sedition, using language which Charles considered contemptuous of his person. On the 8th the King suddenly relieved him of his command, and gave it to Goring, who had just joined his army. Wilmot's chief confederate, Henry Percy, the inefficient General of the Ordnance, was replaced by Hopton, who was obviously an excellent choice.

Goring was a less obvious selection, but he had done much to efface the evil impression caused by his conduct at Portsmouth in 1642. One of the few Cavaliers who enhanced their reputations at Marston Moor, he was at this period *persona grata* with Rupert.

The Committee of Both Kingdoms, realizing the Earl's danger, voted £20,000 for pay and provisions to be sent to Plymouth for his army and ordered Waller's Lieut.-General, Middleton, with 2,000 horse and dragoons to march to his relief. A further £10,000 was voted for Waller, but by 27 August Sir William had got no farther than his old quarters at Farnham, a place that seems to have had a fascination for him.

Meanwhile the Cavaliers were closing in. On 11 August Grenvile with 2,400 men forced his way into Bodmin. Next day he secured Respryn Bridge three miles north of Lostwithiel, thus ensuring his communications with the King. He then occupied Lord Robartes' house at Lanhydrock, between Bodmin and Lostwithiel.

On the 13th Goring and Sir Jacob Astley reconnoitred the east bank of the river Fowey southwards to the sea and next day posted 200 foot with two or three guns, at Polruan Fort at the mouth of the river and at Hall, Lord Mohun's house by Bodinnick Ferry. Colonel Sir Charles Lloyd's regiment was posted at Cliffe opposite Golant to guard that ferry.

Essex made no attempt to hold these important positions or to recapture them. The Royalists now overlooked and menaced Fowey harbour, and it is strange that the Roundheads did not try to dislodge them from Hall and Polruan by landing a party from ships' boats.

Meanwhile on 14 August Middleton's force, which had penetrated as far as Bridgwater, had been defeated by Sir Francis Doddington and had fallen back to Sherborne.

For about a week nothing of moment took place at Lostwithiel, though on the 17th the King, whose headquarters were at Boconnoc, made a personal reconnaissance from the 'fair walk' which still runs below Hall House. He came under fire, a fisherman standing near him being slain. Charles was in every respect the commander in the field.

THE BATTLE OF BEACON HILL, 21 AUGUST 1644

On 21 August the Royalists carried out a well-synchronized general advance along their whole front from Lanhydrock to Boconnoc, a distance of four miles. Such an operation was most unusual in those days and has a very modern look.

Zero hour was 7 o'clock. Grenvile on his side stormed the ruined but still formidable Castle of Restormel, which was held by some of John Weare's Devonshire regiment. The Roundheads retreated without orders either from Essex or their colonel.

It was a misty morning, and the forces of Maurice and the Earl of Brentford, Lord Forth's new title, took possession of Beacon Hill, overlooking Lostwithiel, and Druid's Hill without serious opposition – the mist covering them like a smoke-screen. Prince Maurice then sent a column, 1,000 strong, to take the hill north-east of Lostwithiel on the north side of the road to Liskeard.

Towards nightfall the main body of the King's foot penetrated into the fields on the hillside on both sides of the Lostwithiel–Liskeard road. Colonel Matthew Appleyard with 1,000 men held Beacon Hill, while Prince Maurice's army held the more northerly hill.

Essex was completely taken by surprise and offered little resistance. Not until the afternoon did he send a force to oppose Grenvile's further advance. It is not surprising that Charles' Secretary-at-War, Sir Edward Walker, found it difficult to understand Essex's failure to fortify Beacon Hill, for it is indeed the key to Lostwithiel. The Cavaliers worked all night raising a redoubt twenty yards square to secure this vital ground.

On the following two days the situation remained unchanged, and there was only sporadic fighting. Essex, it seemed, had accepted defeat. On the 24th so little movement could be detected that the King's entourage suspected a Roundhead withdrawal to Fowey.

The King planned a general advance for the 25th, and half the cavalry were sent across Respryn Bridge to support Grenvile on the west bank of the Fowey. During the morning reconnaissance disclosed that the Roundheads were not gone; they were merely taking cover from the Royalist battery, all ready to receive the Cavaliers if they should advance.

Seeing this the King changed his plans and postponed the projected attack. Next day, the 26th, he sent Goring to the west with 2,000 horse and 1,000 foot under Maj.-General Sir Thomas Bassett to post himself at St. Blazey so as to stop the Roundheads landing provisions at Par, four miles west of Fowey, and to prevent their foraging. On the same day supplies, including 100 barrels of powder, reached the Cavaliers from Dartmouth and from Pendennis Castle.

The Roundhead army was now in a desperate plight, bottled up in a narrow tract of land five miles long and two miles wide. With his sea communications practically severed Essex could not find subsistence for his 10,000 men. Even so, five days went by before the King had any assurance that by dividing his forces as he had done he had produced any good effect. He too had his anxieties; the weather was turning foul and provisions were growing scarcer. His 16,000 men were strung out on a 15 mile front. The country was intricate and badly roaded, and messengers were prone to lose their way. Even with wireless and the weapons of the present day he would have been taking risks. With seventeenth century means of inter-communication Charles' dispositions were of a remarkable boldness. At last on the evening of 30 August two deserters were brought to the Royal headquarters at Boconnoc and disclosed Essex's plans. During the night his horse were to break out, while his infantry were to fall back to Fowey and embark.

Instantly the King gave orders that both his own army and Prince Maurice's should stand to their arms all night. The two armies were little more than a musket shot apart and in the event of the Roundhead cavalry trying to escape they had orders to fall upon them. A cottage beside the Lostwithiel-Liskeard road half-way between the two main Royalist bodies was fortified and manned by 50 musketeers. All the various detachments of the army were alerted and Sir Edward Waldegrave's regiment of horse, stationed near Saltash, was ordered to break down the bridges across the Tamar. The Lifeguard, quartered at Lanreath, received the information at about 1 a.m. and rode in to Boconnoc.

About 3 o'clock in the morning the Roundhead cavalry, led by the redoubtable Sir William Balfour, sallied out of Lostwithiel, and made their way up the Liskeard road. It was a hazardous venture and few of them can have expected to get through. But the musketeers in their cottage were presumably asleep for they did not fire a shot. However, the movement of so great a body, about 2,000 horse, could not be accomplished in complete silence. The trampling hooves, the clashing armour, the muttered orders – and oaths – roused the Cavaliers' gunners who fired a few rounds into the darkness, but they did little damage, and that probably moral rather than physical.

Except for Cleveland's brigade there were few cavalry at hand to deal with this eruption, and they could do little until daylight. Then with about 500 horse Cleveland pursued over Braddock Down and Caradon Down to Saltash, where Balfour managed to beat off Waldegrave, and to ferry his men across into Devonshire, reaching Plymouth with the loss of about 100 men.

The Royalists were mortified by Balfour's escape, and Clarendon (writing in about 1671) laid the blame on Goring, alleging that 'he was in one of his jovial excesses when the order to pursue reached him', but this is quite untrue and the accusation must be put down to malice or carelessness. Goring at St. Blazey could do nothing to stop Balfour. The Royalists by adopting a cordon system laid themselves open to an attempt of this kind, but by no other means could they prevent Essex obtaining provisions. Nevertheless it was a sparkling achievement on the part of Balfour, and is a good example of the adage 'Nothing venture, nothing gain'.

THE BATTLE OF CASTLE DORE. 31 AUGUST 1644

Many of the Royalist foot were straggling about the country-

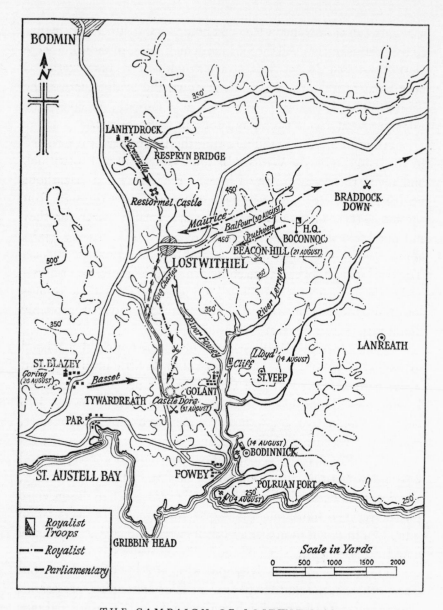

THE CAMPAIGN OF LOSTWITHIEL

side in search of provisions, but with what men he had at hand the King now lost no time in marching on Lostwithiel. He could see the colours of the Parliamentary rearguard on the hill south of the town, where Major-General Skippon was covering Essex's withdrawal. In his despatch the Earl reported that the narrow lane leading to Fowey was 'so extreme foul with excessive rain, and the harness for the draught horses so rotten as that in the marching off we lost three demi-culverins and a brass piece ... thirty horses were put to each of them, but could not move them, the night was so foul and the soldiers so tired that they were hardly to be kept to their colours'. Thus Essex explains his plight, but he does not excuse it. He had been at Lostwithiel for four weeks and he should have known the state of the roads and of the harness of his gun-teams.

While Essex was reeling backwards the King, who never showed more vigour and ability than now, was moving in for the kill. At 7 a.m. 1,000 Royalist foot entered Lostwithiel without much opposition, driving off some Roundheads who were breaking the bridge. Immediately after Charles ordered up two or three guns and planted them 'in the enemies' leaguer' to command the hill where Skippon's rearguard was posted. On this the Roundheads fell back, the Royalist infantry 'following them in chase from field to field in a great pace'.

About 8 o'clock the King at the head of his Lifeguard moved westwards from the redoubt on Beacon Hill and forded the river Fowey south of Lostwithiel finding everywhere evidence of a disorderly retreat; first a cartload of muskets broken down in the mud and then five cannon in different places, '2 of them being very long ones' (demi-Culverins).

The King was in aggressive mood, fully realizing that the enemy were on the run. 'With this small force', Symonds wrote in his diary, 'his Majesty chased them two miles, beating them from hedge to hedge. Being come near that narrow neck of ground between Trewardreth[1] Bay and St. Veepe pass,[2] the rebels made a more forcible resistance. . .' to Grenvile's foot who were now leading the vanguard.

The Cornish Cavaliers retreated hastily but rallied on a body of foot commanded by Lieut.-Colonel William Leighton of the

Guards. The scene of this rearguard action, which took place between 11 and 12 o'clock, can still be identified. It is the hedges and fields just west of Trebathevy Farm.

Charles now launched his Lifeguard to the attack, who inspired by his personal leadership were not to be denied. Major Brett 'led up the Queen's troop, and most gallantly in view of the King charged their foot and beat them from their hedge, killing many of them, notwithstanding their muskets made abundance of shot at his men : he received a shot in the left arm in the first field ... yet most gallantly went on and brought his men off. ....' As the Major was riding back to have his wound dressed 'the King called him and took his sword which was drawn in his hand, and knighted Sir Edward Brett on his horse's back', in the very forefront of the battle. One cannot recall a similar action by a King of England in our history.

A lull followed, for the foot had been far outpaced, but by about 2 o'clock the Royalist infantry, advancing fast, came up in force. Sir Thomas Basset from St. Blazey fell on the enemy's left flank, and about the same time the King's own infantry with Colonel Appleyard leading the van, made a frontal attack, gaining ground in the face of heavy musketry.

It was probably about 4 o'clock when Essex organized a counter-attack by two or three troops of horse, which he had retained, and 100 musketeers. Captain Reynolds and the Plymouth horse charged bravely, driving the Royalist foot back for two or three fields and taking a colour. Lieut.-Colonel John Boteler of Essex's own foot regiment supported Reynolds well and took a colour with his own hand. Then seeing the King's Lifeguard approaching they fell back again.

Goring with his cavalry arrived about this time and was ordered by the King to pursue the Roundhead horse towards Saltash, which he proceeded to do.

At 6 o'clock the Roundheads put in a more serious counter-attack, trying to regain the high ground north of Castle Dore, an Iron Age fort. They drove the Cavaliers back for two fields, but after an hour's fighting, during which Northampton's brigade of horse came up to support the Royalist foot, the Roundheads were beaten right back to Castle Dore. Night was falling fast as the

Cavaliers charged forward, and although they could see signs of disorder in the Roundhead ranks east of the earthwork, they pursued no farther.

Castle Dore, now the centre of the Parliamentary position, is a double entrenchment and commands the roads east to Golant, west to Tywardreath and south to Fowey. Five or six regiments held this front, two to the west, and three or four to the east of the ancient earthwork. So small a force could not hope to hold this extensive position indefinitely, even under favourable circumstances. By now the morale of the Parliamentary infantry was at its lowest. Abandoned by their cavalry, tired and hungry after a hard day's fighting the regiments began to disintegrate in the dusk. Weare's regiment, which had put up so feeble a resistance at Restormel on the 21st was one of the first to go. There was now a great gap in the Roundhead line east of Castle Dore : the Cavaliers had an open road to Fowey.

To Skippon the position must have seemed hopeless indeed, but he was determined to save the situation if he could, and sent officers to seek instructions from the Lord General. His messengers did not reach Essex until about an hour before dawn, and then they received not orders, but a few words of ambiguous advice. The Earl advised Skippon to bring the train to Menabilly, and with the army to secure that place and Polkerris. If that could not be done he should draw up the foot round the train and, by threatening to blow it up, obtain the best conditions he could.

Essex had had enough. 'I thought it fit to look to myself, it being a greater terror to me to be a slave to their contempts than a thousand Deaths. . . .' Accompanied only by Robartes, the author of his downfall, he set sail for Plymouth in a fishing boat.

Skippon was made of sterner stuff. Calling a Council of War he proposed that the foot should cut its way out as the horse had done, but his officers, who, as is often the case, knew better than Skippon how exhausted and demoralized their men were, considered this impossible.

The King supped and spent the night under a hedge amid his foremost troops, with complete absence of ceremony. The night was a stormy one, but Charles was in a happy frame of mind, for the wind would make escape for the enemy by sea out of the question. There was some desultory firing during the night, one shot falling close to the King, but the next day was a quiet one ; the monarch was biding his time, for he knew that the enemy were caught like rats in a trap, and he wished to avoid useless loss of life.

On 1 September, while the Cavaliers were preparing for a final effort the Roundheads, still nearly 6,000 strong, asked for a parley. Next day they surrendered, being allowed to march away with their colours ; the officers with their swords, and one carriage to each regiment, but a total of 42 guns, a mortar, 100 barrels of powder and 5,000 arms, fell into the hands of the victors. Harried by the revengeful Cornish peasantry the remnant of Essex's army eventually found its way to Portsmouth.

Thus Essex's invasion of Cornwall ended in disaster. The King had now got the better of both his opponents : Waller at Cropredy Bridge and Essex at Lostwithiel, but Waller's defeat, though it put his army out of action for most of the summer, was not nearly as serious as that suffered by Essex, though the army that surrendered at Fowey was a far more homogeneous force than that commanded by Waller. The victory at Cropredy had been if not a soldiers', a brigadiers' battle. But in Cornwall the King's personal intervention had been decisive in every phase of the fighting. He had been Generalissimo in practice as well as in name. From his headquarters at Boconnoc he controlled the whole wide-flung front. His energy and careful arrangements ensured the harmonious co-operation of the various columns – not an easy feat when we consider the intricate nature of the terrain, the absence of roads and the primitive nature of his intelligence service. For example, the co-ordinated advance on 21 August could only be achieved by a strict adherence to a pre-arranged plan for there was no means of intercommunication save by galloper. And yet Charles' generals managed to carry out a well synchronized attack.

Essex exhibited none of the skill which he had shown in the relief of Gloucester, nor of the dogged courage he had displayed at Newbury. On the contrary, his indecision, infirmity of purpose and finally his abrupt abandonment of his army are painful to contemplate.

In glaring contrast, the King, who had noted the Earl's lack of resolution on the morrow of Edgehill and had taken the measure of his man – a mark of the good general – deliberately and rightly decided to take risks. He conducted the campaign with cool confidence in himself, awaiting in patience the day – August the 21st – when he judged it was time to strike. And he judged right. The more deeply one examines this little studied campaign the clearer stands out the firm grip on the situation that Charles possessed. In short, the campaign of Lostwithiel was a triumph for the King of England and the biggest success obtained by the Royalists in the whole of the war.

[1] Tywardreath. The O.S. calls it St Austell Bay.
[2] Golant ferry.

The Second Battle of Newbury

THE CAMPAIGN

1644

15 October	*King Charles takes the offensive and enters Salisbury.*
18 October	*Goring drives Waller out of Andover.* *The Parliamentarians raise their siege of Donnington Castle.*
22 October	*The armies of Essex, Manchester and Waller join forces at Basingstoke.*
25 October	*The relief of Banbury Castle.*
27 October	*The second battle of Newbury.*
9 November	*The King offers battle and withdraws his guns from Donnington Castle.*
19 November	*The relief of Basing House.*

THE BATTLE

27 October, 1644

BY ALL THE rules of the military art the summer of 1644 should have seen the destruction of the King's 'Oxford' Army, an event which could have shortened the war by a year. In the south midlands the Parliamentarians could pit two armies, those of Essex and Waller, against one. They had only to concentrate and victory would be as certain as anything in the realm of History and of War can be. But at this point personalities wrecked every possible combination. Neither Essex nor Waller had the least intention of co-operating one with the other, and in consequence they gave the King the opportunity to defeat them in detail.

Charles achieved the first success of his campaign when he inflicted a sharp reverse on Waller at Cropredy Bridge (29 June). He then turned against Essex. The Earl, ever a fumbling strategist, now excelled himself by marching down into Royalist Cornwall, where he succeeded, as one would expect, in getting himself cut off not only from London, but from the friendly fortress of Plymouth. Charles with his own army and the Western Cavaliers surrounded Essex at Lostwithiel.

After these brilliant successes one would expect that Charles might once more have made a thrust at London. He did no such thing. After summoning Plymouth to surrender, and being refused, he marched slowly back toward Oxford with no more ambitious plan than to relieve the beleaguered garrisons of Donnington Castle, Banbury Castle and Basing House, before going into winter quarters.

Parliament, fearful lest the Royalists should now attack the capital, concentrated three armies to meet the threat, those of Manchester, Waller and Essex. Since the last two were but thin by this time, a brigade of the City of London Trained Bands was added to the force.

The eve of Second Newbury found the King ensconced in a sound defensive position north of the Kennet with his forces disposed in a rough triangle, whose strong points were Shaw House, Donnington Castle and Speen Village.

His army was only 9,000 strong for he had sent the Earl of Northampton and his brigade of 800 horse to relieve his brother, Sir William Compton, at Banbury Castle.

The Parliamentarian armies, 19,000 strong, reached Thatcham, 3 miles east of Newbury, on 26 October. They outnumbered the Royalists by more than two to one, the greatest numerical superiority that either side ever enjoyed in a major battle of the First Civil War. It was a grave disadvantage that they had no generalissimo to command their three armies, but that had not proved fatal at Marston Moor. Altogether they now had as fair an opportunity to destroy the King's army as they had ever had, or were likely to have.

As usual King Charles commanded in person. Brentford was still Lord General, but wounds, age and gout had somewhat impaired his vigour. Besides his 'Oxford' Army the King had a contingent of the Western Army under Prince Maurice.

It is practically impossible to name all the regiments that were present at Second Newbury, for many were very weak, and the brigades were little more than strong regiments. Still the army was a veteran one, and many of the regiments had fought at Edgehill.

The Horse

Lt.-General Lord Wilmot had been relieved of his command and replaced by Lord Goring, who, though no disciplinarian, was a robust fighter always at his best in an emergency. He had four brigades[1] of old Royalist horse at his command. There was also some Western cavalry with Maurice.

The Foot

Lord Astley[2] commanded the three brigades[3] of the 'Oxford' Army. The organisation of the Cornish army is obscure. It too may have been organised in three brigades, but, if so, they were probably very small.

Artillery

Lord Hopton, who, with the possible exception of Prince Rupert, was the best of the Royalist generals, now commanded the Artillery in place of Lord Percy. He does not, however, seem to have confined his activities to gunnery.

Earlier in the month one of Sir Samuel Luke's spies 'saw and told 29 brass pieces of ordnance on their carriages marching along to Salisbury, and above 200 carts and wagons with ammunition, and 10 wagons besides laden with clothes for soldiers'.[4] With the guns taken at Lostwithiel the Royalist artillery was unusually strong at Second Newbury.

In the absence of Essex, who was sick, the chief commanders were the Earl of Manchester and Sir William Waller. Manchester, who was no soldier at the best of times, had become half-hearted in his prosecution of the war; Waller on the other hand was a skilful tactician with a good eye for country.

The Horse

According to Ludlow the Parliamentarians still had 7,000 mounted troops on the day after the battle. The best of these were the 3,500 who belonged to Manchester's Army of the Eastern Association, including Lt.-General Cromwell's famous double regiment of Ironsides. Essex's cavalry and dragoons, commanded by Balfour, the hero of Edgehill, had numbered no more than 3,205 when mustered at Tiverton[5] *before* the Lostwithiel fighting, nevertheless Waller is said to have had 6,000 mounted men when he faced the King west of Andover. These were from his own army and Essex's.

Local regiments which belonged to none of the three main armies swelled the number, including Ludlow's from Wiltshire and Norton's from Hampshire.

The Parliamentarians seem to have had at least 8,000 horse and may have had considerably more.

The Foot

Manchester's foot, commanded by Crawford, were 4,000 strong, and Sir James Harrington's brigade of the London Trained Bands numbered at least 3,000. To this must be added 'the poor handful of my Lord General's old foot', as their commander, Skippon, called them. These numbered about 2,000, and were

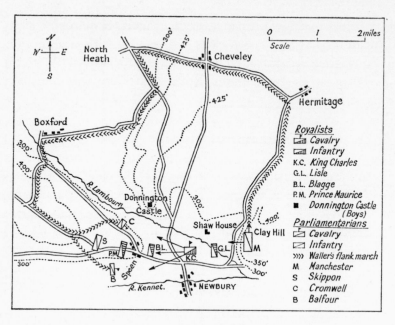

THE SECOND BATTLE OF NEWBURY, 1644

organised in two brigades under Henry Barclay and Edward Aldrich, Essex's own regiment being unbrigaded. None of the authorities give the strength of Waller's contingent, but it can scarcely have been weaker than Essex's for his army had not been through nearly as much; 11,000 seems a conservative estimate of the Parliamentarian infantry.

Artillery

The Parliamentarians had 24 pieces of ordnance.[6]

	Royalists	Parliamentarians
Horse	4,500	8,000
Foot	5,000	11,000
Guns	29	24
	9,000	19,000

The Parliamentarian generals were well informed about the Royalist army for Sir John Urry, who had just changed sides for the second time,[7] had given them full information as to its condition, and particularly its diminished numbers. The plan they hatched in consequence was an ambitious one, devised to make the fullest use of their numerical superiority. It was indeed the boldest and most original plan made by any Parliamentarian army during the whole war. In nearly all the other big battles, except Marston Moor, they were content to take up a defensive position and await events, but at Second Newbury, they elected to divide their army and attack simultaneously from east and west.

Waller with 12,000 men was to march by night round the north of the Royalist position, and attack Speen village, while Manchester with the other 7,000, including 1,500 horse, was to put in a simultaneous attack on Shaw House. We are not told who conceived this plan, but Waller's record shows that he was capable of such an enterprise. On the other hand Balfour or Skippon, with memories of the King's enveloping movements at Lostwithiel, may have been for beating him at his own game.

Two points were essential if the plan was to succeed. First, the outflanking march must be a complete surprise, and, second, Manchester's attack must be properly synchronised with Waller's. The solution to this seemed simple : Manchester's men would go in when they heard the guns firing at Speen. But in war even the simple is very difficult.

No contemporary plan exists to show the dispositions of the Royalist Army, but the salient points are clear. Prince Maurice with his Cornish army and the Duke of York's Regiment of foot held Speen, with Blagge's tertia in support. Donnington Castle was garrisoned by the Earl Rivers' regiment, 200 men with four guns, commanded by Lt.-Colonel Sir John Boys. At Shaw House, where by tradition the King is said to have spent the previous night, was George Lisle's brigade, supported by some cavalry and dragoons. Sir Barnard Astley's brigade seems to have been split up, with part holding the line of the Lambourn south of Shaw House, while part held the passage of the Kennet at Newbury.

The main body of horse was kept in reserve in the fields called Speenhamland.

The fighting began at break of day. During the night Manchester's army had made a bridge across the Lambourn. A tertia of 1,000 foot in two bodies came down Clay hill without being discovered and forced the guard of 'the pass' near Shaw House. The Cavaliers fell back to the next guard, and Sir Barnard Astley counter-attacked, leading up a good body of musketeers, who drove the Roundheads back in such confusion that they routed their own supports and lost 40 prisoners.

Manchester probably intended this attack as a feint. After it was over things remained peaceful for the greater part of the day, in the words of Richard Symonds 'they lay quiet till 3 afternoon, only our cannon and theirs played.'

About 3 p.m. Waller was seen approaching 'on the top of the hill towards Welford . . . where we had a work with 4 piece of cannon and 400 foot'.[8] It seems that Waller had surprised an outpost of 300 horse and 200 foot under Sir John Douglas stationed at Boxford to guard the Lambourn, and that Maurice's men were surprised, 'never imagining that they would at that time of day have attempted a quarter that was thought the strongest of all'.[9] Still the fighting was fierce for a time. The Royalist guns swept off many of the assailants, but Skippon's men were not to be denied. Major Alexander Urry,[10] nephew of the turncoat, led the forlorn hope : eager to avenge Lostwithiel they fell furiously on the redoubt, clapping their hats over the touch-holes of the cannon,[11] which included some lost in Cornwall. Skippon was soon in possession of Speen village, and the survivors of Maurice's foot 'retired to the hedge next the large field between Speen and Newbury (Speenhamland), which they made good'.[9]

With Speen securely in his hands about 4 o'clock Waller began to exploit his success with his cavalry. On his right a force under Balfour was to advance between Speen and the Kennet ; on his left another under Cromwell was to make its thrust between Speen and Donnington Castle.

Thus far Manchester had made no move. It is not impossible that he found it difficult to distinguish the cannonade at Speen, which was supposed to be the signal for his attack, from the desultory bombardment that had been going on all day. Half-hearted though he was, it seems unlikely that his delay was deliberate. Probably he had not thought it neccessary to keep his men standing to their arms all day and a certain amount of time was consumed in assembling them and giving out orders. Be that as it may, it seems that his attack went in about an hour late. Not until Skippon's gallant assault on Speen had already succeeded did Manchester launch the assault on the Shaw House sector.

The defenders were only 1,400 strong, but had been posted by Lord Astley with 'great contrivance', according to John Gwyn, who was one of them. Lt.-Colonel Richard Page[12] held Shaw House itself with 800 foot; 400 musketeers in the dry moat and the rest in support in the garden. In an adjacent field was Colonel Anthony Thelwall with 400 more foot, some of them deployed in a quickset hedge. In support, in the interval between Page and Thelwall, was the Prince of Wales' regiment of horse, 200 strong, under Sir John Browne. The whole sector was commanded by Lord Astley and Colonel George Lisle. Some horse under Lord Hopton were to act as a reserve, but they were soon moved to meet the threat from Speen.

Gwyn tells us that Astley 'from his great experience and quick apprehension had no sooner cast his eye upon' the Shaw House position than he saw how to take advantage of it. Thelwall was ordered to make up the gaps in his hedge and to deepen the ditch, and while he, Lisle and Page 'were fixing of themselves, as well as they could at their posts' Astley had a great body of horse out skirmishing with the enemy, so as to cover the position. Thelwall was ordered not to open fire until the enemy came within a pike's length of him.

When at length the attack came it was a two-pronged thrust. Manchester sent in 3,000 foot supported by 1,200 horse. One great column attacked Page's position at Shaw House and the other attacked Thelwall. They came on singing psalms, and despite a heavy fire each column met with some success at first, driving 40 musketeers from a hedge, and clearing some little houses.

The Prince of Wales' Regiment immediately charged the Roundheads who had won the hedge and 'did good execution upon them',[13] but seeing a body of Parliamentarian horse ready to charge them, prudently retired to the Royalist foot in the garden of Shaw House. Page's men fired on the Parliamentarian horse, 'whereof very many fell', and as they wheeled about, Sir John Browne fell upon their rear, killing many. He was able to maintain his original position all day.

Thelwall's men galled the Roundhead foot with several volleys playing 'through the quickset hedge in their teeths'[14] and after causing a heavy slaughter fell on them with the butt-ends of their muskets, beating them from the hedges and quite out of the field.

The momentum of the attack on Shaw House was soon lost, for after driving the Cavaliers from the houses back to a breastwork Manchester's infantry were held up and spent an uncomfortable hour and a half in a fire-fight. They were caught at close range in a cross-fire from the breastwork and from Shaw House. Page with some leatherguns, 'loaden with key-shot', and his musketeers in the dry moat caused havoc in the ranks of the Roundheads, and though Ludlow brought up his regiment of horse almost within pistol-shot of the Royalists' works, so as to encourage and support the foot, in the end they broke and fled in confusion. Page pursued them up Clay Hill 'with a notable execution'. The Parliamentarians left 500 dead 'upon a little spot of ground', lost several colours, among them one of Major-General Crawford's,[15] and also two drakes, which were drawn into the house.

Ludlow, unfortunately, tells us very little about this fighting except that he 'had divers men and horse shot, and amongst the rest my own'. In a letter Colonel Richard Norton says that Ludlow's horse broke its bridle, 'so that he was fain to quit', and that in leading up Ludlow's Regiment he himself 'received a fair admonition (by musket-shot in my leg) for meddling where I had no charge. . . .' It may be that this movement was an attempt to cover the withdrawal of Manchester's foot. Ludlow cannot have been away from his regiment for very long for he himself withdrew it as night came on, perceiving to his evident disgust that his major 'had secured his troop in the rear of all', adding sarcastically that he had 'taken care that all the regiment might not be lost in one engagement'.[16]

Thus by the skill of Lord Astley and his veteran officers and men the Shaw position was held against odds of at least three to one. The hero of the defence was George Lisle, who fought stripped to his shirt, so as to ensure that in the failing light his men should know him, and who, according to *Mercurius Aulicus*, was taken by the Roundheads for a witch!

Meanwhile about 4 o'clock Balfour and Cromwell had launched their attacks into Speenhamland, where a series of cavalry charges took place.

Balfour came round under Speen hill with 100 musketeers in the van of his wing, and got into the open field. Although a good body of Royalist cavalry was drawn up there, they received his attack in some disorder. The King himself with Prince Charles and many noblemen, besides his staff, was in the middle of the field, but 'could not by his own presence restrain those horse . . . from shamefully giving ground'. History does not name the runaways, perhaps they were the horse of the Western Army. Balfour's men now charged a regiment made of sterner stuff, the Queen's, commanded by Sir John Cansfield, 'which stood them most gallantly'.[17] The King's Lifeguard under Lord Bernard Stuart, was nearby and drove at the Roundheads making them wheel off in confusion, and following them in the chase for half a mile. Most of Balfour's musketeers were killed and very many of the horse as well. The Lifeguard fell on some musketeers that had lined the hedges and 'played upon us in the chase till we cut their throats'. It seems unlikely that this success was achieved by no more than two small regiments, and there is evidence that it was due in part to Sir Humphrey Bennet's brigade.

Meanwhile Cromwell, his left flank harassed no doubt by the guns of Donnington Castle, had advanced towards the north side of Speenhamland. He made even less progress than Balfour, so that afterwards Manchester and others were to assert that Oliver performed no service in this battle. Deeply dissatisfied as he was with the conduct of the war there is ground for the suspicion that as Colonel Burne put it,[18] 'he sulked that day—just as Stonewall Jackson did when fighting under Lee at White Oak Swamp'. But whatever his mood a simpler explanation is possible: that the Ironsides, for once, were routed, and it is this view that receives the support of contemporary writers such as Walker and Clarendon.

Before Cromwell's men had actually deployed in Speenhamland, Goring put himself at the head of Cleveland's brigade, 800 strong, and gave orders for a charge. The old Earl, seeing the King himself in danger, told his men they must now charge home,[19] and they went to work with such vigour that he forced the first wave of Ironsides back in great confusion over a hedge. Charged by a fresh body Goring and Cleveland routed that in turn, killing many.

Although the Cavaliers 'endured the shot' of three bodies of Parliamentarian foot both in their pursuit of Cromwell's men and in their return, their most serious loss was the Earl of Cleveland, who was taken prisoner when his horse was shot.

With the failure of their two great cavalry attacks the Roundheads had shot their bolt. The firing went on into the night, but the battle was over. Still the Royalists' position was untenable and their generals knew it. With only one hedge between them and Skippon's men on Speen Hill they could not afford to be found in Speenhamland when the next day should dawn.

About an hour after dark the King sent for his Lifeguard and rode up to Donnington Castle, whence for half an hour, he saw the infinite shooting of muskets on both sides in all places.[20] That night he rode for Bath, which he reached at 4 p.m. next day, a remarkable march of 50 miles.

It fell to Prince Maurice and Lord Astley to conduct the retreat. The Cavaliers drew off their guns, carriages and many of their wounded, including Lord Brentford, to the shelter of Donnington Castle, and set out for Wallingford.

Gwyn describes how 'my Lord Astley marched away with us by moonshine[21] and of necessity through a narrow filthy pass of puddle and mire just by the hedgeside that parted us and the two armies'. Sir Humphrey Bennet, 'who had behaved himself very signally that day', brought up the rear with his brigade. The Parliamentarians, 'well enough pleased to be rid of an enemy that had handled them so ill,'[22] made no attempt to interfere with the withdrawal.

We have little reliable information as to the casualties at Second Newbury. Clarendon, who asserts that very many more of the Parliamentarians were killed than of the King's army, estimates that they had 1,000 slain, which is not impossible, but his claim that the Royalists had only 100 common soldiers killed hardly seems probable. On the Shaw House front Manchester seems to have lost at least 500 men, and the Cavaliers, being under cover most of the time, probably had few men hit.

The killed on the Royalist side included Lt.-Colonel Sir William St. Leger[23] and Lt.-Colonel William Leake.[24] Among the wounded were the Lord General, the Earl of Brentford, who was wounded in the head; Sir John Cansfield; Sir John Grenvile; Lt.-Colonel Page, who received three wounds; and Cleveland's brigade-major, Captain William Alford,[25] who died of his injuries. Eight officers and 39 troopers of Cleveland's brigade were captured when he charged into Cromwell's ranks.

On the other side the killed included Lt.-Colonel Knight, Major Urry[26] and Captain Gawler.[27] Captain Charles Doyley, commander of Essex's Lifeguard, said to have been killed by Sir Humphrey Bennet, was still alive in 1647, when in a petition he mentioned having been 'many times dangerously wounded',[28] once perhaps on this occasion. Among the wounded were Colonel Norton and Lt.-Colonel Walter Lloyd.[29]

The Parliamentarian commanders had little reason to be satisfied with their performance at Second Newbury. The King, outnumbered by two to one, had escaped from their trap after inflicting rather more damage than he had suffered himself. Reinforced by Rupert, Gerard and Langdale he returned and offered battle on 9 November. The Parliamentarians refused the challenge and Charles was able to withdraw his guns from Donnington Castle unmolested. The bitterness with which the commanders, particularly Manchester and Cromwell, now attacked each other is the measure of their ill-success. The root of the trouble lay in their clumsy command set-up. There was no single generalissimo to command the three armies. It is not impossible that, had he been Captain-General, Waller might have been capable of imposing his will on the unwieldy host. Yet it is hardly to his credit that with only 7 miles to march he failed to attack Speen until 3 p.m.[30]

If Cromwell showed to less advantage here than in any of his other battles it is going too far to accuse him of any misconduct. But the same applies to Manchester. It was not his failure at Shaw House that wrecked the Parliamentarian plan so much as the breakdown of the promising attacks by Balfour and Cromwell. Indeed there is considerable uncertainty as to how late Manchester was in putting in his attack. And even if he had synchronised it precisely with Skippon's attack, there is no reason to suppose that it would have made much difference, since the King so far from reinforcing Shaw actually drew away the Horse under Hopton that had been intended as Lisle's reserve. Of the Roundhead generals only Skippon added to his laurels.

On the Royalist side things went ill at first. Sir John Douglas failed in his duty and the Western Army, particularly their horse, it seems, failed at Speen. But great credit is due to Goring and the cavalry who restored the fortunes of the day by routing Balfour and Cromwell, to Astley, Lisle and the defenders of the Shaw position, and to Maurice and Astley for their conduct of a difficult withdrawal.

But when all is said and done the Parliamentarians profited from Second Newbury. As a direct result of the quarrels that followed, they reorganised their forces into the New Model Army and made the hard-fighting Sir Thomas Fairfax its General.

1 Lord Goring, Lord Wentworth, Earl of Cleveland and Sir Humphrey Bennet.
2 The veteran Sir Jacob Astley was created a baron in 1644.
3 Colonel Thomas Blagge, Colonel George Lisle and Sir Barnard Astley – son of Lord Astley.
4 W. Robinson's report of 21 October 1644.
5 Symond's Diary, p. 73.
6 Money, 112.
7 He was to do so again, before he went to the gallows with Montrose.
8 Symonds.
9 Clarendon.
10 Lord Robartes' Regiment. (Redcoats).
11 Ludlow.
12 Sir James Pennyman's Regiment.
13 Clarendon.
14 Gwyn.

[15] Money, 137.
[16] Money, 142.
[17] Symonds.
[18] Burne and Young, p. 187.
[19] Lloyd's Memoirs.
[20] Symonds.
[21] The moon was in its first quarter and set just after midnight.
[22] Clarendon.
[23] Duke of York's Regiment. Foot.
[24] Sir Edward Ford's Regiment. Horse.
[25] Colonel Dutton Fleetwood's Regiment. Horse.
[26] Lord Robartes' Regiment. Foot.
[27] Earl of Essex's Regiment. Foot.
[28] Firth and Davies. I. 47.
[29] Colonel Edward Aldrich's Regiment. Foot.
[30] Sunset was 4.26 p.m.

The Battle of Naseby

THE CAMPAIGN

1645	
April	*The New Model Army begins to form at Windsor.*
7 May	*King Charles moves out from Oxford.*
21 May	*Fairfax before Oxford.*
30 May	*The Royalists storm Leicester.*
5 June	*Fairfax breaks up from before Oxford.*
14 June	*The Battle of Naseby.*
18 June	*Fairfax recaptures Leicester.*
10 July	*Fairfax defeats Goring and the Western Army at Langport.*

THE BATTLE

14 June, 1645

'Oh wherefore come ye forth
In triumph from the North
With your hands and your feet
And your raiment all red?
And wherefore doth your rout
Send forth a joyous shout
And whence be the grapes of the
Winepress that ye tread?'

MACAULAY

WHATEVER YOU MAY think of Macaulay's verses his instinct

was sure when he saw in Naseby the decisive battle of the First Civil War. Far more men were engaged at Marston Moor, but at Naseby the stakes were higher.

The strategy of the 1645 campaign should have been equally clear to either side. A Naseby was essential. Neither could hope to do any good without first trying conclusions with the other's main army in the field.

For the Royalists the best plan was to concentrate as big an army as they could and seek out the new Model with all speed. Early in May the King left Oxford and joining forces with Rupert and Goring, who now commanded the Western Army, mustered at least 5,000 foot and 6,000 horse at Stow-on-the-Wold. At this time Fairfax, as yet not master in his new house, was marching by order of the Committee of Both Kingdoms to the relief of Taunton.

The two armies were practically equal in numbers, and it would have been greatly to the King's advantage to have brought on a battle at this stage, before the New Model had had time to get into its stride.

By this stage in the war King Charles considered himself no mean general. His campaign of 1644 had gone well enough. At Cropredy Bridge and Lostwithiel he had scored good success. At Second Newbury he had extricated himself from a position that could have been fatal. Yet he lacked the decision to impose his will on his Council of War. Rupert and Langdale, eager to avenge Marston Moor, wanted to march North. Goring and Digby, quite rightly, wanted to settle with the New Model. Though the latter plan was the better, either would have been better than the one actually adopted. This was to permit Goring and his forces to return into the West, while the rest marched north. Goring was jealous of his independence, but this was the moment for the King to assert his authority.

Fairfax relieved Taunton on 11 May, and the Committee now ordered him to besiege the King's capital, Oxford. But this move would not necessarily bring on the decisive battle, which was so much to be wished for. The two main armies pursued their separate ways, rather like chess players, who content themselves with snapping up pawns and pieces, without thinking out a combination to checkmate the opposing King.

Charles' next move was to take Leicester (30 May), a town that he had done very well without for three years. The capture of this piece galvanised the Parliamentarians. The horrors of the storm were greatly exaggerated, one officer even comparing it with the sack of Magdeburg. Fairfax was given a free hand, Cromwell was appointed as his second-in-command, the New Model broke up from before Oxford, and, with a new-found certainty in its movements, marched to meet the King.

Hearing of Fairfax's advance Charles, who had further weakened his army by leaving a garrison in Leicester, fell back to Market Harborough, making for the Royalist fortress of Newark. But Fairfax was moving fast and on the evening of 13 June his vanguard dashed into the village of Naseby and surprised some Cavalier troopers drinking at the inn. At a Council of War, hurriedly assembled at midnight, the King's commanders resolved to hazard a battle. Well before 8 o'clock in the morning the army was in position on the high ground two miles south of Market Harborough.

Rupert, who was now General in place of old Brentford, sent out his Scoutmaster, Dudley Rouse, to observe Fairfax's dispositions, but after a time this officer returned to say that he had been out two or three miles, but could see nobody. Rupert was dissatisfied with this report and escorted by a body of cavalry rode forward to have a look for himself.

In the early hours of the morning Fairfax had broken up his camp, and when the two armies eventually caught sight of each other in the distance the New Model was coming up the Naseby ridge, about 4 miles south of Charles' position on the East Farndon ridge.

Rupert, no doubt, had a good view of the New Model deploying on the ridge north of Naseby; bringing forward the King's army he marshalled it on Dust Hill.

THE ROYALIST ARMY

King Charles not only commanded his army in person as was his custom, but on this occasion rode at the head of the reserve, a body of horse and foot, which, with memories of Edgehill in mind, was posted behind the centre. When Brentford was Lord General he usually remained at the King's side in battle, but Rupert instead of exercising the proper functions of his office, led the right wing of horse, a task for which his brother, Maurice, should have been perfectly adequate.

The army was a veteran one, with a high proportion of officers. Its great weakness was simply that it was too small.

According to Lord Digby the Cavaliers 'were all carried on at that time with such a spirit and confidence of victory as though he that should have said "consider" would have been your foe....'[1]

The Horse

The horse consisted of four[2] brigades and certain unbrigaded units. The numerous regiments varied very much in size, but they were divided into more or less equal squadrons.

Sprigge shows nine squadrons in the front line of the right wing, but there were probably only seven.[3] In the second line he shows six, but there may only have been five.[4] Langdale's wing he also shows with nine squadrons in first and six in second line. The Northern Horse were the remnants of about twenty regiments, but it seems unlikely that 1,500 men would have formed more than twelve squadrons at most. These Northern Horse, diehards who had not given up the struggle after Marston Moor, had recently shown their mettle in a famous exploit: Sir Marmaduke Langdale's relief of Pontefract Castle (1 March, 1645).

Colonel Thomas Howard's brigade was in close support of Astley's infantry. His 880 men formed three bodies, one behind Astley's centre, and the other two separating the three divisions of infantry of his second line.

There were three bodies of horse in the King's reserve. On the flanks were two bodies of the Newark horse, totalling 800. In the centre was the Lifeguard, which Walker says was 500 strong.

The Foot

Lord Astley commanded the foot, who were organised in three brigades under Sir Barnard Astley, Sir Henry Bard and Colonel George Lisle, two regiments being unbrigaded; the King's Lifeguard and Prince Rupert's.

Although elements of 24 regiments were present the foot were organised in nine more or less equal bodies or divisions. Sir Barnard Astley's brigade consisted of three divisions, Bard's and Lisle's of two each ; two were in the reserve. Rupert, as was his custom, drew out 400 musketeers and placed them in bodies of 50 to support the outermost bodies of horse on each wing.

Artillery

The train consisted of 2 mortars and 12 pieces of ordnance, including two demi-cannons, and two demi-culverins. The rest seem to have been sakers. Sprigge's map shows two pieces with the reserve, four with Astley's second line, and six with his first. They were employed in pairs.

THE PARLIAMENTARIAN ARMY

The establishment of the New Model Army was eleven regiments of horse, each 600 strong ; one regiment of 1,000 dragoons ; and twelve regiments of foot each of 1,200 ; a total of 22,000. Not all these units were present, nor were they all up to strength, even so Sir Thomas Fairfax found himself at the head of a formidable army.

The Horse

The horse were divided into two wings under Lt.-General Oliver Cromwell and Commissary-General Henry Ireton. There was no brigade organisation. Besides the General's Lifeguard, which if Sprigge's plan is accurate was as strong as a regiment, there were ten regiments of the New Model and in addition a unit called The Associated Horse, 200 strong, which presumably came from the Eastern Association.

Cromwell's wing was rather stronger than Ireton's, having thirteen squadrons to the latter's eleven, but the dragoons were all on Ireton's flank. Ireton, though an intelligent officer, had no previous experience of commanding a large body of cavalry.

There had been no difficulty in filling the establishment of the horse with volunteers from the cavalry of Essex, Manchester and Waller. Officers for whom there was no room in the New Model were content to serve as troopers. It seems, therefore, that the Parliamentarian cavalry numbered nearly 6,000, and the squadrons must have averaged about 250.

The Foot

Like the horse the foot had no brigade organisation. Sprigge's plan shows them in three lines, the first consisting of five regiments, the second of three, and the third of a detachment from one of those in second line. A forlorn hope of about 300 musketeers was placed in front at the left of the line of infantry, 'down the steep of the hill towards the enemy.'[5]

In theory the eight regiments should have numbered 9,600, but it seems that they were considerably below establishment. The three old armies had provided only 7,174 foot for the New Model; 7,226 had to be produced by impressment. How successful this had been is uncertain, but it is unlikely that the regiments averaged much more than 800 – a total of 6,400.

With many recruits in the ranks the foot were by no means as good as the horse.

Artillery

Lt.-General Thomas Hammond commanded the Ordnance. If Sprigge's plan is a reliable guide the Parliamentarians brought only nine guns into position, though oddly enough he shows two more in the waggon-lager. Four pairs were in the intervals of the front line, and the odd gun was near the centre of the second line.

	Royalists	New Model
Horse	5,490	6,000
Foot	4,300—4,700	6,400
Dragoons	—	1,000
	9,790—10,190	13,400

Fairfax's position was a large fallow field on the north-west side of Naseby, flanked on the left by Sulby hedge. When the Royalists came in sight the front line ran along what Sprigge calls 'the ledge' of the hill. But Fairfax drew his line back 100 yards so that the Cavaliers 'might not perceive in what form our battle was

209

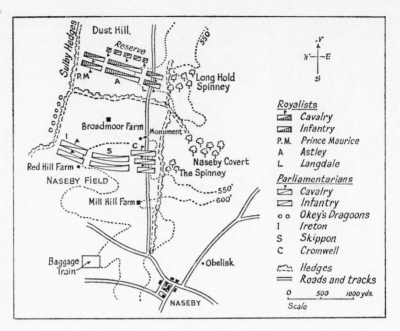

THE BATTLE OF NASEBY, 1645

drawn, nor see any confusion therein. . . .'[5] The Cavaliers thought this move portended a retreat to Northampton, and hastened forward to engage.

The Parliamentarians were not quite ready when the Royalists came in view. Colonel Okey tells us that he was 'half a mile behind in a meadow giving my men ammunition' when Cromwell rode up 'and caused me with all speed to mount my men, and flank our left wing'. He goes on 'by that time I could get my men to light, and deliver up their horses in a little close, the enemy drew towards us which my men perceiving, they with shooting and rejoicing received them. . . .'

The battle began about 10 o'clock when the Royalists made a general advance. As they came on Fairfax marched his men back to the brow of the hill, and the forlorn hope went forward rather more than carbine shot[6] ahead of the front line with orders to fall back if hard pressed.

Rupert's men were coming on fast, but seeing Ireton lead his squadrons down over the brow of the hill to meet him, they 'suddenly made a stand, as if they had not expected us in so ready a posture. . . .' Probably Rupert did not want to get too far ahead of Astley. Ireton now halted also, partly because of some rough going and partly to let his squadrons 'recover their stations'.[7] Thereupon Rupert's men advanced once more and Ireton sounding a charge fell upon them.

Ireton's three right-hand squadrons, his own regiment, and the right of Vermuyden's charged those opposite them, which must mean the left squadron of Rupert's regiment, and the regiments of the Queen and Prince Maurice. The centre of the three Parliamentarian squadrons 'charged not home', but the other two routed their opponents. The Queen's regiment, though not charged, was carried away by the disordering of its neighbours.

Fortunately for Rupert Ireton now saw Sir Barnard Astley's brigade 'pressing sore' upon Skippon's foot, and, instead of following up his advantage against the opposing cavalry, led his right squadron in a charge against some Royalist foot – presumably the Duke of York's regiment. This ended disastrously for him. His horse was shot under him, a pikeman speared him through the thigh, a sergeant wounded him in the face with his halbert, and he became a prisoner.

His command, though left leaderless, had not quite shot its bolt. Vermuyden's right squadron pressed on and broke some of the Royalist second line, no doubt men of Sir William Vaughan's regiment, but there were more Royalist squadrons at hand – Vaughan's and Northampton's and these countercharged and drove back the Parliamentarians in disorder. The rest of Ireton's wing was less successful. The two left hand squadrons of his front line – Butler's regiment – were 'more backward' and the opposing Cavaliers, the Lifeguards of the two Princes, though far less in number, advanced upon them and, despite the flanking fire of Okey's dragoons, overbore them. Sprigge attempts to excuse Butler's men by saying that they had 'much disadvantage, by reason of pits of water, and other pieces of ditches that they expected not, which hindered them in their order to charge.' But the Cavaliers had the same ground to cross. In Colonel Okey's opinion 'had not we by God's providence been there, there had been but a few of Colonel Butler's regiment left. . . .' His stout-hearted dragoons took the departure of the Parliamentarian horse in a resolute spirit : 'we gave up ourselves for lost men, but we resolved every man to stand to the last. . . .'

It is impossible to relate with any degree of accuracy the details of a cavalry fight ; the mêlée, charge and countercharge with every man hacking, thrusting and pistolling for dear life, hardly makes for accurate reporting. Still it is clear that the main body of Rupert's regiment – two squadrons – must have overthrown the left 'division' of Vermuyden's regiment and, pressing on, routed Fleetwood's. One may suppose that Northampton's and Vaughan's came up in support and clinched the business. Vaughan himself – known to the Roundheads of Shropshire as 'the Devil of Shrawardine' – broke right through Ireton's wing.

Thus 1,600 men put 2,700 to rout ; a splendid achievement.

'The enemy,' writes Chaplain Sprigge, 'having thus worsted our left wing, pursued their advantage, and Prince Rupert himself having prosecuted his success upon our left wing, almost to Naseby town, in his return summoned the Train, offering them quarter.'

Rupert has been much condemned for pursuing the routed Parliamentarians from the field as if this was an act of recklessness. What would his critics have had him do ? Permit the broken enemy to depart peacefully and without further casualties ? Yet it is after the foe are routed that the execution takes place. Allow the Roundhead troopers to rally ? Rupert had disposed of a force much stronger than his own. Had he really done so badly ?

By this time the Prince was probably aware of the success of Cromwell's wing. At any rate he retreated in great haste and rejoined the King. He was followed up by such of Ireton's wing as had managed to rally, though probably at a respectful distance.

Meanwhile in the centre Astley's attack had gone well. Walker says the rebels only discharged five pieces at them, which 'over shot them', as did their musketeers. 'The Foot on either side hardly saw each other until they were within carbine shot, and so only made one volley ; ours falling in with sword and butt-end of the musket did notable execution ; so much as I saw their colours fall, and their foot in great disorder.' The front line of the Parliamentarian foot, except for Fairfax's regiment, which had no Royalist body to oppose it was pressed backwards. Skippon himself was badly wounded by a shot which drove a piece of his breast-plate into his side, and 'a great piece of rag of his waistcoat'. The tough old veteran[8] stayed at his post till the field was won. Lt.-Colonel Francis, who commanded Skippon's regiment on the left of the front line, was killed as the Duke of York's regiment drove his men back, and it must have been now that Ireton made his ill-fated attempt to relieve the pressure. The Royalist cavalry of Thomas Howard's brigade were at hand and no doubt drove off the survivors of Ireton's squadron.

Fairfax's regiment, 'not being much pressed upon' stood firm, but almost all the rest of the front line 'gave ground and went off in some disorder, falling behind the reserves. . . .' The officers did their best to rally them but finding their efforts fruitless joined the second line with their colours, 'choosing rather there to fight and die, than to quit the ground they stood on'.

The second line, Rainsborough's, Hammond's and Harley's regiments, now advanced and came to push of pike. Astley had done well enough, for he like Rupert was heavily outnumbered. Sprigge indeed confesses that his men 'were not wanting in courage', and he could no doubt have held his own, but for the fact that his left flank was now in the air.

Langdale, a dour Yorkshireman, had advanced at the same time as Rupert and Astley, leading the Northern horse and, according to Walker, some of the Newarkers as well. Cromwell, like Ireton, did not wait to be attacked. Whalley's regiment, one of those formed from the famous Ironsides, charged two divisions of Langdale's Horse 'who made a very gallant resistance, and firing at a very close charge, they came to the sword'.[9] In the mêlée that followed Langdale's men were routed and driven back as far as Prince Rupert's bluecoats, 'whither indeed they fled for shelter and rallied': Cromwell, who seems to have been with his second line, now ordered Sheffield's regiment[10] to second Whalley, which they did resolutely. Meanwhile Cromwell's other squadrons advanced with some difficulty, their movements cramped by furze bushes on the right: moreover the ground was uneven and they had to march over 'a Cony-warren . . . which put them somewhat out of their order, in their advance'. Despite these Royalist rabbits,

Cromwell's men were able to outflank the rest of Langdale's wing and to put the Cavaliers into great confusion, routing everybody they charged, and forcing them to fly beyond all the Royalist foot. Astley's left flank was now exposed, and Cromwell, dividing his command, sent four regiments to follow Langdale, and launched the rest against Astley's foot.

The King still had fresh horse in hand, his Lifeguard and probably some of the Newark Horse. A charge now and he might still win the day. There are those who think it heresy to question any military action of Oliver Cromwell's, but it may be that his charge against Astley was a trifle premature. What if the King had now counter-attacked? He very nearly did.

'At this instant,' says Walker

> 'the King's Horseguards and the King at the head of them were ready to charge those who followed ours, when a person of quality, 'tis said the Earl of Carnwarth, took the King's Horse by the bridle, turned him about, swearing at him and saying, *Will you go upon your Death?* and at the same time the word being given, *March to the right hand*, which ... (as most concluded) was a civil command for everyone to shift for himself, we turned about and ran on the spur almost a quarter of a mile, and then the word being given to make a stand, we did so; though the body could never be rallied. Those that came back made a charge, wherein some of them fell.'[11]

It is unrewarding to speculate on what would have happened in other circumstances, but nobody can suppose that the Royalist reserve would have failed to charge had Rupert remained at their head and left Maurice to oppose Ireton. As it was Cromwell was permitted to deal with the unfortunate Royalist infantry without interference. Okey saw how things stood, and ordering his men to mount charged into the Royalist foot, taking, he claims, 500 prisoners. Ireton offered his captor his liberty and was himself released.

Still one Tertia,[12] Lisle's perhaps, held out against Cromwell's horse, 'standing with incredible courage and resolution',[13] although attacked from all sides.

Fairfax, who had had his helmet beaten off, was riding up and down bareheaded to see how things stood. Coming up to his own Lifeguard its commander, Charles Doyley told him 'that he exposed himself to too much danger, and the whole army thereby

... and so many bullets flying about him. ....' Doyley offered his own helmet to the general, who refused it, saying, 'It is well enough, Charles.' He then asked Doyley if he had charged the Tertia that still resisted and was told that he had done so twice but could not break them. Fairfax then ordered Doyley, when he gave the signal, to attack the Royalist front, while he himself took 'a commanded party' and charged their rear at the same time.[14] He also called up his regiment of foot which joined in the assault.[13]

The charge was successful and Fairfax and Doyley met in the midst of the Royalist Tertia where the General killed an ensign. A trooper seized the colour, and bragging of the exploit, was chidden by his captain. Fairfax told Doyley to let the trooper alone saying, ' "I have honour enough, let him take the honour to himself." This done the General made haste to put his army into order again, rallying the disordered foot, and hastening them forward to join those horse, who were observing the King whereby there was framed, as it were in a trice, a second good Batalia at the latter end of the day.'[15]

Rupert was back with the King by this time, but his horse 'having done their part ... could never be brought to charge again ... and so after all the endeavours of the King and Prince Rupert, to the hazard of their persons, they were fain to quit the Field'.

They were pursued to within sight of Leicester. In the pursuit Cromwell's troopers cruelly killed 100 soldiers' wives and other women, 'some of them of quality'.

The three hour battle of Naseby was the end of the King's old Oxford Army. All the foot, and artillery were lost, the casualties among the cavalry included 100 officers and gentlemen. Sprigge puts the prisoners at 4,962. All the 200 carriages, 8,000 arms, 40 barrels of powder, 200 horse with their riders, and nearly 100 colours were captured. Roundhead soldiers had for their reward 'the riches of the court, and officers, the rich plunder of Leicester'. Not the least prize was the King's Cabinet with all his correspondence, which when published revealed to friend and foe alike his devious negotiations with the French and the Irish.

The war was to linger on for more than a year, but Naseby was decisive. Had the King destroyed the New Model he could have joined forces with Goring for another march to London. But with his veteran army destroyed it was only a matter of time before his numerous fortresses and towns would be reduced.

Sir Thomas Fairfax was a modest and inarticulate officer. His second-in-command was far readier with tongue and pen, and too many historians have given him the credit for the victory. But it was not Cromwell that bore the heaviest burden of responsibility at Naseby, bravely though he fought.

Much has been heard of the indiscipline of the Royalists and in the bitterness of defeat Clarendon and Walker were not backward in condemning Rupert for his conduct on this day. Perhaps they did not dare to criticise their royal master. That Rupert's place was with the reserve is evident, but once he had been permitted to ride off to the right, the command of that body rested squarely on the King himself. How ill he managed it we have seen. Yet he was by this time a general of some experience, the victor of Cropredy Bridge and Lostwithiel. Maybe the charge that Carnwarth prevented would have ended only in disaster and death –– not that death on the battlefield is any worse than death on the block.

There was an instant during the battle of Naseby when King Charles' crown might have been saved. It was the King himself and no other that let the moment pass.

---

[1] Warburton. III. 127.

[2] Two southern brigades under the Earl of Northampton and Colonel Thomas Howard; two northern under Sir Marmaduke Langdale and Sir William Blakeston.

[3]
1. Prince Rupert's Lifeguard	140
2. Prince Maurice's Lifeguard	120
3, 4, 5. Prince Rupert's Regiment	400
6. The Queen's Regiment	150
7. Prince Maurice's Regiment	150

[4]
1 and 2. The Earl of Northampton's Regiment	250
3, 4, 5. Sir William Vaughan's Regiment	400

TOTAL 1,610

[5] Sprigge.

[6] 60 yards?

[7] Sprigge.

8 The House of Commons sent two surgeons to attend him and he was at the siege of Oxford in 1646.

9 Sprigge.

10 By 'the Reserves to Colonel Whaley' Sprigge must mean this regiment.

11 Walker.

12 Possibly Rupert's Regiment is meant. It was the strongest regiment present, 500, but only one officer is named in the list of prisoners (Peacock).

13 Sprigge.

14 Bulstrode Whitelock, p. 448-449. Memorials of the English Affairs (1853).

15 Sprigge.

The Campaigns of Montrose

JAMES GRAHAM, 5th Earl of Montrose (1612-1650) was appointed Lieutenant-General of the Royalist forces in Scotland and created a Marquess in February 1644. In August of that year he raised the Royal Standard at Blair Atholl against no less than three Covenant armies : Lord Elcho at Perth, Argyll and the Campbells in the west, and Lord Burleigh at Aberdeen.

Montrose decided to move against Elcho first, and Sunday 1st September found him encamped three miles west of Perth, on Tippermuir, faced by Elcho and the Covenant army of 700 horse, 7000 foot and 9 guns.

Montrose himself had 3200 foot soldiers and 500 bowmen under Lord Kilpont. He had no cavalry or artillery. Elcho's left wing of cavalry charged first at Montrose's thin line but were dispersed by the infantry fire and volleys of stones from the Athol Highlanders. Retreating, they disordered the ranks of infantry and, seeing his chance Montrose charged with the whole of his force and completely broke the Covenant foot. Of Elcho's 7000 foot, 2000 were killed in the ensuing rout.

It was now Montrose's task to prevent Argyll and Burleigh[1] from joining forces, and he moved his depleted army of 44 horsemen and 1500 foot (many of the Highlanders having gone home with their plunder) towards Aberdeen. Opposing him on 13 September he found Burleigh's force of 500 horse and 2000 foot south west of the city on a hillside near Aberdeen. Montrose's Irish troops cleared the opposing forlorn hope before the Covenant left wing charged Montrose's right. However, after discharging their pistols they retired to the main body. Burleigh's right then attacked Montrose's left flank with 100 horse and 400 foot but were held by the Gordon horse until a mixed force of cavalry and bowmen were transferred from the Royalist right. Under this pressure the Covenant attack was shattered and, after an unsuccessful charge by the Covenant left wing, their army broke and fled.

Montrose then led raids on Argyll's Campbell lands until, in January 1645 he reached the Great Glen. Here he found his way north barred by a force of 5000 at Inverness, and Argyll with 3000 men forming to the south at Inverlochy. Montrose, with only 1500 men, marched through the hills south to Roy Bridge, then over the northern slopes of Ben Nevis until on the evening of 1st February they were one mile from Inverlochy Castle. Argyll's force, under Duncan Campbell of Auchinbrech, believing that the force could only be a raiding party, did nothing until attacked the following morning by the whole of Montrose's army. Campbell attempted to form up his men but they were shattered by the impetus of the attack. In the ensuing slaughter 1700 of Campbell's 3000 foot were killed. Argyll, who had not hazarded his person, fled in his galley.

A new field army under Baillie had been formed by the Covenanters. Baillie formed a scheme whereby he believed if he split his army he could ensnare Montrose in a pincer movement. Accordingly, 3600 foot and 400 horse were detached from the main army and given to Sir John Urry. Probing after Urry's cavalry screen, Montrose, with 1400 foot and only 250 horse, finally halted on 8 May at Auldearn, two miles east of Nairn, after being lured by Urry into Covenant territory. Early the next morning Urry attacked the Royalist positions, beating back an initial thrust by Macdonald's foot. However, Montrose had placed the greater part of his force (some 800 men and the horse) out of sight, and these he now led in an attack on Urry's right flank. Taken by surprise the Covenant foot began to waver, and after a renewed frontal attack by the Gordons and Macdonalds, Urry's force crumbled, his cavalry and 1600 local troops fleeing without offering battle. Out of a force of 4000, he returned to Baillie with a mere 100 horse.

After this victory Montrose went in search of Baillie's army, and 2 July 1645 found him on Gallowhill south of the present Bridge of Alford. On that date Baillie's army also appeared on the opposite bank. The river was crossed in 1645 by a ford only, then by a causeway over marshy land. Baillie allowed himself to be persuaded into crossing these obstacles with his force of 500 horse and 2000 foot. After the horse had deployed beyond the causeway, and while Baillie's foot were still disorganised crossing the stream. Montrose's force of 2000 men and 250 horse fell upon them, Baillie's screening cavalry were driven off and the whole of his infantry destroyed in the encounter. He repaired to Perth where yet another Covenant army had been formed, and then marched south to link up with Lanark and a force of 1000 foot and 500 horse. Montrose outmarched him and on 14 August, with 500 horse and 4400 foot was one mile north east of Kilsyth, where Baillie must pass him on the journey south. Baillie's 800 horse and 6000 foot appeared on the 15th on the high ground overlooking Montrose's position. To prevent Montrose escaping, the Covenant forces began marching across the Royalist front to gain some high ground to the north. As they did so Montrose's centre charged into them, piercing their line. Baillie's right attacked Montrose's left, but after being reinforced by the horse from the right wing and the cavalry reserve the Covenant army began to melt away. Caught by the devastating flank attack scarcely 100 of Baillie's 6000 foot escaped.

After Kilsyth Leven, besieging Hereford, sent David Leslie north to deal with Montrose, and he arrived in Scotland with a force of 3000 horse, 1000 foot and 2000 dragoons. Montrose had but 1200 horse and 500 foot, for the Highland clans had begun to return home, not wishing to campaign in the lowlands. On 12 September, believing Leslie to be far north of him, Montrose was at Selkirk, his men camped at Philiphaugh west south west of Selkirk just below the junction of the Yarrow and the Ettrick to take Montrose in the rear. All but 150 of the Royalist cavalry fled as soon as Leslie's forces were seen, and despite a desperate charge by Montrose, the Royalists were completely overwhelmed. At the end of the battle the Royalist army numbered no more than 50 horse and 50 foot.

The Covenanters sullied their victory by a massacre of prisoners, who had accepted quarter.

Montrose's operations were not unlike Commando raids. He did not command sufficient forces to control all Scotland, but the victories won by his skill, leadership and *élan*, affected the fighting in England, by drawing off considerable detachments from Leven's Army.

The Battle of Dunbar

THE CAMPAIGN

1650

22 *July*	*Cromwell crosses the border.*
29 *July*	*The English before Edinburgh.*
30 *August*	*Cromwell decides to retreat to Dunbar.*
31 *August*	*Action near Haddington.*
1 *September*	*Leslie occupies Doon Hill.*
3 *September*	*The battle of Dunbar.*
4 *September*	*Lambert occupies the city of Edinburgh.*
24 *December*	*Surrender of Edinburgh Castle.*

THE BATTLE

3 September, 1650

'The Lord has delivered them into my hands.'
CROMWELL

IN WAR THE good tactician often has the better of the good strategist. Military history offers us numerous examples to support this contention. At Waterloo Napoleon, perhaps the greatest master of the Art of War that the world has yet seen, suffered defeat at the hands of Wellington, the foremost tactician of his day. This is not so strange when one considers that the battlefield is the province of the tactician, while strategy is the managing of the campaign. Before Dunbar David Leslie had Cromwell in a strategical situation that was seemingly hopeless. But the tactical *coup de grâce* remained to be given.

Other things being equal numbers are bound to tell in battle. Yet at Dunbar Cromwell defeated an army almost exactly double the size of his own. This seems incredible for there would seem to be no special reason why one Englishman should be worth two Scots. The solution to this problem is a simple one. In June 1650 the standing army in Scotland numbered but 2,500 horse and 3,000 foot. Fully three-quarters of the 22,000 men who fought – or failed to fight – under Leslie at Dunbar were newly levied men, many of them with as little as three months' service. Leslie's army was considerably better, no doubt, than the two that had faced each other at Edgehill eight years before. But Cromwell's army was something entirely different from the unruly mob that had followed Essex in 1642. Years of service and iron discipline had moulded it into the finest fighting machine in the Europe of the day. At Dunbar Cromwell commanded troops that the great Gustavus himself would have been proud to have led.

In the early stages of the campaign the cold, wet, hunger and the flux did more damage to Cromwell's army than the Scots did. The 16,354 men he led across the border on 22 July had sunk to 12,080 by 3 September : some 4,000 had succumbed to sickness, and on the very day before the battle we find Cromwell writing from Dunbar : 'Our lying here daily consumeth our men, who fall sick beyond imagination. . . .' The army was supplied by sea, and contrary winds had interfered with the regular arrival of provisions. Up until 13 August the men had no tents and the summer was a very wet one. Even an Ironside's constitution could not always endure such conditions.

And so on the night of 30 August, at Musselburgh, Cromwell held a council of war which decided to retreat to Dunbar and fortify the town. He hoped this would provoke Leslie to give battle. In addition the town would be able to accommodate his sick, and would be 'a place for a good magazine'. Reinforcements were expected from Berwick, and Dunbar would be a convenient place to land them.

On the 31st the English marched to Haddington, hotly pursued by Leslie, who put Cromwell's rearguard into some disorder. Fortunately for the latter 'the Lord by his providence put a cloud over the moon', and enabled the rear brigade of horse to escape with little loss. At midnight the eager Scots made an attempt on Cromwell's quarters at the west end of Haddington, but after an hour's fight were repulsed by Colonel Charles Fairfax's regiment.

Next day, after offering battle for about four hours, during which time they sent away their waggons, the English fell back to Dunbar. Once more Leslie pursued very closely, but there was no serious fighting. The evening found the Scots strongly posted on Doon Hill, about 2 miles from Dunbar. From this position Leslie could if he chose advance on the town, bar Cromwell's road to Berwick via Cockburnspath, or, if he allowed him to march that way, fall upon his rear. On Doon Hill he himself was practically unassailable.

Cromwell, expecting an attack, encamped his army in the fields between Doon Hill and the town. All the next morning (2 September) his army 'stood in battalia in the field' unable 'to engage the enemy by reason of the hill. . . .'[1] But the Scots did not come down.

That afternoon as Cromwell puts it :

'The enemy . . . gathered towards the hill, labouring to make a perfect interposition between us and Berwick, and having in this posture a great advantage, through his better knowledge of the country; which he effected by sending a considerable party to the strait pass at Copperspath [sic] where ten men to hinder are better than forty to make way.'

Leslie's best plan was to stay in his strong position and await events. If Cromwell tried to embark his army he would probably lose his train, his horses and his reargaurd. If he tried to march on Berwick he would have the Scots army on his flank and his road blocked at Cockburnspath.[2]

But Leslie was not master in his own house : the clergy were. As Cromwell puts it ; 'the ministers pressed their army to interpose between us and home, the chief officers desiring rather that we might have way made, though it were by a golden bridge. But the clergy's counsel prevailed'. Leslie was persuaded to move down Doon Hill and take up a position along the Brox Burn. It seems that this move began before daybreak on the 2nd and went on all

day. The Scots captured an outpost of Pride's regiment in an isolated farm about 250 yards from the place where the modern road
crosses the Brox Burn. The English now 'marched as close to the
dike (burn) as they possibly could ; placing two field pieces in each
regiment of foot, expecting that night the enemy would have
fallen on'.[3]

But Cromwell, not content with a passive defence, was watching events closely, and seeking for an opening. 'Upon Monday
evening,' he writes, 'the enemy drew down to their right wing
about two-thirds of their left wing of horse . . . shogging also their
foot and train much to the right, causing their right wing of horse
to edge down towards the sea. We could not well imagine but that
the enemy intended to attempt upon us, or to place themselves in
a more exact condition of interposition.' He goes on to describe
how Lambert and he went to Broxmouth House, and reconnoitred
Leslie's position, both simultaneously observing a tactical weakness that gave them 'an opportunity and advantage to attempt upon
the enemy'. Sending for Colonel George Monck, a former
Royalist colonel who was an older soldier than either of them, they
showed him their idea, and he confirmed their opinion.

What precisely was this chink in Leslie's armour? The
question can only be answered if we consider the ground.

Between the two armies lay the Brox Burn, running down
from Doon Hill to the sea. The burn, though swollen by the recent
rains, was fordable, but it ran between steep banks, which made it
a formidable obstacle, particularly in its upper reaches. There it
runs through a ravine, not unlike a railway cutting, but further
down the banks become lower, and below Broxmouth House,
where Cromwell had established an outpost, the stream was not
much of an obstacle. The two points that must have struck the
English commanders were that Leslie's left, jammed in between
Doon Hill and the Brox Burn, had about as much room to manoeuvre as a sword has in its scabbard ; while between Broxmouth
House and the sea there was little enough to impede the advance
of cavalry.

About 9 o'clock that night Cromwell held a council of war,
but exactly what the main arguments were cannot be said. We have
only one detailed account, and that was written in about 1680 by

John Hodgson, who was only a lieutenant at Dunbar, and was, therefore, certainly not an eyewitness.[4] It seems that some of the colonels were for embarking the foot, and letting the horse try to cut their way through to Berwick. This was not very practical, for there can hardly have been shipping for 7,000 men. Hodgson credits his commanding officer, 'honest Lambert', with opposing this suggestion and pointing out the weaknesses of the Scots' position. He asserted that 'if we beat their right wing we hazarded their whole army, for they would be all in confusion, in regard they had not great ground to traverse their regiments between the mountain (Doon Hill) and the clough (Brox Burn)'. Moreover the Scots 'had left intervals in their bodies upon the brink of the hill, that our horse might march a troop at once, and so the foot ; and the enemy could not wheel about nor oppose them, but must put themselves in disorder'. In addition the English 'guns might have fair play at their left wing while we were fighting their right'. These points then were the substance of the appreciation made by Cromwell and Lambert. Monck also spoke in favour of giving battle, and the council proceeded to work out the details of the plan.

Meanwhile Leslie had been interrogating a one-armed veteran taken when Cromwell's outpost was cut off. 'How will you fight,' the Scots general asked, 'when you have shipped half your men and all your great guns?' 'Sir,' the Englishman answered, 'if you will please to draw down your army to the foot of the hill, you shall find both men and great guns too.' Whether this stout reply pleased Leslie, or whether he hoped to impress his enemy by his confidence and strength, the prisoner was permitted to depart, and reported to Cromwell who rewarded him with two gold pieces.

THE SCOTS ARMY

David Leslie, who commanded the Scots army, was an officer of good experience, who had distinguished himself, as we have seen, at Marston Moor. His victory at Philiphaugh (1645) had put an end to the great Montrose's astonishing series of successes. Cromwell had not previously commanded an army opposed by a general with so high a reputation.

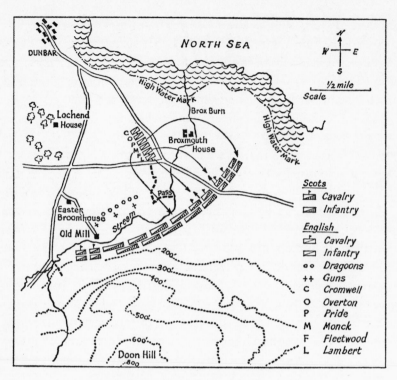

THE BATTLE OF DUNBAR, 1650

Leslie had not less than 6,000 horse and 16,000 foot; his 22,000 men outnumbering Cromwell's army by nearly two to one. But this great host lacked the discipline and battle experience of the English. Moreover the covenanters had dismissed many of their old soldiers and the English Cavaliers as 'Malignants', in order to officer their army with 'ministers' sons, clerks, and such other sanctified creatures, who hardly ever saw or heard of any sword but that of the spirit'.[5]

THE ENGLISH ARMY

Cromwell had no more than 3,500 horse and 7,500 foot, but the majority were veterans, and he had the assistance of experienced generals. His second-in-command was the stout-hearted Yorkshireman, Major-General John Lambert; Lt.-General Charles Fleetwood commanded the horse, while the three brigades

226

of foot were under Colonels George Monck, Robert Overton and Thomas Pride. The army had been afflicted with much sickness, and an 'honourable commander' describes 'Our bodies enfeebled with fluxes, our strength wasted with watchings ; want of drink, wet, and cold, being our continual companions'. . . .

Leslie had shown Cromwell his hand by moving in daylight. Cromwell's counterstroke was prepared in the darkness. All through the night the English commanders toiled away shifting their dispositions so that when day should dawn everything would be in order. Leslie had shown them a strong right wing of horse on the gentle slopes that run down to the Great North Road and the sea. With this, it was obvious, he meant to advance across the easily fordable lower reaches of Brox Burn. Here then Cromwell massed the bulk of his cavalry, six veteran regiments. Moreover, Cromwell resolved to get his blow in first.

It was a night of wind and wet, the best possible for Cromwell's purpose for all noise of his movements was drowned. He 'rid all the night . . . through the several regiments by torchlight, upon a little Scots nag, biting his lips till the blood ran down his chin without his perceiving it, his thoughts being busily employed to be ready for the action now in hand'.

In the Scots camp there was no such diligence. Early in the night there were a couple of alarms. Thereafter the Committee proposed that they might take some rest, and the men were stood down. It is said that Major-General Holbourne gave orders to put out all the matches save two in a company. The foot made themselves shelters of the new reaped corn and went to sleep. Many of the troopers went off foraging, while others unsaddled their horses. Many of the officers left their men and went off in search of cover.

Cromwell's plan was to attack at daybreak. In the vanguard the six regiments of horse were to be commanded by Lambert and Fleetwood ; they were to be supported by Monck with three and a half regiments of foot. The brigades of Pride and Overton and the two remaining mounted regiments were to bring up the rear.

About 4 o'clock on the morning of Tuesday, 3 September, the attack went in, though the troops were only just formed in time.

The Scots were taken completely by surprise, in a position that they had chosen not for defence but as the start-line for an attack.

The first onset was made by Lambert with a brigade of horse about 1,400 strong[6] supported by two regiments of foot. They fought their way across the Brox Burn where the old Dunbar-Berwick road crossed it and established themselves on the other bank. Surprised as they were the Scots rallied and fought back well. 'The enemy made a gallant resistance,' wrote Cromwell, 'and there was a very hot dispute at the sword's point between our horse and theirs.' Some Scottish horse, their front rank men armed with lances, charged down the hill very resolutely, and Lambert's brigade was forced to give way a little. Major Rokeby[7] was mortally wounded, Colonel Whalley cut in the wrist, and Major Christopher Lister was taken.[8] The commander of this Scottish counter-attack seems to have been a Colonel Strachan, who was wounded. His success was short-lived.

Meanwhile Fleetwood's brigade must have been engaging other bodies of the Scottish horse, of whom there were about 4,500 on Leslie's right.

Monck's brigade, perhaps 3,000 strong, had engaged the mass of infantry in the Scottish centre. 'Our first foot,' Cromwell wrote, 'after they had discharged their duty (being overpowered with the enemy) received some repulse, which they soon recovered.' It may be that all or part of Overton's brigade had crossed to their support, and enabled them to rally. If so it must have been left to Okey's dragoons to provide the escort for Cromwell's artillery.

Meanwhile Cromwell himself, with his own regiment of horse and Pride's brigade of foot, had crossed the Brox Burn between Broxmouth House and the sea, to strike the stroke that was to decide the day. Wheeling to the right he fell upon the flank of the Scots, who were already fully engaged in attempting to overpower his vanguard.

'My own regiment,' he writes, 'did come seasonably in and at the push of pike did repel the stoutest regiment the enemy had there merely with the courage the Lord was pleased to give ; which proved a great amazement to the residue of their foot.' These stout Scots were evidently the Highlanders of Campbell of Lawers.

Their lieutenant-colonel, another Campbell, was killed by a sergeant of Cromwell's, but his men 'stood to the push of the pike and were all cut in pieces'.[9] The musketeers of this regiment were armed not with matchlocks but with 'firelocks' which partly accounts for their good resistance.

Pride's regiment determined to avenge the cruel usage of their fellow soldiers taken the previous day, seconded Cromwell's. Oliver himself rode up to the rear of Lambert's regiment, and gave the order to 'incline to the left; that was, to take more ground to be clear of all bodies'.[10] Thus the Scots were completely out-flanked. One eyewitness wrote: 'I never beheld a more terrible charge . . . our foot alone making the Scots foot give ground for three-quarters of a mile together.'

Lambert had rallied the cavalry of the vanguard and returned to the charge, while Packer, a veteran Ironside, led Cromwell's regiment in from the flank. In Cromwell's own words: 'The horse . . . did with a great deal of courage and spirit beat back all opposition, charging through and through the bodies of the enemy's horse and their foot; who were, after the first repulse given, made by the Lord of Hosts as stubble to their swords. . . .' Leslie's right wing disintegrated. The horse fled in all directions, some took the Berwick road, others made for Haddington. Hodgson describes how Lambert's regiment of foot pushed on up the hill preventing the straggling parties that had been engaged from reforming – or from 'bodying' as he puts it.

Some few of the Scots still 'stood very stiffly to it', notably the regiment of Sir John Haldane of Gleneggies; its colonel, lieutenant-colonel and major were all numbered among the slain. This was probably the body which 'would not yield though at push of pike and butt-end of musket, until a troop of horse charged from one end to another of them, and so left them to the mercy of the foot'. But the great majority of the Scottish infantry were far less resolute. Throwing down their arms they took to their heels, or surrendered where they stood. The left wing, which had not fired a shot, departed without more ado. 'And, the sun appearing upon the sea,' Hodgson wrote, 'I heard Noll say, "Now let God arise, and his enemies shall be scattered,"[11] then, "I profess they run." '

In the brief space between 4 o'clock and the time when the

rising sun dispersed the mists of morning, Cromwell had broken Leslie's army.

Oliver lost no time in putting his men in order once more. As he formed them up they broke into the 117th Psalm:

O give you praise unto the Lord,
All nations that be;
Likewise you people all accord
His name to magnify.

For great to us-ward ever are
His loving-kindnesses;
His truth endures for ever more:
The Lord O do ye bless.

Two verses of a psalm and a good body of Ironsides had got together. Cromwell launched them in pursuit, and for eight miles they rode, cutting down the hapless fugitives. Cromwell puts the killed at 3,000, the majority of whom, no doubt, were slain after their regiments broke.

The prisoners numbered 10,000, about half of whom, 'almost starved sick and wounded', were released. The trophies included 30 guns, and 208 colours. Cromwell for his part claims that he 'lost not above thirty men'. This would be well-nigh incredible were it not that he had arranged things so that the Scots had more or less 'routed one another'. Cromwell's tactical skill was never more clearly demonstrated than at Dunbar.

At Dunbar the Scottish field word had been 'The Covenant', the English 'The Lord of Hosts'. Both in fact made their appeal to the Almighty. Only a month earlier Cromwell had beseeched the General Assembly of the Kirk of Scotland: 'in the bowels of Christ, think it possible you may be mistaken'. Now they were appalled by this 'dreadful appearance of God. . . .'

Leslie and Holbourne were both exonerated by the Scottish Parliament on 23 December, but the former, who was probably one of the type described by Napoleon as *bon général ordinaire*, might just as well have been dismissed for all the good he was capable of doing thereafter.

Dunbar shook the political tyranny of the Kirk, and allowed

King Charles II to loosen their control, and to build up a new army which was as much Royalist as Presbyterian.

Cromwell had saved his army from a position nearly as bad as that of Essex at Lostwithiel in 1644. He was now able to capture Edinburgh, but the war dragged on. His triumph was spectacular but incomplete.

1 Hodgson, p. 276. *A True Relation*.
2 Pease Bridge?
3 Cadwell.
4 Captain John Hodgson. *Memoirs*.
5 Walker.
6 Lambert's, Whalley's and Lilburne's regiments.
7 Lambert's regiment.
8 Lilburne's.
9 Gumble, *Life of Monck*.
10 Hodgson.
11 Psalm 68.

The Battle of Worcester

THE CAMPAIGN

1651

4 August	*Leith: Cromwell outlines his strategy.*
5 August	*The Scots cross the border near Carlisle.*
14 August	*Haslemoor. Harrison and Lambert join forces.*
15 August	*Derby lands at Wyre Water.*
22 August	*Charles II at Worcester. Cromwell at Mansfield.*
26 August	*Lilburne defeats Derby at Wigan.*
28 August	*Skirmish at Upton-on-Severn. Massey wounded.*
29 August	*Cromwell bombards Worcester. Royalist night sortie.*
3 September	*The Battle of Worcester.*
15 October	*King Charles II sails from Shoreham Creek.*

THE BATTLE

3 September, 1651

'It is, for aught I know, a crowning mercy.'
OLIVER CROMWELL. 4 SEPTEMBER 1651

ENGLAND HAS HAD her share of warrior kings, though Charles II is not usually accorded his place among them : it is not for his martial exploits that he is remembered. . . . Indeed, much of his character, gallant yet realistic, seems to have been an inheritance from his grandfather, King Henri IV of France. Henry of Navarre, victor of Arques and Ivry, had been one of the foremost warriors of his day. At Worcester, with an indifferent army and opposed by Oliver in person, Charles showed that his soldiership was not to be despised.

Cromwell, for his part, had displayed his tactical skill in a score of fights. In the Worcester campaign we see more of him as a strategist. His problem was straightforward. In Scotland his army simply was not strong enough to bring the war to an end. If he could lure the Scots into England, he could rely on all the forces serving at home and could concentrate an overwhelming strength. On 4 August he wrote to Speaker Lenthall from Leith:

> 'I do apprehend that if he (Charles II) goes for England, being some few days march before us, it will trouble some men's thoughts, and may occasion some inconveniences . . . we have done to the best of our judgments, knowing that if some issue were not put to this business, it would occasion another winter's war, to the ruin of your soldiery, for whom the Scots are too hard in respect of enduring the winter difficulties of this country; and . . . the endless expense of the treasure of England in prosecuting this war. It may be supposed we might have kept the enemy from this, by interposing between him and England; . . . but how to remove him out of this place, without doing what we have done, unless we had had a commanding army on both sides of the river Forth, is not clear to us. . . .'

Cromwell goes on to affirm that 'this enemy is heartsmitten by God', and not so considerable as the Scots army that had fought at Preston.

> 'Major-General Harrison . . . shall attend the motion of the enemy, and endeavour the keeping of them together, as also to impede his march, and will be ready to be in conjunction with what forces shall gather together for this service. . . . Major-Gen. Lambert, this day, marched with a very considerable body of horse, up towards the enemy's rear. With the rest of the horse, and nine regiments of foot (most of them of your old foot and horse), I am hasting up; and shall, by the Lord's help, use utmost diligence. I hope I have left a commanding force under Lt.-Gen. Monck in Scotland.'

Thus Oliver laid his trap.

The Scots crossed the Border on 5 August, and next day, near Carlisle, Charles II was proclaimed King. He issued a promise of pardon to any who would join him,[1] but scarcely enough Englishmen enlisted to make up his losses from desertion and 'purple fever'. The desperate mood of the invading army may be seen in a letter from the Duke of Hamilton (8 August): 'We have quit Scotland, being scarcely able to maintain it; and yet we grasp at all, and nothing but all will satisfy us, or to lose all. I confess I cannot tell you whether our hopes or fears are greatest; but we have one stout argument, despair; for we must now either stoutly fight it, or die.' He concluded by saying that all were 'laughing at the ridiculousness of our condition. . . .' This letter was intercepted by Harrison, and Parliament lost no time in publishing it to the discouragement of English Cavaliers.

The position was indeed desperate. The Parliamentarian forces were converging from every direction. Lambert was following them, Harrison blocked their path. In Yorkshire Fairfax was organising the militia. Cromwell himself left Leith on 6 August and moved southwards with extraordinary speed. Meanwhile the Council of State supported him with feverish activity, concentrating troops at Barnet and Reading. Lambert and Harrison joined forces on 14 August and when two days later they joined the militia of Cheshire and Staffordshire at Warrington they had 17,000 men, and already outnumbered Charles. Derby, who had landed at Wyre Water on the previous day (15 August), only brought 250 foot and 60 horse to his support.

That August was exceedingly hot yet Cromwell was pressing southwards at the rate of 20 miles a day, his men in shirt-sleeve order, their coats, arms, and armour carried on country horses pressed for the service. By the time the Scots reached Worcester, where the King was received with 'all the demonstrations of affection and duty that could be expressed'[2] (22 August), Cromwell was near Mansfield, and his net was closing. On the 24th Cromwell was at Warwick, where he held a council of war with Fleetwood and Desborough.

On the 26th Cromwell wrote to London asking that 5,000 shovels, spades and pickaxes, 30 tons of match and 400 barrels of powder should be sent to Gloucester. Clearly he expected to have to besiege Worcester, where that same day King Charles had a rendezvous of his English subjects. Lord Talbot, Sir John Packington, Sir Walter Blount, Sir Ralph Clare came, and with them a number of those old Cavaliers whose long and gallant defence of Worcester in the First Civil War had won it the title of 'the loyal city'. Even so his army numbered no more than 16,000, about 2,000 being English. Cromwell now had at least 28,000 men at his disposal. The same day Colonel Robert Lilburne routed Derby's followers at Warrington. 'It was,' wrote Cromwell, 'a comfortable success.' On 27 August Cromwell was at Evesham, about 16 miles south-east of Worcester. Confident of victory he ordered Lilburne to Shrewsbury so as to cut off the Scots from home.

At dawn on the 28th the King sent Major-General Edward Massey[3] to break down the bridge at Upton-on-Severn, some 10 miles south of Worcester. Cromwell, who intended to operate on both banks of the river, sent Lambert with a party of horse and dragoons to force the passage. According to the Royalists Massey was outnumbered. It seems certain that he was surprised, for some of Lambert's dragoons were able to seize the church, which should have served him as a strongpoint, and held it against the Royalist counter-attack. Massey was badly wounded in the hand and arm and had his horse killed, but was able to withdraw to Worcester in good order, while Lambert repaired the bridge. Only 6 or 7 Royalists were killed in this affair.

On the 29th, as a Royalist writer[4] puts it, 'Sultan Oliver appear'd with a great body of horse and foot on Redhill within a mile of Worcester, where he made a bonnemine, but attempted nothing. . . .' Despite this gibe the English occupied Perry Wood on the low range of hills a mile east of Worcester, planted their cannon and played 'pell mell into the city' all day. Cromwell had now set up his headquarters in Judge Berkeley's house at Spetchley, two miles south-east of the city. In a letter to Lenthall he outlines his plans :

'I hinted to you in my last, that we had taken the pass over Severn, Upton-bridge. Lt.-General Fleetwood, with his brigade of horse and foot lies there, and is ready to enterprise any design upon the enemy on that side, as opportunity shall be offered. We know not as yet which way the enemy will draw, our intelligence tells us that he is yet at Worcester, and in the parts adjacent, on the other side Severn. We are this morn advancing towards that city: And I suppose we shall draw very close to it. If they will come forth and engage with us we shall leave the issue to God's providence, and doubt not to partake of glorious mercies. If they avoid fighting, and lead us a jaunt, we shall do as God shall direct, in the mean time, let us live under the exercises of faith and prayer. . . . The enemy hath raised a fort[5] on this side of the town, and burnt down divers out-houses.'

As was his wont Cromwell made a thorough reconnaissance of the enemy position, and the surrounding country. Visiting

Fleetwood's men at Upton he 'was entertained with abundance of joy by extraordinary shouting from each regiment, troop and company, as he went to salute them'.

But in the Royalist camp morale was not so high. During the march the Duke of Buckingham, who, according to Clarendon, 'had a mind very restless', had told the King that 'the business was now to reduce England to his obedience, and therefore he ought to do all things gracious and popular in the eyes of the nation; and nothing could be less (so) to it than that the army should be under the command of a Scotch general.' He did not hesitate to recommend himself for the post!

David Leslie, for his part, oppressed no doubt by the memory of how Oliver had dealt with him at Dunbar, had shown himself 'sad and melancholic' during the whole march, and had told the King privately that 'he well knew that army, how well soever it looked, would not fight'. Charles, who did not believe this, had very sensibly kept it to himself.

To make matters worse Leslie was jealous of Lt.-General John Middleton, an excellent officer who was doing his best to keep up the spirits of the rest. The unfortunate Massey, in great torment from his wound, could not stir from his bed, at the time 'when his activity and industry was most wanted'. When on 28 August Charles assembled his council of war at the Commandery[6] to discuss whether to offer battle; to bring in provisions and to lie still; or to rise and march on London, Hamilton offered a fourth alternative: a march into Wales. After some discussion the King resolved next night 'to give the grand rebel a camisado, by beating up his quarters that night with 1,500 picked horse and foot under Middleton and Sir William Keith. Every man was to wear his shirt over his armour for distinction. This promising enterprise was betrayed by one Guise, a tailor 'and a notorious sectary', who swung for it next day, but not before his treachery had led to a repulse, in which the Royalists lost nine or ten killed, and some prisoners.

On the 30th Fleetwood crossed the Severn at Upton and advanced up the west bank to Powick. Here he was faced by a brigade of horse and foot under Major-General Robert Montgomery and Colonel George Keyth, but there does not seem to

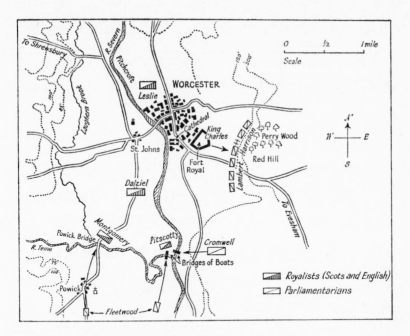

THE BATTLE OF WORCESTER, 1651

have been any fighting that day, and Fleetwood seems to have fallen back to Upton.

The Earl of Derby, sore wounded in the mouth at Wigan, arrived at Worcester on the 31st.

Meanwhile Cromwell's soldiers, fortified by forty barrels of strong beer, sent up by the city fathers of Gloucester, that Roundhead stronghold of the First Civil War, were busy collecting bridging materials. Cromwell sent Major-General Richard Deane, to reinforce Fleetwood and by the morning of 2 September all was ready. But, with a trust in omens unexpected in so pious a person he selected the anniversary of Dunbar[7] for his day of battle.

Early in the morning, about 5 or 6 o'clock. Fleetwood set out from Upton, but 'by reason of some hindrance'[8] he did not reach the Teme until between 2 and 3 o'clock in the afternoon. The Scots evidently defended Powick village for the marks of drake and musket shot can still be seen on the south wall of the church tower.

The King holding a council of war on the tower of Worcester Cathedral observed the firing at Powick, and could also see Crom-

237

well's men making a bridge of boats over the Severn 'under Buns-hill, about a mile below the City towards Team mouth. . . . His Majesty presently goes down, commands all to their arms, and marches in person to Powick Bridge to give orders, as well for maintaining that bridge, as for opposing the making the other of boats. . . .'[9]

The English were actually making two bridges of boats, using 'twenty great boats[10] with planks' for the purpose. One spanned the Severn and the other the Teme, and we are told that they were within pistol shot of each other. Cromwell's forethought is here apparent. Not only could he keep touch with Fleetwood, but he could surprise the Scots at Powick Bridge, who having broken down one of the arches[11] naturally thought themselves secure.

Soon after Charles left Powick Bridge the English made a furious assault. The Scots defended it well until with Montgomery wounded, and their ammunition spent, they made a disorderly retreat into Worcester, leaving Colonel Keyth a prisoner at the bridge.

Meanwhile Cromwell, having 'with much celerity' finished his bridges, led across a column headed by Ingoldsby's regiment and was himself the first man to set foot on the other bank. Major-General Pitscotty, a veteran of Marston Moor, opposed him with 300 Highlanders who were very much outnumbered, and were driven back from hedge to hedge. Major-General Dalziel's brigade posted in reserve between Powick Bridge and Worcester did not intervene to support either Montgomery or Pitscotty.

The Royalist chronicler maliciously comments that Cromwell after he had marched over a considerable number of his men, 'said (in his hypocritical way), the Lord of Hosts be with you, and returned himself to raise a battery of great guns against the Fort Royal. . . .' But in fact by returning to his command post, a cottage in Perry Wood, he was resuming his responsibilities as commander-in-chief. It was hardly for him to do the work of a brigade commander by leading the attack on Pitscotty.

At this juncture King Charles showed his mettle. Seeing that Cromwell had shifted much of his strength to the west bank of the Severn, he determined to make an attack on the east. Gathering together a body of horse and foot he sallied 'out at Sidbury Gate by the Fort Royal, where the rebels great shot came frequently near his sacred person.'[12] Buckingham, and Lord Grandison[13] with some cavalry; Hamilton with his own troop and some Highlanders, and Sir Alexander Forbes' regiment of foot, made up this force. Leslie's cavalry drawn up in Pitchcroft were still fresh.

To oppose the Royalist onslaught Lambert and Harrison had at least seven regiments.

The King and Hamilton managed their business with some skill. Pouring out of St. Martin's as well as Sidbury Gate, with covering fire from the guns of Fort Royal, they drove Cromwell's men back up Red Hill and actually overran some of his great guns. The doubtful fight raged for three hours, but Cromwell eventually was able to turn the tide by bringing men back across the bridge of boats. 'Here His Majesty gave an incomparable example of valour to the rest by charging in person, which the Highlanders especially imitated in a great measure, fighting with the butt-ends of their muskets, when their ammunition was spent; but new supplies of rebels being continually poured upon them, and the main body of Scotch horse not coming up in due time from the town to His Majesty's relief, his army was forced to retreat in at Sidbury Gate in much disorder.' Hamilton, his leg broken by a cannon shot, was carried back to the Commandery. Sir John Douglas was mortally wounded, and Forbes, shot through the calves, lay in Perry Wood all night and was taken prisoner next morning.

Thus ended the second phase of the battle. Cromwell was quick to exploit his advantage, pushing past the Fort Royal into the city close on the heels of the retreating Royalists. But all resistance was not at an end, and when Cromwell, who 'did exceedingly hazard himself', rode up and down offering quarter to the Royalist foot 'they returned no answer but shot'. The garrison of Fort Royal also refused quarter, but the place was stormed and they were slaughtered by the Essex militia, who turned the guns on the city.

Had Leslie intervened the city might still have held out for a time, but he could only ride up and down 'as one amazed'.

Charles himself riding back into Sidbury Gate found his

passage barred by an ammunition cart, which had overturned when one of its oxen was killed. Dismounting, the King entered the city on foot, and reached Friars' Street, where he took off his heavy armour, and mounted a fresh horse. Some of the foot were beginning to throw down their arms. Hat in hand Charles rode up and down among them 'entreating them to stand to their arms, and fight like men . . .' but they had had enough. 'I had rather you would shoot me,' the young King is reported to have said 'than keep me alive to see the sad consequences of this fatal day.'

Meanwhile Fleetwood's men had occupied St. John's suburb, and Dalziel's brigade, without much resistance, had laid down their arms. All chance of escape to the west was thus cut off. And indeed it was time for the King to think of escape, for Cromwell's men were in possession of Sidbury Gate.

At this time, when all seemed lost, the English Cavaliers fought a brave rearguard action, led by the sixty-year old Earl of Cleveland, the hero of Second Newbury, they rallied what force they could and charged up Sidbury Street, giving the King time to make his escape, about 6 o'clock, through St. Martin's Gate. In this affair Sir James Hamilton was desperately wounded.

About this time the Earl of Rothes, who with a party of Scots had resolutely maintained the Castle Hill, was compelled to surrender. The last stand was made by some of the English Cavaliers at the Town Hall. Then while Harrison with some of Cromwell's cavalry pursued the Royalists through the summer night, others of his soldiery 'fell to plundering the city unmercifully, few or none of the citizens escaping but such as were of the phanatique party'.[14] While King Charles was making the first stage of the astonishing escape, which was to take him safely to France, his opponent sat down to pen his despatch : 'Being so weary, and scarce able to write'. . . . It had been 'a very glorious mercy, and as stiff a contest, for four or five hours, as ever I have seen'.

The losses, as one would expect, fell very heavily upon the Royalists, while Cromwell had less than 200 men killed, though these included his Quartermaster General, Moseley ; Captain Charles Howard, the commander of his Lifeguard was seriously wounded, and Lambert had his horse shot under him.

The story of the King's escape may be read elsewhere[15]. Suffice it to say that though 'a tall black man, six feet two inches high' he made his way safely to the Sussex coast where a remarkably efficient Cavalier Colonel, George Gounter, procured a vessel which took the King and Lord Wilmot to France. Perhaps it was as well for Cromwell that Charles escaped : it was enough to have the blood of one King on his hands.

It is hard to estimate the Royalist losses. Perhaps 2,000 were killed and wounded. The final total of prisoners was reckoned at about 1,000, including 640 officers. Among them were Hamilton, who died of his wound ; Derby, who was beheaded ; Cleveland, Leslie, Montgomery and Massey. The trophies included 158 colours. The prisoners were driven like cattle to London ; many perishing for want of food and from disease. The survivors were sold to the plantations. The names of some of the officers confined in Windsor Castle may still be seen where they carved them on the walls of their prison.

If his prisoners could complain of their treatment, none of Cromwell's supporters were too humble to receive his attention. We find him writing to Lenthall from Evesham (8 September) on behalf of 'some honest men', who

'. . . suffered by your soldiers; which could not at that time possibly be prevented, in the fury and heat of the battle.

'I also humbly present to your charity the poor distressed wife and children of one William Guise, . . . who was barbarously put to death by the Enemy for his faithfulness to the Parliament. The man (as I am credibly informed) feared the Lord;. . .'

His 'crowning mercy' permitted Oliver at last to sheathe his sword. Never again while he lived could the Royalists raise an army against him. The most serious of the risings, under Colonel John Penruddock in 1655, was put down by one troop of horse.

Though 53 years old and feeling his years, his energy was still astonishing. Leaving Leith on 6 August he was before Worcester on the 28th. With only one day's rest his men had covered some 300 miles in 22 days – how astonished some of the generals of the eighteenth century must have been, if they ever troubled to read of his campaigns! There was truly something almost Napoleonic about it all, and surely the Emperor would have approved of the enveloping movements designed to ensure that the Royalist army should be netted complete. It is true that one thinks of Cromwell as a tactician but both in 1648 and 1651 he gave evidence of strategic insight. At the tactical level one is compelled to admire his forethought and his imagination in providing the bridge of boats, the key to his victory. Bridging operations in the teeth of the enemy are not easy.

What of the Royalists? There were excellent officers among them, Cleveland, Massey and Middleton; and gallant men too, like Hamilton and Derby, but Leslie was the general, and he, poor man, had lost his nerve. When the crisis came, the King took command himself. The iron nerve, which never failed him during his forty-one-day journey to Shoreham creek, is already evident in his conduct of the battle. As destiny would have it King Charles II's military career ended at the age of 21. Had he gone on soldiering he might today have ranked with Rupert and Hopton as one of the outstanding Royalist generals of the Civil War.

[1] Excepting only Cromwell, Ireton, Bradshaw, who had presided at the trial of King Charles I, and John Cook, the barrister who had prosecuted him.

[2] Clarendon.

[3] The Parliamentarian governor of Gloucester in the First Civil War.

[4] Boscobel.

[5] Fort Royal, built by the Royalists in the First Civil War and repaired in 1651.

[6] It is now a museum run by the City.

[7] Curiously enough he was to die on 3 September, 1658.

[8] Fleetwood's letter in the *Perfect Diurnall* for 8 September.

[9] Boscobel.

[10] These were doubtless trows, craft of some 70 tons burthen, which plied upon the Severn in those days.

[11] The repairs can still be clearly seen.

[12] Boscobel.

[13] A troop commander in Prince Rupert's regiment of horse in the First Civil War.

[14] Boscobel.

[15] See, for example, the admirable account in Arthur Bryant's *King Charles II* (1931).

1651—1685

THERE WAS NO significant difference between the Royalist army of 1685 and those of the Civil Wars.

King James' redcoats may have presented a rather more uniform appearance than those who fought at Worcester, but the only important change was that the pikemen had now lost their armour and were dressed like the musketeers. The introduction of grenadiers, important in the siege warfare of Marlborough's day, made little difference in the Sedgemoor campaign.

Monmouth's ill-equipped army one imagines would have cut but a sorry figure on the battlefields of the Civil War.

The Battle of Sedgemoor

THE CAMPAIGN

1685

1 *June*   *Monmouth sails from the Texel.*

11 *June*   *Monmouth anchors off Lyme.*

14 *June*   *The skirmish at Bridport.*

18 *June*   *Monmouth reaches Taunton.*

20 *June*   *Monmouth proclaimed King at Taunton.*

25 *June*   *Monmouth at Keynsham, near Bristol.*

27 *June*   *The action at Norton St. Phillips.*

3 *July*   *Monmouth at Bridgwater.*

6 *July*   *The Battle of Sedgemoor.*

8 *July*   *Monmouth captured by the Sussex Militia, near Horton, Dorset.*

15 *July*   *Monmouth executed on Tower Hill.*

THE BATTLE

6 July, 1685

WHEN ON 6 FEBRUARY, 1685, King Charles II died his last words are generally believed to have been : 'I am sorry to be such an unconscionable time a dying. Let not poor Nellie starve.' A monarch more burdened by the gravity of the situation might on his death-bed have shown some concern as to the succession, for Charles, while not backward in imparting his vigorous warmth, had omitted to provide a legitimate heir. In consequence it was his fifty-two year old brother, the Duke of York, who now ascended the throne as King James II. Lacking his dead brother's subtlety, James had never concealed that he was a Roman Catholic.

Besides the throne Charles had left his brother a truly tiny professional army of about 3,000 horse and foot – for the most part famous old regiments that are still with us – and also a serious rival for the crown in his thirty-six year old illegitimate son, James Scott, Duke of Monmouth. Monmouth was a Protestant.

England, therefore, might well have to choose one day between a King who was legitimate but a Catholic or one who was illegitimate but a Protestant. In seventeenth-century England nine out of ten detested the Catholics. A bastard here or there excited nobody.

When Charles died Monmouth was in exile at The Hague and not too discontented with his lot, for with his lovely mistress, Lady Henrietta Wentworth, to dally with he had no great itch to be stirring. He was, however, surrounded by a group of unscrupulous adventurers and exiles who gradually worked on him to try a throw for the crown. The Duke of Argyll would land in the Highlands, and raise the great clan Campbell, while Monmouth himself would land in the West Country, where he had been much courted and acclaimed during a Progress he had made – much to his father's annoyance – five years earlier, in 1680.

After blowing hot and cold several times – as he was wont to – Monmouth eventually decided to risk his head; Lady Wentworth pawned her jewels so that arms might be purchased and the Duke gathered his pathetically slight expedition. Lord Grey of Wark; Anthony Buysse, a mercenary from Brandenburg; Nathaniel Wade, a Bristol lawyer; altogether a mere 83 fighting men, including a detachment of Dutch gunners to serve four light field-pieces; 1,500 foot arms; 1,500 cuirasses for the cavalry he hoped to raise. All this with two small ships cost nearly £3,000. For £5,000 more Monmouth hired and equipped the *Helderenberg* a Dutch fifth-rate of 32 guns to escort the expedition, for, although Charles II had lacked the means to keep a large fleet in being, about a dozen vessels including the *Oxford* (54 guns) were in commission. It was a crippling blow to Monmouth to have to spend so much of his capital in this way.

The expedition sailed from the Texel and dropped anchor off Lyme Regis on 11 June, having encountered no hostile sail during the course of the 400-mile voyage which had taken eleven days.

There was no question of an opposed landing, though one Samuel Dassell tried in vain to persuade the captain of a merchant vessel riding in the shelter of the Cobb to fire two great guns at Monmouth's boats as they landed on the steep shingle beach. The Mayor of Lyme, Gregory Alford, who had been captain of a troop of horse[1] in the Royalist army in the days of the First Civil War, had time to get clear away to Honiton, warning Albemarle at Exeter and sending an urgent letter to the King. Dassell and a colleague escaped to London, which they reached on the 13th – receiving £20 apiece for their pains.

Once ashore Monmouth knelt a short time on the beach then unfurled his colours, a deep green flag with the words *Fear Nothing but God* embroidered in gold, being welcomed with cries of 'A Monmouth, the Protestant Religion!' By the 12th he already had 1,000 men. His stores were landed, except for the cavalry armour which, unaccountably enough, was left aboard his two smaller vessels to be captured five days later by the British sixth-rate man-o'-war *Saudadoes* (16 guns) off Lyme.

On hearing the news from Lyme James II, who was himself an experienced officer, immediately sent a small force to the West to observe Monmouth's movements. This consisted of six troops of horse and dragoons and five companies of foot, under Brigadier John Churchill, the future Duke of Marlborough and victor of Blenheim. The Lords Lieutenant of the Western and Southern counties, meanwhile, had called out the militia and while Monmouth was still at Lyme those of Dorset advanced to Bridport. Worsted in a skirmish there many of them joined the Duke's ranks.

On 18 June Monmouth reached Taunton, which like Lyme had been a great Parliamentarian stronghold in the Civil War. Here he was enthusiastically received. Recruits poured in until he had perhaps as many as 8,000 men. The foot were organised in five regiments – Red, White, Blue, Yellow and Green; Wade commanded the Red; Holmes the Colonel of the Green was a tough old Cromwellian veteran. Eight hundred mounted men under Lord Grey, ill-armed, variously mounted and untrained, could hardly be called cavalry. There were not enough muskets for all the foot and about 500 were armed with scythe heads mounted on poles like a mediaeval bill – a formidable enough weapon at close quarters. The daughters of some of the leading citizens of Taunton busied themselves with making 27 colours for the regiments and on 20 June the Duke had himself proclaimed King in the market place of Taunton, the text of the proclamation alleging that James II had poisoned his brother Charles.

By rapid marches through Bridport and Axminster, Churchill reached Chard on the 19th, and once more made contact with the rebel rearguard. Monmouth sent an emissary to Churchill hoping to seduce him from his loyalty to King James, but these overtures met with a cold reception. On the 21st Churchill was reinforced by further companies from the Queen Dowager's Regiment under their Colonel Percy Kirke, who had marched 140 miles in eight days to join the royal advance guard.

Monmouth had seen a good deal of military service and his strategy was not to be despised, as his next move shows. It was an attempt to capture Bristol, then the second city of the Kingdom. It was touch and go. Monmouth reached Keynsham on 25 June. So far there had been no more than a few skirmishes between his army and Churchill's force.

Lt.-General Louis Duras, Earl of Feversham, a French officer, with the main Royalist army perhaps 2,000 strong, had just reached Bath, while the Duke of Beaufort, that pillar of the Stuart dynasty, who was Lord-Lieutenant of Gloucestershire, had thrown his militia into Bristol to strengthen the wavering civic authorities. Although seventeenth-century Bristol was strongest on the Somerset side, as the sieges of 1643 and 1645 had shown, it is not impossible that a bold thrust now would have carried the place for the rebels. Indeed, the Bishop of Bristol considered that without Beaufort's presence the city would have been a 'cheap and easy prey'. But as chance would have it Captain John Parker, an enterprising officer of the Horse Guards, swam the Avon with a party of horse and got between Monmouth and Bristol. With an initiative that does him the greatest credit he 'staggered' the rebels 'with great sound of trumpets, drums and hautboys'. Colonel

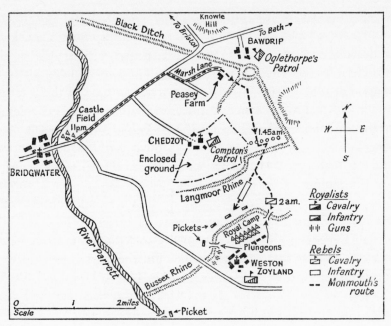

MONMOUTH'S NIGHT MARCH BEFORE
THE BATTLE OF SEDGEMOOR

Oglethorpe of the Life Guards took the rebel horse by surprise in the streets of Keynsham and in a confused skirmish the Royalists had 6 or 8 casualties and the rebels 14 killed. 'This disappointment and allarum . . . broke all their measures.' The upshot of this apparently trifling affair was extraordinary. Monmouth's morale broke. Instead of attempting Bristol, where he could have rested his men, recruited, and formed a base, he determined to retreat. A rebellion on the defensive must fail.

Monmouth arrived once more at Bridgwater on 3 July after getting rather the better of a fierce action at Norton St. Phillips, where the Duke of Grafton yet another of Charles II's sons was prominent on King James' side. The climax of this three and a half week's campaign was now at hand.

Here is the position on the eve of the battle of Sedgemoor. Oddly enough, Monmouth had now decided to make another attempt on Bristol, when a local man named Godfrey arrived with the information that the Royalist army, as viewed from the tower of Chedzoy Church, kept but poor guard. In fact their outpost arrangements were good, but Monmouth chose to believe Godfrey and struck on a truly astonishing plan. He would attempt to carry the Royalist camp by a night attack. Now in one way this was an excellent idea, for despite desertions Monmouth still outnumbered Feversham by at least two to one, and, therefore, if he could get into a mêlée in the dark, he would have a great advantage. Once Feversham's army was cut to pieces King James would have no other to oppose Monmouth's march on London. The crown of England hung on that night's work. And the two chief instruments of fate were to be not Dukes or Earls, Captains or Colonels, but a humble countryman, Godfrey, and an unknown trooper of the Blues.

The rebels set off up the Bristol road with strict orders to move in the greatest silence; should any man make a noise his neighbours were to cut him down at once. The rebels passed Peasey Farm where they left their baggage train and had successfully negotiated the Black Ditch when the jingle of approaching cavalry was heard and the army froze as Colonel Oglethorpe clanked past on the other side of what is now the King's Sedgemoor Drain at the head of a strong patrol.

The mist rose from the fenny fields as the host tramped through the night, and reached the Langmoor Rhine. Here Godfrey found himself at fault, unable for a time to find the crossing, the column closed up like a shunting train, and it was now that the trooper of the Blues, posted in the corner of the field, detected it, loosed off his pistol, and galloped off to Chedzoy to warn his troop commander, Sir Francis Compton, who immediately sent him post haste to alarm the Royal Camp. The trooper rode as fast as he could in the dark to the edge of the Bussex Rhine and called out twenty times at least, 'with all imaginable earnestness, "Beat the drums, the enemy is come, for the Lord's sake, beat the drums." ' The main guard beat to arms and the men began to seize their muskets and run to fall into line on their alarm posts.

Meanwhile, after their fatal delay, for which Godfrey must undoubtedly bear the blame, the rebels were coming on again. Grey took his mob of horsemen to seize the plungeons over the Bussex Rhine, and clashed with Compton who had wasted no time in falling back to the main position, and was in time to beat off an

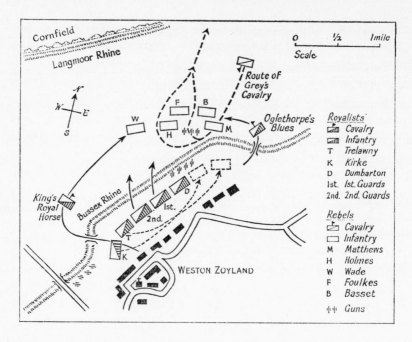

THE BATTLE OF SEDGEMOOR, 1685

attack of 300 rebel horse under Captain Jones, a London cabinet-maker, who tried to cross the Upper Plungeon.

Grey's men did not figure for long in the action. Received by musketry most of them panicked, and after riding along their side of the Rhine, they wheeled off causing considerable confusion among their own infantry, who by now were breasting up to the Royalist position. Instead of pushing on across the Bussex Rhine, which was practically dry, they now began to develop a fire-fight. Monmouth, on foot with a half-pike in his hand, and Wade did their best to persuade them to advance, but shaken by the knowledge that they had failed to gain surprise they would not budge.

The Dutch gunner guided by the glow of the matches from Dumbarton's Regiment brought his three brass guns up within 160 paces of that regiment and poured in a destructive fire. The regiment had all but four of its officers hit.

Churchill was soon on the scene and brought the regiments of Kirke and Trelawny from the left to equalise the Royalist front with that of the rebels.

Meanwhile the Royalist artillery parked near the main road lay idle for the simple reason that the drivers, who were hired civilians, had cleared off. Bishop Peter Mews[2] of Winchester, an old Cavalier soldier, rose to the occasion. He ordered his servants to harness his coach horses to the guns and dragged four of them into action. Sergeant Weems of Dumbarton's later received a reward of £40 from King James for his service in siting of 'the great guns'.

His enemies said that Feversham played but little part in the proceedings because he was looking for his wig, but in fact when he came up he gave the very sensible order that the Royalists were not to cross the Bussex Rhine until it was full daylight.

When the time came he attacked both flanks of the rebels with his cavalry. As his infantry crossed the ditch it is said that they raised a great shout. Considering how near the King had been to being completely surprised their morale was creditably high.

As for the rebels it was the end. Only a few hundred of Wade's Taunton men, the Red regiment stiffened perhaps by some of Blake's[3] Roundhead veterans, left the field in a body.

Monmouth divesting himself of his armour, rode off with Buysse leaving his army to be mopped up. He himself fell into the hands of the Sussex militia two days later.

This is not the place to describe the doings of Kirke's Lambs or Judge Jeffrey's Bloody Assize. Suffice it to say that the rebellion was crushed with a heavy hand. Not less than 230 were legally executed, besides those hanged out of hand immediately after the battle – the Dutch gunner, a tribute to his efficiency, being among the first. Deportation was the lot of at least 800. Dame Alice Lisle was beheaded for harbouring a fugitive and the maids of Taunton paid for their zeal with heavy ransoms. Monmouth himself, after a craven appeal for his life, met his end with fortitude, though it took Jack Ketch six blows of the axe to finish him.

The horrors of the aftermath must not blind us to the real efficiency of the small Royalist army. James II himself remarked that his soldiers had 'showed themselves to be old troops, and what difference there is between such and new raised men'. They were not particularly well-conducted in quarters or on the march, but in action they had proved as steady as one could wish, the true forerunners of the army that was to conquer the French at Blenheim, Ramillies and Oudenarde.

That is the story of Sedgemoor and of how James Scott staked his head to gain a crown. Poor Henrietta Wentworth might have done better to keep her jewels. She pined away and died the next year of a broken heart.

There are few traces of these stirring events to be found today in the quiet countryside around Weston Zoyland. The churches that stood as mute witnesses of the battle in July 1685 still stand today – but the view from their towers and spires bears but a limited resemblance to that of two and a half centuries ago. Both the Bussex and the Langmoor Rhines have long been filled in – and their original course can be detected only from air photographs. The line of the Black Ditch was subsequently absorbed into the larger Sedgemoor Drain, but the River Parret and the area of enclosed ground to the South of the village of Chedzoy remain very much the same as they were represented on maps made at the time.

To remind the casual visitor of the last battle fought on English soil, a memorial in grey stone has been erected, and bears the following inscription :

> 'To the Glory of God, and in memory of all those, who, doing the right as they saw it, fell in the Battle of Sedgemoor, 6th July, 1685, and lie buried in this field, or who, for their share in the fight suffered death, punishment or transportation, PRO PATRIA.'

[1] Sir John Berkeley's Regiment.

[2] Peter Mews (1619-1706) as a lieutenant in the Lifeguard of Foot was taken prisoner at Naseby. He is said to have been wounded nearly thirty times during the Civil Wars!

[3] Robert Blake (1599-1657), afterwards admiral and general at sea, had made an obstinate defence of Taunton in 1644 and 1645.

1685—1745

THE MILITARY ART saw many changes between the reigns of James II and George II. The British Army built up a great reputation under Marlborough, and confirmed it at Dettingen and Fontenoy, though it failed to distinguish itself at Sherriffmuir, the one important engagement of the '15 Rising.

Cavalry had not changed radically since the days of Rupert and Cromwell, but infantry were now much more formidable. The iron ramrod, introduced about 1720, had greatly increased the musketeer's rate of fire. It was now possible for a well-drilled regiment to fire three effective volleys in a minute. The introduction of the ring-bayonet, about 1700, had made every musketeer his own pikeman, and had done away with the need for two types of private soldier in the same unit. The infantry fought in a three-deep line.

The Royal Regiment of Artillery had been formed in 1716, and although its drivers were still civilians, was now more mobile, and effective for field operations, than the artillery of the seventeenth century. No doubt this can be attributed to the influence of the great Duke of Marlborough, whose victory at Blenheim was due in part to efficient gunnery.

The Highlander of 1745 was a formidable warrior just as his ancestor of 1644-1645 had been under Montrose. Even so he belonged to a bygone age, an excellent partisan, but ill-equipped and ill-trained to fight pitched battles against a disciplined 'modern' army.

On 12 January, 1746, General Hawley issued what would now be called a Training Instruction. It gives a lively, if prejudiced, idea of the Highlander and how to dispose of him.

> 'They commonly form their front rank of what they call their best men, or True Highlanders, the number of which being always but few, when they form in battalions they commonly form four deep, and these Highlanders form the front of the four, the rest being lowlanders and arrant scum.
>
> 'When these battalions come within a large musket shot, or three score yards, this front rank gives their fire, and immediately throw down their firelocks and

253

come down in a cluster with their swords and targets making a noise and endeavouring to pierce the body, or battalions before them, becoming 12 or 14 deep by the time they come up to the people they attack.

'The sure way to demolish them is at 3 deep to fire by ranks diagonally to the centre where they come, the rear rank first; and even that rank not to fire till they are within 10 or 12 paces, but if the fire is given at a distance you probably will be broke for you never get time to load a second cartridge, and if you give way you may give (up) your foot for dead, for they being without a firelock or any load, no man with his arms, accoutrements &c., can escape them, and they give no Quarters [*sic*], but if you will but observe the above directions, they are the most despicable enemy that are.'

Hawley had fought at Sheriffmuir and knew with whom he had to deal.

The Battle of Culloden

THE CAMPAIGN

1745

4 July   *Prince Charles Edward sails from Belle Ile in the privateer Du Teillay.*

25 July   *The Prince lands at Moidart.*

19 August   *The Prince raises his standard at Glenfinnan.*

17 September   *The Highland army captures Edinburgh.*[1]

21 September   *The battle of Prestonpans. The Highland Army defeats Lt.-General Sir John Cope.*

14 November   *Carlisle surrenders to the Prince.*

6 December   *The retreat from Derby begins.*

20 December   *The Highland Army crosses the Esk into Scotland.*

1746

10 January   *The Highlanders besiege Stirling Castle.*

17 January   *The Battle of Falkirk. The Highland Army defeats Lt.-General Henry Hawley.*

18 and 19 February   *The Highland Army reaches Inverness.*

16 April   *The Battle of Culloden.*

20 September   *Prince Charles Edward sails from Loch nan Uamh.*

THE BATTLE

17 April, 1746

'Death itself were dearly bought,
All for Scotland's King and Law.'

CULLODEN WAS THE last scene of the struggle between the
Houses of Hanover and Stuart, and since the leading actors were
young Princes of the rival houses, one might imagine that it was
a dramatic and even romantic affair. Legend has indeed trans-
formed Prince Charles Edward, 'Bonnie Prince Charlie', into a
figure of romance, though in fact he was an arrogant and stupid
young man whose chief assets were a strong constitution and almost incurable optimism. His victorious opponent, Lt.-General
William Augustus, Duke of Cumberland, K.G., – 'Billy the
Martial Boy' or 'The Butcher' according to political taste – has
few admirers. Yet, though no match for the great Marshal Saxe,
who defeated him at Fontenoy (1745), and Lauffelt (1748), he
was a firm and efficient officer of at least average ability. The Young
Pretender, on the other hand, besides being himself no soldier,
distrusted his ablest general, Lord George Murray, and chose to
lean on his hare-brained Quartermaster-General, John William
O'Sullivan.

Lord George, who was 51, was a son of the first Duke of
Atholl. Commissioned into the Royal (Scots) he had served in
Flanders in 1712. In the '15 he had commanded a regiment of
Atholl Highlanders fighting for the old Pretender. In 1719 he took
part in the Glenshiel expedition, but was pardoned and returned
to Scotland in 1724. Lord George was certainly outspoken, and
perhaps headstrong. Unfortunately for his cause, the Prince and
his entourage took a dislike to Murray from the first.

In 1745 the pick of the British Army under the Duke of
Cumberland was in Flanders. The French had much to gain from
a Jacobite diversion in Scotland, but, although they provided the
Prince with shipping, even after his capture of Edinburgh they
sent him very few troops. His invasion of England was a failure

because the English, grown prosperous under Walpole's government, were no longer interested in the restoration of the House of Stuart. The Prince has been much condemned for his retreat from Derby and it is true that a rebellion on the defensive cannot succeed. But it should be remembered that Charles I with more that 15,000 men had failed to take London in 1642. Was it likely that 5,000 Highlanders would have succeeded in 1745? And indeed the Young Pretender himself was the only one of the Jacobite hierarchy who wished to go on.

By April 1746 the prospects of the Highland Army were black. The men were unpaid, the commissariat was defective, and desertion was rife. All operations were bedevilled by discord among the leaders. Their chief asset, no doubt, was the memory of Prestonpans and Falkirk where the British Army had shown itself far less steady than its traditions and discipline demanded. But with Cumberland in the field, and the veterans of Fontenoy to reckon with, there was little reason to hope for a repetition of these fiascos.

Cumberland had followed the retreating Jacobites to Perth and thence to Aberdeen, where he remained, waiting an improvement in the weather until 8 April, when he marched out at the head of an army reported to number some 10,000 men. He reached Banff on 10 April, crossed the River Spey two days later, and on the 14th arrived at Nairn.

Early on the morning of 15 April, the Highland Army marched out to take up a battle position on some irregular ground which had been reconnoitred by O'Sullivan the previous day, and which lay about a mile to the south-east of Culloden House. At this juncture some of the staunchest units, including part of the MacDonalds and the MacPhersons, were absent. This, and desertion, left the army much weaker than it should have been – probably not more than 5,000 strong. The troops were drawn up to await the expected British advance, but no enemy materialised. The supply services, if such they could be called, had now completely broken down and, as time wore on, more and more men stole off to seek food and drink. At headquarters the general officers joined battle on a variety of topics.

Lord George Murray thought the ground unsuitable for the

Highland Army, and he was certainly right. It was too favourable for cavalry, an arm in which Cumberland had a great superiority, and the open moor would give the Royal Artillery clear targets. Late that afternoon a formal Council of War of senior officers and Chiefs assembled – the first since Derby. After some deliberation it was determined to make a surprise attack at dawn on Cumberland's camp at Nairn.

This plan, somewhat reminiscent of Monmouth's for Sedgemoor, was devised by the Prince and O'Sullivan. The Duke of Perth disliked it, and the Irish officers thought it 'a desperate attempt', but Lord George Murray, though 'very sensible of the danger should it miscarry', came round to it, probably because he preferred it to fighting on the open moor.

The chief drawback was that Nairn was eight miles away, rather too long a march to put in between dusk and dawn, and the night proved an exceptionally dark one.

From the first things went badly. About 7 o'clock it was found that a third of the men were away foraging, and when mounted officers were sent out to bring them back many said that they were starving and that the officers 'might shoot them if they pleased, but they could not go back till they got meat. . . .' But the Prince, optimistic as ever, announced that 'had he but a thousand men he would attack'. And so some 4,500 men set out to attack a force that the unpredictable O'Sullivan put at 18,000. Their best hope, as Lord George Murray said, was that as the 15th had been Cumberland's 25th birthday his men would be 'drunk as beggars'.

The Highland Army set off about 8.30 p.m. in two columns, making their way in single file through 'trackless paths, marshes and quagmires'. It is astonishing that under these conditions even the Highlanders could manage to cover two miles an hour. Soon a gap began to open between them and the French troops bringing up the rear, who were weighed down with the paraphernalia of continental warfare and unused to marching in the heather. The Prince now showed his inexperience by sending to Lord George to slacken the pace. A night march cannot be controlled from the rear.

Many of the Highlanders, faint from want of food, fell out

as Lord George passed through Kilravock wood, and thinking himself too weak to attack he sent Lochiel to tell the Prince it was useless to continue.

Once again the disadvantage of the commander being behind is apparent. Unable to see for himself how things really stood the Prince sent Lochiel back with positive orders to go on. But by this time there was a gap of half a mile in the column. Soon after a drum was heard in the English camp. Lord George gave the order to retreat. Riding forward Charles met Perth's men retiring. 'Where the devil are the men a-going?' he demanded angrily, and then hearing that they had been ordered back to Culloden House, he cried, 'Where is the Duke? Call him here. I am betrayed! What need have I to give orders when my orders are disobeyed?'

Eventually Perth, who had got lost in the dark, reported to the Pretender that Lord George had turned back three-quarters of an hour before. 'Good God!' cried the Prince, 'What can be the matter? What does this mean? We were equal in numbers and could have blown them to the devil. Pray, Perth, can't you call them back yet? Perhaps he has not gone too far?' After this outburst Perth and Lochiel persuaded the Prince to return to Culloden, which he did, convinced that Lord George had intentionally wrecked his plan. But nobody who reads of the Prince's own activities that night can suppose that he had the least idea of how to control a military operation.

Exhausted and starving the clansmen trailed back to Culloden, where most of them flung themselves down on the ground to sleep. Many had thrown away their targets. Those who were not too tired scattered in search of food. This was the state of the army when the alarm was raised that Cumberland was in full march towards them. Orders were immediately given to rendezvous on Drummossie Moor, where they had been drawn up on the previous day.

The English army had set off at daybreak, marching in three divisions, each consisting of five battalions of infantry, with cavalry on the left flank, and the train of artillery and the baggage following on the right rear of the foot.

Approaching Culloden the advanced guard – Kingston's Light Horse and the Argyleshire Highlanders – became aware that the Highland Army was on the move and appeared to be taking up its position. After a short reconnaissance, during which the main body halted, the bulk of Cumberland's army moved forward in very good order and deployed into line, finally appearing some five hundred yards from the Jacobites, now arrayed in battle order.

The most strenuous efforts of the Highland officers had been required to get their men together and for once the thrilling call of the pipes had little result, many who had taken part in the night march failing to rejoin in good time.

THE BRITISH ARMY

Cumberland's infantry was drawn up in three lines. The first under the Earl of Albemarle and Brigadier Sempill consisted of Pulteney's, which was ordered up from the reserve before the action began, so as to prevent the line being outflanked, the Royal, Cholmondeley's, Price's, the Royal Scots Fusiliers, Munro's and Barrel's regiments.

The second under Major-General John Huske was composed of Battereau's – originally with the reserve – Howard's, Fleming's, Bligh's, Sempill's, Ligonier's and Wolfe's regiments. The last named was moved out and placed *en potence* so as to cover the front of Barrel's regiment. (See Map.) The reserve under Brigadier Mordaunt originally consisted of Pulteney's, Battereau's and Blakeney's but by the time the fight started the first two had been moved forward.

The cavalry were under Lt.-General Henry Hawley and Major General Bland. Somewhat to the rear and to the right of the front line were a squadron of Cobham's Dragoons and Kingston's Light Horse. On the left were Lord Mark Kerr's and the rest of Cobham's Dragoons. The Argyleshire Militia and Loudoun's Independent Company were behind some walls to the left front of the army.

In the intervals between the regiments in the front line were five pairs of 3-pounders, and in front of the second line were two coehorn mortars.

Less than half Prince Charles' army were true Highlanders. The rest, except for the three small regiments from the French service, were recruited from the North East counties of Scotland and other districts outside the 'Highland Line'.

On the right of the front line – commanded by Lord George Murray – was the Atholl Brigade, the Camerons and the Stewarts of Appin, all three numbering together less than 1,200 men. Lord John Drummond commanded the centre, his regiments, from right to left being the Frasers – about 300 strong – then the Mackintoshes[2] (the old Clan Chattan) – some 500 strong – followed by the Farquharsons, a small unit of probably not more than about 100 men (who may indeed have formed part of the Mackintosh regiment). On their left was the combined Mac-Lachlan – MacLean regiment – maybe 300 all told ; then came the regiment, raised around Edinburgh, commanded by an adventurer named John Roy Stuart, and the only non-clan unit in the front line. It may have numbered 200. The left wing consisted of the MacDonald regiments – Keppoch, Glengarry (with whom were included the Grants of Glenmoriston) and Clanranald, the whole probably about 700-800 strong. Somewhere in the line was a small body of Clan Chisholm. It is variously positioned by different writers and memoirists, but it may have been between John Roy Stuart and the MacLachlan – MacLean unit.

Behind this front line – at a distance of not less than 60 yards – was the Jacobite second line, consisting from right to left of Lord Ogilvy's regiment of two battalions (possible 500) ; Lord Lewis Gordon's two battalions (400?) ; then Gordon of Glenbucket's – Gordons and Grants from the Highlands of Aberdeenshire and Banffshire – maybe 200, then the Duke of Perth's regiment (200), and finally the *Royal Ecossais* (200) and the Irish Picquets (150).[3] Behind the second line was what remained of the Jacobite cavalry, many of them ignominiously dismounted and serving as infantry, their horses having been taken over by the Prince's Lifeguard and the squadron of Fitz-James' Horse (70). In addition there was a handful of troopers, still mounted, who made up the units commanded by Lords Balmerino and Elcho.

Along the front line had been distributed the 12 guns, pieces of varying calibre, served by inexperienced gunners, and no match for the heavier metal of the Royal Artillery.

The Highland Army's position lay between the walls of Culloden House and those of Culwinniac Farm, at a slight angle to Cumberland's line, its left being further from them than the right, but while the right wing more or less rested on the walls of the farm, there was an appreciable gap between the left and the walls around Culloden House. It was the right wing enclosures round the farm that had troubled Lord George Murray, and he had directed the two battalions of Lord Lewis Gordon's regiment, commanded by Moir of Stonywood and Gordon of Avochie, to move to a position facing and parallel to the enclosures, to deal with any enemy troops attrmpting to outflank the Highland Army by pulling down the dry stone walls. This Lord George thought a sufficient precaution against any incursion from that direction.

At Culloden the Highland Army did not muster more than 5,000 at most.

The weather, which that morning had promised to be fair and sunny, quickly deteriorated, and shortly after midday, the sky had clouded over, while a strong wind blew from the north-east into the faces of the Highlanders, bringing with it squalls of cold rain, to dampen their clothes and their ardour. The regulars, with their backs to it, were less affected.

Cumberland seems to have anticipated that the Jacobite attack would come on his right, he moved two infantry battalions – Pulteney's and Battereau's – from the reserve to prolong his first and second lines and conform with the Highland front, which somewhat overlapped his right. Wolfe's regiment was moved from the extreme left of the second line to take up a position at the end of the front line, facing inwards, next to and at right angles to Barrel's, military speaking, *en potence* to it, and apparently partially protected by a turf wall, from which position it could fire at an attacker moving forward against Barrel's regiment in the front line. Behind and to the left, in advance of Hawley's dragoons, came the Argyleshire Highlanders, who, as they made their way towards the right flank of the Jacobites, with the Nairn on their left, came to a point where they were out of sight of both armies, by reason of the slope of the ground towards the river, and there they found themselves against the east wall of the enclosures which stretched between the Highland right and Cumberland's left.

These walls appeared to prevent any outflanking movement by Hawley's cavalry. But the Argyleshire men were ordered to pull down the dry stone walls and admit the dragoons so that they could strike the Jacobite right or even rear. This was speedily undertaken by the Campbells assisted by Loudoun's Independent Company – also Campbells. This seems to have taken place out of sight of the Highland Army, but as the Campbells and the dragoons moved up towards the north-west of the enclosures they were observed. However, no counter measures were taken, and the battalions posted to watch that side were not even moved up to the walls from which they could have fired with advantage. Some firing broke out as soon as the Highlanders appreciated the fact that they were being outflanked, but events here were rapidly overtaken by those in the centre of the battlefield.

The rain was increasing when shortly after one o'clock the Jacobites opened fire from the four-gun battery in their centre. One round it seems narrowly missed the Duke of Cumberland – no mean target, nearly eighteen stone astride a big grey horse; another 'took off two men exactly before him.'

Two minutes later Cumberland's guns began to reply. Colonel Belford had two laid upon the group of horsemen about the Prince's Standard. Several roundshot fell about them, and one carried off the head of his groom, Thomas Caw. Some gentlemen from Inverness, who were watching the proceedings from a nearby hill, lost their appetite for things military, and departed in haste. The Prince and his retinue moved out of the line of fire, but the ground where he had stood was soon covered with the bodies of Murray of Broughton's Hussars.

Belford's guns played 'very briskly' on the 'ill-served and ill-pointed' guns of the Jacobites, who, it seems fired as few as one shot to every twenty from the Royal Artillery. Colonel Sir Joseph Yorke, Cumberland's A.D.C., recollected that 'when our cannon had fired about two rounds I could plainly perceive that the rebels fluctuated extremely and could not remain long in the position

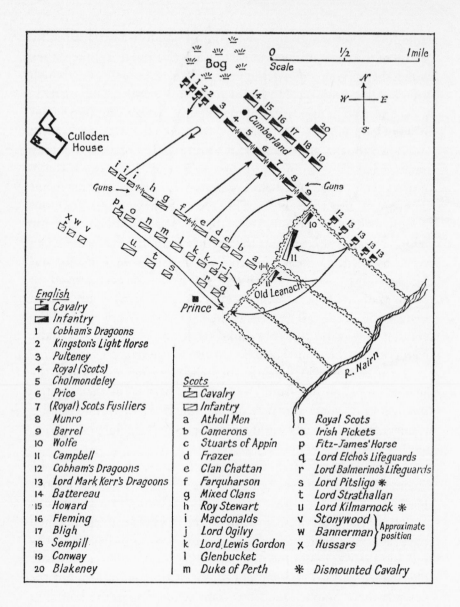

Bog

Scale
0   ½   1 mile

Culloden House

Cumberland

Guns →

← Guns

Old Leanach

R. Nairn

Prince

English

⊟ Cavalry
◨ Infantry

1 Cobham's Dragoons
2 Kingston's Light Horse
3 Pulteney
4 Royal (Scots)
5 Cholmondeley
6 Price
7 (Royal) Scots Fusiliers
8 Munro
9 Barrel
10 Wolfe
11 Campbell
12 Cobham's Dragoons
13 Lord Mark Kerr's Dragoons
14 Battereau
15 Howard
16 Fleming
17 Bligh
18 Sempill
19 Conway
20 Blakeney

Scots

⊟ Cavalry
◨ Infantry

a Atholl Men
b Camerons
c Stuarts of Appin
d Frazer
e Clan Chattan
f Farquharson
g Mixed Clans
h Roy Stewart
i Macdonalds
j Lord Ogilvy
k Lord Lewis Gordon
l Glenbucket
m Duke of Perth

n Royal Scots
o Irish Pickets
p Fitz-James' Horse
q Lord Elcho's Lifeguards
r Lord Balmerino's Lifeguards
s Lord Pitsligo ✳
t Lord Strathallan
u Lord Kilmarnock ✳
v Stonywood ⎫
w Bannerman ⎬ Approximate position
x Hussars ⎭

✳ Dismounted Cavalry

THE BATTLE OF CULLODEN, 1746

264

they were in without running away or coming down upon us'. Lord George Murray's opinion of the battlefield was being confirmed only too plainly. Cumberland 'finding his cannon rapidly thinning the Jacobite ranks, without experiencing any loss in return', was in no hurry to come to close quarters. Belford's guns made 'a strange slaughter-house' of the battery in the Jacobite centre. Towards the end of the cannonade he had the guns charged with grape, swept the field 'as with a hail storm' so that the Highlanders 'were greatly surprised and disordered. . . .'

Every minute that they had to endure this bombardment diminished the Prince's chance of success. His own gunnery was doing no good. The Royal Artillery was tearing great gaps in the six-deep ranks of the clan regiments, now swollen by returning foragers.

It is evident that the Prince, as during the night advance on Nairn, was stationed too far to the rear to control events. It is equally certain that, since all depended on the wild charge of his Highlanders, he should have launched them much sooner.

To escape the artillery fire some of the clansmen flung themselves on the ground, some called out for a charge, others took to their heels. Lochiel now informed Lord George Murray that he could not hold his men much longer. Thereupon Lord George sent 'to know if he should begin the attack, which the Prince accordingly ordered'.

It was high time. As the Duke of Perth was further from Cumberland's line than Murray he was ordered to begin the attack, but when he gave the order the MacDonalds refused to obey him. A man of 32 the Duke was a tactful and obliging person, but evidently not the man to exact obedience from the unruly clansmen. He was unfortunate in having feeble lungs. But his courage was beyond question. Seizing Clanranald's colours he cried that if only they would show their usual courage he would change his name from Drummond to MacDonald. All was in vain.

Lord George Murray was made of sterner stuff. When he led he did not have to look over his shoulder to see if his men were following, for the charge was already under way. Galled by the fire from Cumberland's guns, swept by wind and rain, and infuriated by their own inaction, the centre of the Highland line suddenly and spontaneously surged forward, the Mackintoshes in the lead, but followed within a minute or two by all the regiments of the right – Frasers, Stewarts of Appin, Camerons and the Atholl Brigade, as well as by the Maclachlans and Macleans on their left, and possibly the Farquharsons (if indeed they were an independent unit). Despite the wind, the enemy was wreathed in cannon smoke, and the onrushing Highlanders could see little enough of the red-coats. It was difficult for them to keep their direction without inclining to right or left. As it was, probably because a heavier fire came from their left, the attacking regiments, led by the Mackintoshes, swerved to their right. Now the smoke round Cumberland's men grew denser, the guns firing grape as rapid volleys rang out from the long line of infantry. With the pressure of the Mackintoshes on their left, Camerons, Stewarts and Atholl men crowded closely upon one another, as Hawley had predicted, forming a dense mass, an excellent target for Wolfe's regiment, so admirably placed to enfilade them as they dashed past. Great gaps appeared in the masses of Highlanders, chief after chief fell as they approached, but there was no hesitation and swiftly the leading clansmen struck Cumberland's infantry.

A British soldier, Edward Lunn, who was probably in Price's regiment, describes the attack :

'Their spirited advance lasted but a short time with any kind of warmth, and they shifted away to our left. They came up very boldly and fast all in a cloud together, sword in hand. They fired their pieces and flung them away; but we gave them so warm a reception that we kept a continued close fire upon them with our small arms; besides two or three of our cannon gave them a close fire with grape-shot, which galled them very much. . . . They thought it was such a bad day that our firelocks would not fire, but scarce one in our regiment missed firing, but (we) kept them dry with our coat laps.'

Barrel's took the brunt of the Highland charge but some of it fell on Munro's – one of the runaways of Falkirk. This time, determined to win back their name, they did not flinch, but holding their fire until the Highlanders were within 30 yards gave them a volley in their teeth. At that range it was hard to miss.

Lord George Murray relates that many of the clansmen 'could not fire as some of their own men were betwixt them and the enemy. This was a vast loss for the fire of Highlanders is more bloody than that of any regular troops whatever'.

Even so Barrel's regiment was borne backwards by the sheer weight of the mass of charging men. Captain Lord Robert Kerr received a Cameron on his spontoon, as his men gave way, and was cut down by Major Gillies MacBean of the Mackintosh regiment, his head 'cleft from crown to collar-bone'. Lt.-Colonel Robert Rich of Barrel's was terribly wounded, six cuts in the head, his left hand lopped off, and his right arm nearly severed above the elbow. Ensign Brown was wounded defending a colour. But Barrel's fought back like heroes, Michael Hughes, a volunteer in Bligh's regiment, could see the officers, 'some cutting with their swords, others pushing with their spontoons, the sergeants running their halberts into the throats of the enemy, while the soldiers mutually defended each other . . . ramming their bayonets up to the socket.'

The two cannon between Barrel's and Munro's regiments were so well served, that when the Highlanders were within two yards of them 'they received a full discharge of cartridge shot, which made a dreadful havoc', before the guns were overrun.

The officer commanding the grenadiers on the left of Munro's had 18 casualties in his platoon and himself narrowly escaped as the Highlanders swept through the gap. He tells us that he had six balls through his coat :

'In the midst of the action, the officer that led on the Camerons, called to me to take quarter; which I refused, and bid the rebel scoundrel advance. He did, and fired at me; but providentially missed his mark. I then shot him dead, and took his pistol and dirk, which are extremely neat. No one that attacked us, escaped alive; for we gave no quarter, nor would accept of any.'

Meanwhile, Major-General John Huske, on orders from Cumberland, had moved Bligh's and Sempill's some 50 yards forward. Crowding through the English front line the Highlanders 'received a full fire from the centre of Bligh's regiment'. Sempill's, renowned for its good musketry, added to the slaughter. Few indeed reached the second line. The Highlanders, trapped between Barrel's and Sempill's, were cut down to a man. Amid the din Huske was heard shouting, 'Give them the bayonet.' It is said, probably truly, that 'hundreds perished on their points', but it was lead not cold steel that won the day. The wonder is not that the

Highlanders were beaten, but that they got to close quarters at all.

Some of the clansmen got round the left flank of Barrel's only to be shot down by Wolfe's and Ligonier's. The attack had lost its momentum. Even so some desperate Highlanders stood their ground and 'threw stones for at least a minute or two before their total rout began'.

The Highlanders on the left could not bring themselves to emulate the bravery of their comrades. Old John Gordon of Glenbucket's men and John Roy Stewart's at least had the excuse that they had no swords. Lord John Drummond eventually persuaded the MacDonalds to advance within 100 yards of Cumberland's line. Three times they looked as if they were going to charge, 'firing their pistols and brandishing their swords'. The English were unimpressed. Lord John, half-pike in hand, walked between the two armies in a brave attempt to draw their fire, but the officers of the Royal and Pulteney's had their men well in hand. They were not going to loose off their first carefully loaded volley while the Scots were out of range. Even had they done so the time was past when the MacDonalds could have been brought to charge, or when their charge could have been effective. The right wing was already streaming back up the hill, hastened on its way by the fire of two guns and a coehorn mortar. Already the English cavalry were moving forward to outflank them.

Without more ado the MacDonalds fled, throwing down their firelocks. Lord John Drummond strove in vain to halt them. Cumberland's right wing 'advancing some paces gave their fire in so close and full a manner that the ground was soon covered with the bodies of the dead and wounded. . . .' The cannon added to the carnage. O'Sullivan lost his head and galloping up to the Prince's retinue cried, 'You see all is going to pot!'

But if the clan MacDonald as a body left Drummossie Moor without adding to their reputation, there were gallant gentlemen among them. It was at this time, when all was already lost, that they chose to charge, a forlorn hope if ever there was one – forlorn as Keppoch's cry : 'O my God, has it come to this, that the children of my tribe have forsaken me !' In the charge his brother, Donald, was one of the first to fall. He himself was hit twice before he reached the front of Price's, and a shot in the back finished him as he was being helped from the field. Lochgarry came through unhit and Clanranald, though badly wounded in the head, managed to make his escape.

In the midst of those running back from the chaos of the fight was Lord George Murray. He had ridden with the Atholl regiments – his own men – in the attack, and it seems that his horse became unmanageable. However this may be he was far into the Hanoverian line before he dismounted and fought his way back through the mêlée, making his way as fast as he could to the second line. Desperate though matters had now become, he made one more effort to restore the situation. The nearest regiments in the second line were Glenbucket's and the Duke of Perth's. These he ordered forward, to prolong the right of the retreating Mac-Donalds, and they fired a volley, but as Cumberland's infantry had not yet moved forward, it cannot have done much damage. The situation was beyond saving. Already on the right, the Argyleshire Highlanders and Hawley's dragoons were pressing in on the troops observing the enclosures. The mass of men retreating from the fight received several deadly volleys from the Campbells as they raced past. One of Lord Lewis Gordon's battalions, that of Gordon of Avochy, was still in position, forming a front towards the outflanking force. The English dragoons now came on the scene, their only opponents being the skeleton squadron of Fitz-James' Horse, who faced them when they made their way through the tumbled down walls on to the right rear of the Highland Army. The dragoons cautiously forbore to charge, being content to move slowly forward, exchanging pistol and carbine fire with the Jacobites, and allowing them to fall back before them.

The entire Highland Army was now on the point of dissolution. Kingston's Light Horse, from the right of Cumberland's line, were sabring the fugitives. The MacDonalds were in full flight from the field, carrying with them much of the second line, except the *Royal Ecossais* and the Irish Picquets, who held their ground against Kingston's men. In the mêlée, their gallant Brigadier, Walter Stapleton, wearing the uniform of King Louis, was severely wounded. The cavalry soon sheered off, to seek easier victims, and apparently met, somewhere in the centre of the field, the dragoons coming from the south, those who had come through the enclosures. There was still some sporadic fighting round isolated pockets of resistance, but the battle was over, with the dragoons setting off to pursue that part of the beaten army making its way towards Inverness, and cutting down the fugitives almost to the outskirts of the town. Finally Cumberland ordered the infantry to advance – there was no opposition. His opposite number, Lord George Murray – seems to have gathered a few remnants of his regiments about him, and with them made off towards the hills to the south. They had been preceeded by the Prince and some of his friends. How many of his followers had fallen none can say, but the most moderate estimate is 1,200.

Prince Charles reached Gorthlick, some 20 miles from Culloden, that night. Next day he issued his last order to those of his followers who still remained in a body. 'Let every man seek his own safety the best way he can.' Thus briefly and ungraciously he dismissed the men who had fought for him. The Chevalier Johnstone has recorded their sad parting :

'Our separation at Ruthven was truly affecting. We bade one another an eternal adieu. No one could tell whether the scaffold would not be his fate. The Highlanders gave vent to their grief in wild howlings and lamentations; the tears flowed down their cheeks when they thought that their country was now at the discretion of the Duke of Cumberland and on the point of being plundered; whilst they and their children would be reduced to slavery. . . .'

Their worst fears were soon to be realised, for Jeffreys' 'Bloody Assize' is not to be mentioned in the same breath as the atrocities which accompanied 'Billy the Martial Boy's' pacification of the Highlands. But that is another story.

The fate of Prince Charles' followers has been ably dealt with by John Prebble,[4] suffice it here to say that Lord George Murray escaped abroad and died in exile in Germany in 1760. The Duke of Perth, who escaped to France, did not long survive. He was worn out by his exertions in the campaign. Lord John Drummond escaped but died of fever at Bergen-op-Zoom the following year. O'Sullivan got back to France, was knighted, married a wealthy wife, fell out of favour with the Prince, and died about 1761. Lochiel, though wounded in both ankles by grapeshot, escaped to France, only to die of brain-fever in 1748. Lord Balmerino, who had commanded the Lifeguard, died on the scaffold, but made a good end. The Earl of Kilmarnock suffered the same fate. Young Lord Ogilvy, who reached France via Norway, became a general in the French service, where he had formerly held a commission, and lived to recover his estates, surviving until 1802.

Cumberland's losses were not heavy. The official figure is 50 killed, 259 wounded and one missing, a total of 310. Barrel's regiment 438 strong, was the hardest hit, with 17 killed and 108 wounded. Munro's had 82 casualties. Of the cavalry only six were killed. Of about 13,000 present in the battle it has been estimated that only some 3,000 were seriously engaged.

Cumberland's A.D.C., Major Lord Bury of the Coldstream Guards, had distinguished himself by his coolness under fire, and to him fell the honour of taking the Duke's despatch to London. The news had preceeded him, nevertheless the King rewarded him with 1,000 guineas. Cumberland himself did even better. His income was raised by £25,000 per annum ; Handel composed a march in his honour, and a flower, the 'Sweet William', was named after him.

Barrel's regiment was to wear 'Culloden' on its colours for the next 40 years, while Nelson's fleet at the Nile numbered a 'Culloden' among its men-of-war. The defeated Highlanders had given the Hanoverian Government a good fright, and the victory was all the more popular in consequence. But when all is said and done Cumberland and 'Hangman Hawley' marred their victory by the atrocities they permitted, and indeed encouraged, afterwards. Pillage, rape and murder were the order of the day, the innocent suffering with the guilty.

An undistinguished military career lay ahead of the victor, culminating in his defeat at Hastenbeck and the inglorious Convention of Klosterseven (1757). It is more charitable to remember him as the founder of the Ascot Race Meeting(1748).

Prince Charles, after months of wandering in the Highlands, which went far to foster the legends which sprang up round his name, escaped to France. He had 42 years to run, before, a bibulous and unattractive old man, he died, a French pensioner, at Rome.

The honours of the Culloden campaign lie not so much with the leaders as with the led : the gallant clansmen of Clan Cameron and Clan Chattan ; the stout-hearted soldiers of Barrel's and Munro's.

[1] But not the castle.

[2] They had been raised by Lord George Murray's cousin, Lady Mackintosh, whose husband was a captain in King George's army. She was a very pretty young woman of 20, and rode in at the head of her men to join the Prince, wearing a tartan riding-habit and a man's blue bonnet. The English credited 'that bloody rebel Lady Mackintosh' with leading her clan into action at Culloden, and it seems a pity to diøsbelieve such a fine piece of mythology. She was imprisoned after the battle and Hawley, who was fond of hanging people, is quoted as saying at Cumberland's, table: 'Damn the woman, I'll honour her with a mahogany gallows and a silk cord !' But most of the English officers who visited her in prison found her charming.

[3] Detachments from the six Irish regiments in the French service – the Wild Geese. They were redcoated regiments.

[4] Culloden: 1961.

Seeing the Battlefields

HASTINGS

The small town of Battle is approximately 6¾ miles north-west of Hastings on the A2100 at the junction with B2092. Probably the best starting point for the visitor will be Caldbec Hill, the most likely site for the Hoar Apple Tree. From Harold's assembly area the visitor should then move to the high altar within the Abbey grounds, which marks Harold's headquarters during the battle. The left of the English line is obscured by buildings, but the right of the position can be made out fairly easily in the fields and woods. Lastly the visitor might like to walk down to the railway bridge on the A2100 from where he can see the English position as the Normans would have seen it as they deployed.

LEWES

Lewes is 8 miles north-east of Brighton. The battlefield lies north-west of the town. The best way to see the field is to follow in the footsteps of Earl Simon's army, taking the track from Offham which leads on to Offham Hill. The road leading to the Race Course marks the area of heaviest fighting.

EVESHAM

Evesham is 15 miles south-east of Worcester. If the visitor goes to the junction of A435 and B4084 (the Worcester road) north of the town he will be in a good position to explore the battle-field. 'Battle Well', the reputed place where Earl Simon fell, can be found only with difficulty 130ft. to the left of A435 and 200ft. south of B4084. It is now only a shallow depression in the ground.

BANNOCKBURN

The battlefield is 1 mile south-east of Stirling. The best place from which to explore the field is St. Ninians, on the A9. The visitor can either ascend Coxett Hill or walk down the side road past the ruined kirk towards the A905. The spot where this road is crossed by the railway probably lies in the centre of the fiercest fighting of the battle.

FIRST AND SECOND ST. ALBANS

The best place to start looking at the battlefields is from the top of the Bell Tower (see map), which is open to the public for a small fee. The National Provincial Bank stands on the site of the Castle Inn. The position of Key field is marked by a street name, and is easy to find.

The Museum has a collection of arrowheads and spurs found on the battlefield. The visitor should also look at the brass of Sir Antony de Grey in the Abbey in order in see a contemporary representation of the armour of the period.

TOWTON

The battlefield is between York and Leeds, and is bisected by the B1217. The visitor will find that seeing the field presents few problems as the ground is still relatively open. It is still possible to see Lord Dacre's tomb in Saxton parish churchyard.

TEWKESBURY

The battlefield lies just south of Tewkesbury on the A38. A hotel stands on the site of Gubshill Manor. Hedges and fences make it difficult to explore the possible Lancastrian position. Tewkesbury Park has become a Golf Course and Country Club, thus completely altering the scenery.

BOSWORTH

The battlefield is approximately 14 miles east of Leicester by road. The western boundary of the fighting is now marked by the railway line, and the Ashby de la Zouch canal cuts from east to west the ground over which Henry Tudor advanced. King Richard's Well is marked by a stone monument erected in 1813. The best viewpoint is Ambion Hill. Leicestershire County Council have established a Battlefield Centre for the public in the former Ambion Hill Farm.

FLODDEN

Branxton is 2 miles south-east of Coldstream, and can be approached from the town along the A697. A monument 500 yards south-west of Branxton commemorates the battle. Exploring the battlefield is straightforward.

EDGEHILL

The battlefield lies to the west of the A41 road from Warwick to Banbury. A general view of the field may be obtained from the pseudo-Gothic tower of The Castle Inn on the ridge of Edge Hill itself, where the Royalists drew up their lines in the morning.

The actual battlefield is as present controlled by the War Department, and may only be visited by permission of the Commandant of the C.A.D., Kineton, Marlborough Farm Camp, Leamington Spa, Warwickshire. Should such permission be obtained, an excellent 'stand' for viewing the field is the large artificial mound near the south-west corner of Graveground Coppice.

FIRST NEWBURY

The battlefield is somewhat built over, but it is fairly easy to visit the main positions. The best way is to go down the Andover road (A343) from Newbury as far as the Gun Public House. There stands the Falkland Monument – perhaps $\frac{1}{2}$ mile from the place where he fell. To get a clear view of Round Hill one must take a view of the field from the North, somewhere near the bridge across the railway.

MARSTON MOOR

The battlefield lies about 6 miles west of York on the B1224 road and is still much as it was in 1644, even though the cottage in Tockwith, where Oliver Cromwell is supposed to have had his wound dressed during the fight, has vanished – destroyed by a bomb during the Second World War. One may wander at will across the field of Marston Moor, but no particular observation post is better than another.

LOSTWITHIEL

Restormel Castle, North of Lostwithiel is worth a visit. Most of the fighting on 21 August 1644 took place on the high ground NE of the town and astride A.390. The second battle (31 August) took place in the fields near Castle Dore, which stands on the high ground NW of Fowey, and may be approached by B. 3269.

SECOND NEWBURY

Donnington Castle is the best viewpoint from which to survey the Second Battle of Newbury. The castle ruins lie about $1\frac{1}{2}$ miles to the north-west of the town and can be reached by the Oxford road (A34), the castle being about $\frac{1}{2}$ mile to the west of that road. Shaw House is now a Girls' School, Speenhamland is obscured by new roads and houses. The fields west of Speen, where Skippon's men stormed the Royalist battery, appear to be much as they were in 1644, but the earthwork itself is no longer to be seen.

There are models of the battles, and a number of relics, weapons and so forth, at the Museum in Newbury.

NASEBY

Naseby lies between Northampton and Market Harborough but not on the direct road (A508). The best approach is from Market Harborough by B3046. The field is little altered and can easily be toured by anyone following the modern road from Naseby to Tockwith. The Church, which contains several relics of the battle, is worth a visit.

The so-called Naseby Obelisk, erected in 1825, is a full mile from the scene of the engagement. The monument more recently erected by the Cromwell Association indicates the approximate position of his wing at the start of the action.

The battlefield is but little altered, and is accessible from the main Dunbar-Cockburnspath road (A1). It may be that there are rather more trees now than in 1650, but it seems likely that there were some along the banks of the Brox Burn even in those days.

WORCESTER

There is still much to evoke the scenes of 1651. The Cathedral itself, whence the young King viewed the field, still stands in all its majesty. The Commandery, the fine early seventeenth-century house which was the Royalist headquarters, may still be seen. One may walk down to the east bank of the Seven to a point opposite its junction with the Teme. It is no great effort of the imagination conjure up Cromwell's soldiers labouring with barges and planks to build their bridges of boats.

Over at Powick one can still see the splash marks of musket bullets on the south wall of the church tower. It is easy to see, too, where an arch of the old brick bridge at Powick has been broken and later repaired. Here Prince Rupert routed the Roundhead cavalry in 1642.

SEDGEMOOR

The battlefield lies rather less than 3 miles, as the crow flies, south-east of Bridgwater on the A372. The Rhines have been greatly changed and the Langmoor stones have disappeared. The Bussex Rhine itself has been filled in, though its course can still be detected. Yet the general appearance of the battlefield cannot be much different, and the fine old churches of Weston Zoyland, Chedzoy and of Bridgwater help the imagination. At Chedzoy one can still see the place where the Royalist troopers sharpened their swords.

CULLODEN

The battlefield lies about 7 miles east of Inverness and can be reached without difficulty by the B9006. Although it is largely covered with trees, the cairn which marks the burial place of the fallen stands in a clearing. The National Trust for Scotland now has the responsibility for guarding this historic battlefield.

Select Bibliography

General

C. R. B. Barrett, *Battles and Battlefields of England, 1896*

R. Brooke, *Visits to Fields of Battle in England,* 1857

A. H. Burne, *The Battlefields of England,* 1951

A. H. Burne, *More Battlefields of England,* 1952

A. H. Burne, *The Agincourt War,* 1956

R.A. Newhall, *Muster and Review. English Military Administration 1420-1440,* 1940

C. Oman, *The Art of War in the Middle Ages.* 2 Vols, 2nd Edit. 1924

C. Oman, *The Art of War in the Sixteenth Century,* 1937

W. Seymour, *Battles in Britain.* 2 Vols. 1975

Wars of Roses

J. Adair, 'The Newsletter of Gerhard von Wesel, 17 April 1471.' *Journal of the Society for Army Historical Research,* 1968

F. P. Barnard, *Edward IV's French Expedition of 1475,* 1925

J. Gairdner, *The Paston Letters.* 4 Vols. 1910

E. Hall, *The Union of the Two Noble and Illustre Families of Lancaster and York,* 1548. Edited H. Ellis, 1809

G. L. Harriss, 'The Struggle for Calais: an aspect of the rivalry between Lancaster and York.' *English Historical Review,* 1960

P. M. Kendall, *Richard III,* 1955. *Warwick the Kingmaker,* 1957. *The Yorkist Age,* 1962

R. B. Mowat, *The Wars of the Roses 1377-1471,* 1914

J. Ramsay, *York and Lancaster,* 1892

C. Ross, *Edward IV,* 1975

C. Ross, *The Wars of the Roses,* 1971

Civil War

W. C. Abbot, *Writings and Speeches of Oliver Cromwell.* 4 Vols. 1937-1947

A. H. Burne and P. Young, *The Great Civil War: A Military History,* 1959

Earl of Clarendon, *The History of the Rebellion and Civil War in England.* Ed. W. D. Macray. Oxford, 1888

R. Holmes and P. Young, *The English Civil War,* 1974

Battles

Hastings

English Historical Documents, Vol. 2 1042-1189, Ed. D. Douglas, 1953. (Contains most of main sources in English translation)

The Bayeux Tapestry. Phaidon Press, 1957
P. Compton, *Harold the King*, 1961
D. Haworth, *1066, The Year of Conquest.*
C. H. Lemmon, *The Field of Hastings*, 1956

Lewes and Evesham

A. H. Burne, Gives a useful list of main sources in *The Battlefields of England*, p. 298
W. K. Blauuw, *The Baron's War.* 2nd Edition. 1924
C. Bemont, *Simon de Montfort.* English edition. 1930
M. W. Labarge, *Simon de Montfort*, 1962

Bannockburn

J. Barbour, *The Bruce* (written *c.* 1375). Edited W. Mackay Mackenzie, 1909
J. D. Mackie, Article in *Scottish Historical Review*, Vol. 29, 1950
W. Mackay Mackenzie, *The Battle of Bannockburn*, 1913
J. E. Morris, *Bannockburn*, 1914

First St. Albans

C. H. Ashdown, *Battles and Battlefields of St. Albans*
C. A. J. Armstrong, 'Politics and the First Battle of St. Albans 1455' in *Bulletin of Institute of Historical Research*, No. 87. 1960. This article includes an excellent review of the sources

Second St. Albans

C. H. Ashdown, *Supra*
Gregory. *Gregory's Chronicle: The Historical Collections of a Citizen of London.* Edited J. Gairdner, 1876
Victoria County History. Hertfordshire

Towton

Calendar of State Papers (Venice), edited R. Brown, 1844. Nos. 370-374
'Hearne's Fragment' in *Chronicle of the White Rose*, edited by J. A. Giles, 1845
A. D. H. Leadman, *Battles fought in Yorkshire*, 1891

Tewkesbury

Historie of the Arrival of Edward IV in England. Edited J. Bruce. 1838
J. Warkworth, *Chronicle of the First Thirteen Years of the Reign of Edward IV.* Edited J. D. Halliwell. 1839

Bosworth

J. T. Burgess, *The Last Battle of the Roses*, 1872

W. Hutton, *The Battle of Bosworth Field*. 2nd Edition, 1813. Includes important 'Stanley' source

Flodden

A. H. Burne, *The Battlefields of England*, p. 303 for a full bibliography of sources

G. E. T. Leathers, *New Light on Flodden*, 1937

J. D. Mackie, 'The English Army at Flodden'. *Scottish Historical Miscellany*. Vol. 8. 1959

W. Mackay Mackenzie, *The Secret of Flodden*, 1931

Edgehill

Brig. P. Young, *Edgehill 1642 : The Campaign and the Battle*. Kineton, 1967.

First Newbury

A true Relation of the Late Expedition of His Excellency, Robert Earle of Essex for the Relief of Gloucester, with the Description of the Fight at Newbury. On 7 October, 1643, the House of Commons ordered that this account should be published 'and that none shall reprint the same without the further order of my Lo. Generall.' It may, therefore, be called the Parliamentarian Official Account. It is a very full and fair narrative, not entirely devoid of topographical detail and very useful for the organisation of Essex's army. Reprinted in Washburne's *Bibliotheca Gloucestrensis*

A True and Impartiall Relation of the Battaile. L. Lichfield. Oxford. 29 September, 1643. Money and Gardiner thought this was by Lord Digby, but it is not quite clear why

Clarendon. *History of the Rebellion*, Macray's Edition (1888). Not a very detailed account

Sir John Byron, MS. Clarendon. 23. This was written for Clarendon, and is useful for his comments on Royalist strategy and tactics in general, and for his own attack. Printed in Money, but not with complete accuracy

Sergeant H. Foster, *A True and Exact Relation of the Marchings of the ... trained bands of the City of London*. Also in Washburne. Very useful for his own regiment though his view of the battle as a whole was necessarily restricted.

Anon. BM. Add. MSS. 18 980-2. Printed in Money. It is a pity this officer cannot be identified. He gives a number of useful points.

W. Money, *The Battles of Newbury*. Useful for his local knowledge

Professor G. Davies, 'The Parliamentary Army under the Earl of Essex, 1642-5.' *English Historical Review*, 1934. Very useful for the organisation of Essex's army, though our estimate of the number of regiments differs from his

The Hon. H. A. Dillon, A MS. List of Officers of the London Trained Bands in 1643. Westminster, 1890. Invaluable for the London Trained Bands

Lt.-Col. A. H. Burne and Lt.-Col. P. Young, *The Great Civil War*. 1959. Though part-author of The Great Civil War, further study has led me to depart very considerably from the narrative given there

British Museum. E. 69. Several accounts. Useful for details

Mercurius Aulicus. 1643. P. 527. Adds little to E. 69/10

Marston Moor

Brig P. Young, *Marston Moor 1644: The Campaign and the Battle*. Kineton, 1970.

Lostwithiel

Sir E. Walker, *Historical Discourses*. Richard Symonds, *Diary*.

Second Newbury

E. Ludlow, *Supra*

W. Money, *The Battles of Newbury*. London, 1881

R. Symonds, *Diary*. Camden Society, 1859

Sir E. Walker, *Historical Discourses*

Naseby

Sir B. De Gomme, Plan. BM. Add MS. 16370

J. Sprigge, *Anglia Rediviva*. Includes a useful picture map

Sir E. Walker, *Historical Discourses*

Dunbar

C. H. Firth, *Transactions of the Royal Historical Society*, Vol. XIV, gives Payne Fisher's picture map

Worcester

T. Blount, *Boscobel or the History of His Most Sacred Majesty's most miraculous preservation after the battle of Worcester*

O. Cromwell, See W. C. Abbott, *(supra)* for his letters

A. Fea, *The Flight of the King*, 1908. Reprints contemporary narratives

Sedgemoor

A. H. Burne, *The Battlefields of England*, 1951

Peter Earle, *Monmouth's Rebels*, 1977

B. Little, *The Monmouth Episode*, 1956

M. Page, *The Battle of Sedgemoor*, 1930

Sir Edward Parry, *The Bloody Assize*, 1929

Culloden

J. Prebble, *Culloden*, 1961

K. Tomasson and F. Buist, *Battles of the '45*, 1962

Index of Persons

W

Wade, Nathaniel   245, 246, 251
Waldegrave, Sir William   183
Walker, Sir Edward   181, 200, 212, 213-4, 216
Wallace, Sir William   46, 54
Waller, Sir William   3, 178, 180, 188, 190-1, 193-6, 201, 208
Walter the Steward   48, 51
Waltheof, Earl   11
Warwick, Richard Neville, Earl of   62-4, 66-74, 76-82, 83-4
Washington, Henry   136, 138
Watson, Scoutmaster General   173
Weems, Sgt.   251
Wenlock, Sir John, later Lord   63, 67-8, 78, 80, 89-92
Wentworth, Lady Henrietta   245, 251

Wentworth, Lord   141
Wentworth, Sir Philip   63
Whalley, Col. Edward   213, 228
Wharton, Lord   144
Widdrington, Sir William   169
William the Conqueror   7-20
Williams, Richard   98
Wilmot, Lord   133, 136, 139, 142, 159, 179, 192, 241
Wiltshire, Earl of   81
Woodville, Sir Antony   68
Woodville, Sir Edward   96
Worcester, Thomas Percy, Earl of   57, 58

Y

York, Richard, Duke of 59-64, 66-8, 69
Yorke, Col. Sir Joseph   263

Index of Places & Battles

A

Aberdeen	257
Battle of	218
Abingdon	3
Aire, River	5, 76-7
Aldbourne Chase, Battle of	147
Alford, Battle of	219
Ashdown, Battle of	12
Assize of Arms	42
Auldearn, Battle of	219

B

Banbury	131-2, 191, 275
Bannockburn, Battle of	21, 47-54, 273
Barnet, Battle of	84, 93
Basing	5
Battle Abbey	12
Bayeux Tapestry	13, 16, 17, 19
Beacon Hill, Battle of	181-3
Berwick	47, 48, 94
Bloreheath, Battle of	66
Bodmin	179-80
Bolton	164
Bosworth Field, Battle of	4, 95-106, 108, 274
Bothwell Castle	53
Bridgwater	180, 248, 277
Bridport, skirmish at	246
Bristol	4, 248

C

Calais	66-7
Caldbec Hill	12, 273
Castle Dore, Battle of	183-8
Castleford	77
Chester	4
Chilterns	2, 5
Cirencester	147
Commissions of Array	46, 48
Coventry	66, 131-2
Cropredy Bridge, Battle of	188, 191, 205, 216
Culloden, Battle of	255-72, 277-8

D

Derby	257, 258
Derwent, River	10
Dintingdale	78
Dunbar	47, 53
Battle of	221-31, 237, 277
Dunstable	71

E

Edgecote, Battle of	83
place	131
Edgehill, Battle of	123, 127, 128, 130-44, 161, 222, 275
Edinburgh	48, 94, 110, 231, 256
Etall Castle	111, 121
Evesham	235, 241
Battle of	3, 37-45, 273
Exeter	86, 96, 179, 246

F

Falkirk	48
Battle of	46, 48, 257
Ferrybridge	76
Feudal levy	22, 54
Flodden, Battle of	107-22, 123, 275
Fulford, Battle of	10
Fyrd	9, 22

G

Gloucester,	3, 4, 5, 38, 147, 149, 234
Gorthlick	270
Gunners' Glasse, The	128

H

Haddington	222, 229
Halidon Hill, Battle of	55
Hastings, Battle of	6-21, 23, 55, 273
Hedgely Moor, Battle of	83
Helderenberg, The	245
Hereford	38, 39, 131-2, 220
Hexham, Battle of	83
House-carls	9, 14
Hull	4, 129
Humber, River	5